D1524723

Signal

YEARS OF RETREAT
1943-44

YEARS OF RETREAT
1943-44

HITLER'S WARTIME PICTURE MAGAZINE

EDITED BY S. L. MAYER

PRENTICE-HALL, INC.
Englewood Cliffs, N.J.

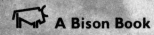 A Bison Book

First U.S. edition published by Prentice-Hall, Inc., 1979

© Copyright 1979 by Bison Books Limited

Produced by Bison Books Limited
4 Cromwell Place
London S W7

ISBN 0 13 810028 4

Library of Congress Catalog Card Number 79 84862

Printed in Hong Kong

Picture Credits
Bison Picture Library: pages 2–3.
US Air Force: pages 5, 6, 7.
Novosti: pages 8–9.

INTRODUCTION
by S.L. Mayer

Signal was the most widely selling magazine in occupied Europe, published by the Wehrmacht under the auspices of the Propaganda Ministry of Josef Goebbels. Its peak sales were in 1943, when it was publishing simultaneously in 20 languages to a readership of over 2½ million. It is ironic that the zenith of *Signal*'s success marked the beginning of the end of the German Reich whose cause it served so well. *Signal: Years of Retreat 1943–44* is the third and final volume in a series which began with an overview of the wartime picture magazine and continued with its sequel *Signal: Years of Triumph 1940–42*. This final volume in the series represents a marked contrast to its predecessors. *Signal* was created with the idea of convincing occupied Europe that Nazi triumphs would continue and therefore that any resistance to the Third Reich was futile and even unpatriotic. Therefore *Signal*'s first years of publication concentrated on Nazi victories, which, at least at the beginning, came thick and fast. The result was that *Signal* presented wartime reportage, most of the time truthfully because there was no reason to lie, in a manner which has seldom if ever been equalled in terms of quality of color photography, thoroughness of coverage from a military angle and imaginative graphics.

Every one of those elements was still available to the *Signal* team in Berlin in 1943–44. However, there were substantive differences. First of all, supplies and quality of paper stocks for the magazine were running thin, as the exigencies of war demanded the use of any and all raw materials for strictly military purposes. Even though the Propaganda Ministry was able to keep supplies of paper adequate to *Signal*'s needs because Goebbels still believed that the magazine with its high

Barrage balloons protect the invasion forces of the United States in June 1944 as the post-D-Day armada loads equipment and men on to Utah Beach.

sales figures was popular, the quality of the paper stock was reduced which damaged the quality of color reproduction. The magazine was forced to reduce the number of pages to meet an increase in demand, which was, in fact, largely due to the inability of other publications to acquire adequate paper stocks. In short there was little else to read and so *Signal* was read.

A second problem arose from the fact that *Signal*'s headquarters were located in the Kochstrasse in Berlin, which did not escape the incessant Allied raids on the German capital during the years of retreat. Undoubtedly these raids prevented the editors and designers from continuing their overly optimistic presentation of the progress of the war as much as the real news from the fronts which filtered through to them. Censorship played a far greater role in the years of retreat as well. The year 1943 was disastrous for the Third Reich. The defeat at Stalingrad and Kursk forced the Axis to retreat over a thousand miles on the Eastern Front. On the Western Front, North Africa and Sicily were overrun by the Allies, Italy was invaded, Mussolini overthrown and re-instated as Hitler's puppet in northern Italy, and at the same time Admiral Doenitz's U-Boats were losing the Battle of the Atlantic to the British and American convoys. *Signal* was not permitted to publish this bad news which obviated the *raison d'être* of the magazine. Therefore it was forced to concentrate on whatever news Goebbels allowed to filter through his propaganda machine. Stalingrad was reluctantly acknowledged about three months after the event, but the fall of Tunisia was not. The fall of Sicily was reported, but only as a tactical withdrawal and the loss of the Battle of the Atlantic was never admitted at all.

Therefore the third great problem of *Signal* during the Nazi years of retreat was

The Zeiss optical plant in Jena in which range finders and gun sights were made before its destruction by bombers of the US Army Air Force.

one of false reportage. Whereas *Signal* initially told a slightly distorted version of the truth, it now had to resort to wild exaggerations and even outright lies. But only when the war was reported at all. Most of the time *Signal* concentrated on activities in the occupied states, painting a glowing picture of co-operation in Eastern Europe which must have disgusted hundreds of thousands of readers in Czechoslovakia and Poland. Slovakia and the Reichsprotectorate of Bohemia and Moravia (all of which had formerly been Czechoslovakia), were given special attention. They were among the few places in Central Europe which did not suffer from the Allied bombing raids. Therefore *Signal* photographers were free to snap their pictures of a peaceful community without the sound of air raid sirens ringing in their ears.

    Signal did not fail to report the bombing itself from time to time. By 1943–44 any attempt to placate British readers in the Channel Islands with stories promoting Anglo-German co-operation had long since been abandoned. Instead the articles concentrated on the inhumanity and brutality of the wanton raids on civilian lives and property, and a strongly anti-Anglo-American bias filled the pages of the magazine as the fortunes of war turned against the Axis. The Americans were portrayed as bewildered and deceived youths who had been forced into a war against their best interests. At a later date *Signal* became blatantly anti-American, picturing the United States as a barbaric, jive-ridden and decadent influence which, if successful, would overrun Europe with the evils of jazz, blacks and crass commercialism. The Nazis, of course, were portrayed as the defenders of European civilization which other civilized peoples like the French should be anxious to defend. The concept of Europe under the swastika standing as the force of culture

The ruins of Goebbels' Propaganda Ministry, under whose auspices Signal *was published, after Berlin was occupied in May 1945.*

Russian soldiers storm into Berlin as the final battle for the existence of the Third Reich was waged in April 1945. Berlin was reduced to rubble by the Allied bombing offensive and the pounding of Soviet guns.

against the twin barbarisms of bolshevism and rampant American capitalism was a theme repeated throughout the pages of *Signal* in its years of retreat.

Although *Signal* continued to publish in German and several other languages, such as Norwegian, Swedish, Danish and Finnish for most of the balance of the war, publication in many languages ceased for obvious reasons in Poland, the Ukraine, Serbo-Croatia and other countries. Only six issues appeared in English in 1944. Originally a bi-monthly publication, *Signal* ceased to publish regularly in 1944. Magazines went undated and were only numbered. They appeared when and as they could. The Paris branch of *Signal*, which helped prepare and distribute the English language version in the occupied Channel Islands, closed in June 1944 after D-Day, although miniature copies of *Signal* were dropped by V-1 rockets over England even after the invasion of Normandy. But it was all in vain, and the editors of *Signal* knew it. Giselher Wirsing, its editor and sometime contributor, moved *Signal*'s offices some 70 kilometers outside Berlin in 1944 to avoid the air raids, and in March 1945, only a few weeks before the capitulation, he ceased publication and moved the archives and personnel of the magazine westward in order to be captured by the Western Allies rather than by the Soviets.

Signal, like the Nazis themselves, was courageous in the face of disaster and fought on regardless until it was impossible to continue. Despite its obvious inadequacies as a journal of truth, it had an element of greatness that must be acknowledged. Its photography and layout were outstanding throughout the war. Its editorial content was not nearly as biased as it could have been and showed considerable restraint not exhibited by many other agencies of the Third Reich. Above all, it was a dim light in the darkness of Nazism which tried to show the war as it really was, and in its way, because of its Wehrmacht connections, was probably the least racist and anti-Semitic of all official German publications during the wartime period. For this reason, more than any other, *Signal* has been remembered and recreated in this trilogy of facsimile volumes concluded by *Signal: Years of Retreat 1943–44*.

E. No.1

SIGNAL · NUMBER 1 · 1944

Signal

Belgium 3 Fr. / Bohemia and Moravia 4 Kr. / Bulgaria 8 Leva / Denmark 50 Øre / Finland 4.50 Mk. / France 5 Fr. / Italy 3 Lire / Croatia 15 Kuna / Netherlands 25 Cents / Norway 50 Øre / Portugal 2 Esc.
Rumania 25 Lei / Sweden 55 Øre / Switzerland 50 Cts. / Serbia 10 Dinar / Slovakia 3 Ks. / Spain 1.50 Pts. / Turkey 15 Kurus / Hungary 50 Fillér / Southern Styria, Eastern Europe 40 Pf.

America's military strategy
Lieutenant-General U. S. Grant, the man responsible for the first total war. SIGNAL tells you about him and the "Anaconda Plan" in this number

ON THE DEFENSIVE

There was little for *Signal* to cheer about in 1943–44 and consequently most of the time the magazine remained silent about the war. In marked contrast to this policy was the decision by Goebbels to publicize Stalingrad as a major but nonetheless indecisive defeat roughly three months after the capitulation of the German Sixth Army. The withdrawal from North Africa was not cited, although the ferocity of the Tunisian campaign itself was grudgingly admitted. The Sicilian campaign was eventually acknowledged, as was the overthrow of Mussolini and his subsequent escape from captivity with the help of Colonel Otto Skorzeny but the overwhelming defeat suffered at the hands of the Russians at Kursk was never mentioned. The defeat suffered in the Battle of the Atlantic was portrayed as a continuing triumph. The bombing missions over Germany and Western Europe were mentioned occasionally, but the readers of *Signal* were receiving reminders of this aspect of the war nightly in any event. Needless to say the concentration camps, genocide, the razing of the Warsaw ghetto and other similar atrocities were never mentioned.

The coverage *Signal* gave to the later stages of the war stand in marked contrast to their blanket coverage of its earlier and for the Reich, at least, happier period. Reportage was sporadic, increasingly blatant and false, whereas previously the accounts were given factually and stoically. It is surprising that no reference at all was made to Goebbels' demand for total war. The editorial staff of *Signal* was caught in a dilemma; either lie or remain silent about the war most of the time. Both policies were followed, but silence remained the keynote, and occasionally the clock was turned back on the causes of the war, the Allied war aims as interpreted by the Nazis, and the effect of victories of at least two years before. The effect on the readership of Hitler's Wartime Picture Magazine's refusing to report the events of the war must have been somber, and no doubt the large non-German population who bought the journal every two weeks must have been able to have read the story which *Signal* failed to tell between the lines: the story of the retreat and coming disaster facing the Third Reich.

FETCHING RATIONS

It is often a perilous journey for the man who fetches the rations, but he is sure of the gratitude of his comrades. Heavily laden, he advances, creeping and dashing, toward the various positions, often very close to the enemy lines. He brings rations, the much awaited mail, and the latest front newspaper to the troops

ALFRED GERIGK

The Soviets came...

...and three European countries lost their culture, their possessions and their existence

The most striking sight I saw during my journey through a country in which the Soviet system had just ceased to rule: Three men in prison garb, white trousers, white open shirts, pale yellowish faces surrounded by black, tousled beards, darkly glowing, fanatical eyes. They all three stood motionless in their narrow prison cell when the door was opened. They remained motionless as the first searching glance fell upon them. They remained motionless when we went towards them and when the first words were spoken to them. They remained motionless, expecting that they would now suffer the fate which they had themselves prepared for hundreds of people.

Three Cheka officials in the Central Prison at Riga, forgotten and abandoned when the Soviets began their wild flight with cars, heavily laden farm carts and vehicles of all kinds. Three Cheka officials, deserted by their Soviet friends, who had been caught attempting to flee, had been arrested and imprisoned. They used to wear the olive-green jacket with the blue tabs, the blue cap with the wide red band— the uniform of the Cheka which everywhere caused fear and trembling whenever it appeared in front of the door of a house, in a home, in an office or business house. They used to receive the lorries which, laden with prisoners, passed through the iron gates of the Ogpu prison on the Road of Liberty.

And now they were standing in their narrow cell, motionless, their eyes glowing like coals. Glowing with fanaticism? Or glowing in fearful expecta-

tion of a fate which, judging by their own past, they consider inevitable? Three Latvian officials of the Cheka— how did they come to wear the uniform with the blue tabs and the blue cap with the red band? Clever propaganda had been made there before the Soviets marched across the frontiers of the Baltic countries. "In the Soviet Union every ambitious and intelligent person has the best chances in the world." A catchword such as that was bound to attract anybody who had not got on in life.

But anybody who had once succumbed to this propaganda, anybody who was once in the service of the Soviets, could never extricate himself again. Each of them was given tasks during the first few days of the Soviet régime which made it impossible for him to turn back. Every single spy was surrounded by a network of spies which held him fast, which made every free action and every free word an impossibility.

Three officials of the Cheka among the thousands who had been unleashed on the Baltic countries, in order to protect and safeguard the system.

What was the system for which these officials of the Cheka spied, for which they imprisoned, abducted, tortured and shot people? The first reconnaissance journey into the Soviet Union, in which I took part, led to countries which for just one year had experienced the system under which more than 180 million people have been living for more than twenty years.

From Virballen we travelled through Lithuania and crossing the Njemenek we passed into Latvia. In Kaunas, Vilna, and in Riga, in tiny villages and country towns, we spoke with the people who as peasants, craftsmen and shopkeepers lived under Moscow's rule. We sought out the official authorities of the countries in order to present the same questions to them which we had asked each of these simple people: What was life under Soviet rule like?

What would have become of Europe if Bolshevism had achieved its principal aim, world revolution? What would have become of the people and of the age-old civilization of the continent which for centuries has been the source of everything which makes life worth living? "Signal's" reporter was one of the first journalists to become acquainted with the nature and the methods of the Soviets in the Baltic States. In his report he gives a sober answer to the question which has continually been asked for more than twenty years, but which has always been suppressed by the terrorism of those in power in Moscow: How did the Soviets bolshevize a country which fell into their hands?

How did the Soviets change these countries into territory under their rule? How did the bolshevization of the. Baltic countries take place?

The former official authorities had disappeared. Those who were quick enough fled abroad before the Soviets entered the country a year ago. Any of the prominent government officials of the pre-Bolshevist period who had remained were banished: "Instructions for a change of residence together with the granting of a pension" was the wording of the official formula. Many who could speak are among the 38,000 people carried off from Lithuania and the 40,000 carried off from Latvia. And anybody who occupied a prominent position under the Soviets naturally fled.

But if they were looked for, people could nevertheless be found who could provide information. A Lithuanian colonel who on the outbreak of war escaped from the Cheka prison. One of the leaders of a Latvian national

Professor Kirchenstein, *the President of the "Soviet Republic of Latvia." He was one of the most zealous champions of incorporation in the Soviet Union and was placed in office when the Bolshevists entered the Baltic countries. Like all the other prominent Soviets, he fled on the approach of the German troops*

society who had been in hiding for weeks. A ministerial director who had sunk from his prominent position to the lowest paid job and was pleased to be overlooked and forgotten in this obscurity. A clergyman who had been kept in hiding by his congregation. And so people were found who were in a position to make observations under the Bolshevist rule, to collect notes and decrees and were able to tell their experiences. And so people were found who were able to supplement and to make a complete picture of what the simple people in the villages and towns had told of their individual fates. And so gradually it was discovered how a country became Bolshevist when it had fallen into the hands of the Soviets.

The Soviets entered the Baltic countries, as it were, as friends. It is true

In front of the gigantic statue of the Moscow tyrant. *It was here that the population of the Baltic countries was forced to assemble for the "elections." In order to guard against painful surprises, the Soviets ordered that the voting was to take place in public*

that great pressure had been exercised in order to obtain in the first place permission to establish Soviet garrisons, in order to form legislative assemblies at the new elections, which requested in Moscow that they should be incorporated in the Soviet Union. But there were certain obligations towards the members of these legislative assemblies. And this was frontier territory where care was necessary. Propaganda had made sure that the peasants expected higher prices, the workers higher wages and improved working conditions. A number of people in military circles had even been persuaded that Soviet Russia would not violate the internal independence of these countries.

The Russians had entered the Baltic countries with the catchwords: "No abolition of private property! No disappropriation of the land! No intervention in internal affairs!" These were the catchwords accompanied by which the Soviet troops took over their garrisons in the Baltic countries. A month later sufficient progress had been made for politicians and deputies to be found who in speeches, in newspaper articles, and by the organization of demonstrations, urgently demanded incorporation in the Soviet Union. And so the process of bolshevization began.

The first stage: No change

The Baltic countries had become Soviet Republics. But it looked as though that would not make much difference to them. It is true that pictures of Stalin, Lenin, and Molotov now appeared and that the façades of public buildings were hung with gigantic Soviet flags. It is true that there were workers' demonstrations with huge placards. It is true that the Soviet Army now occupied barracks which had formerly been Lithuanian or Latvian. It is true that the generals of the Baltic countries were now obliged to take the oath of the Soviet Army, and the Soviet Star made its appearance on the caps of both officers and men. And it is true that the prominent statesmen were sent off to the Soviet Union "with a pension."

But other Lithuanians and Latvians took the place of the former politicians

The Head of the Ogpu in the Baltic countries, Novik. *He reigned in the Ogpu prison in the Street of Liberty in Riga. From his office issued the orders for arrest and transportation of which tens of thousands of Latvians were the victims. As the Soviets, however, had no confidence in a local Communist, Novik was provided with a supervisor from Moscow*
Photographs: D. V.

and statesmen. At the head of the Soviet Republic of Latvia was, for example, the famous Professor Kirchenstein, a biologist and specialist on vitamins, whose activity as a statesman resolved itself into lectures on proper alimentation. The churches continued

How it began: *Immediately after the arrival of the Soviet troops, demonstrations were organized in favour of the incorporation of the Baltic countries in the Soviet Union*

As yet without the Soviet Star. *At the orders of their Bolshevist commanders, the Latvian soldiers marched through the streets of Riga with the pictures of Woroshilov and Molotov to take the oath of allegiance to the Soviet Republic*

to exist. And the functionaries of the Communist Party declared full of sentiment: "Here live religious peoples whose feelings must be respected. They must come to discernment of their own accord." Latvian officials and Lithuanian officials still performed their duties although the ministries were now called People's Commissariats and although everybody who had played a part in the army, in the defence organizations or in politics had been removed from their official positions. The factories continued to work and were merely placed under State supervision. The workers' wages were increased.

It seemed as though the people could be quite reassured or even overjoyed at the change of government.

Second stage: Consolidation of power

Things went on thus for the first six or eight weeks. And then "mistakes" made by the Latvian or Lithuanian officials were discovered. It was time to replace the native pseudo-Communists by reliable men from Moscow. The taking over of the administration gave the Soviets a free hand.

The Commissariat for Home Affairs was rebuilt during this first stage as a Cheka building with interrogation cells and execution rooms. And then one of

the first terrorist decrees made its appearance: the introduction of the rouble currency. That meant a sudden decrease in income. An office girl until then had earned 250 lats. From now on she received 250 roubles, that is to say 25 marks according to the official rate of exchange. Her previous salary had the purchasing power of from 200 to 250 marks. Her new salary had a purchasing power of from 50 to 60 marks. The currency reform was accompanied by the first reforms in industrial and commercial life, in the work performed by the workers and employees. There was the case of a Latvian chocolate factory which received very strict instructions not to produce any more first class quality goods in future but to work according to the recipe of the Soviet sweet factories. Then began the urge for longer working hours, a continually repeated appeal to increase the number of hours voluntarily up to twelve.

The administrative apparatus and the military power were completely in the hands of the Soviets. It was still possible to speak more clearly.

Third stage: Nationalization and transportation

It began in the universities and schools. The universities were suddenly

given a second administrative apparatus; besides the body of professors and teachers there was now the party administration which, with its commissars and political instruction, thrust its way into every faculty, into every course, and into every laboratory. Universities and schools were given a new curriculum. New subjects: the history of Communism, the history of Marxism and so on. In the schools, however, things did not go off so easily. The Latvian and Lithuanian textbooks had become useless. There were no new textbooks as yet. And so the teachers had to give oral instruction with the help of Russian textbooks. And the educational programme was tremendous: "In five years every young Latvian and every young Lithuanian must have a central school education." It was easy to realize this project: a decree converted all the elementary schools into "incomplete central schools."

Autumn 1940: A decree was promulgated according to which all factories and all business houses with a certain turn-over were nationalized, the decree coming into force immediately.

But on the same morning, Soviet commissars appeared in the factories and business houses. An inventory was

SPACE
WITHOUT TERRORS

Just as the U-boats have introduced new forms of naval warfare, the tank armies have introduced new forms of fighting on land. Signal here relates the development of this form of fighting

Tanks were invented during the first World War. It was intended that they should do what the mass employment of infantry and artillery had failed to do, namely, break through the enemy's deep system of positions in such rapid fashion that the enemy had no time to bring up his reserves. The technical development of the new arm continued in the postwar period. Greater speed, increased range and heavier weapons and armament resulted in an improvement of its operative and tactical possibilities. Practical experience, of course, was lacking at first. The German tanks gathered this first experience in the Polish campaign. During the campaign against France tank divisions broke through the Maginot Line and pushed forward as far as Abbeville and later as far as the Spanish frontier. A new tank strategy had thus been born.

Even at that time Soviet military experts paid particular attention to the study of this new kind of operative warfare. Today we know that they adopted this method of employing tanks. But German military experts, specialists in mobile troops, did not rest but continued to develop the weapon which had been so successful. Every weakness was suppressed, the tanks were improved technically, their fire power was increased and their range of communication extended. Changes in organization were made, new battle formations were found, other methods of attack were planned.

The tank battles on the Eastern Front differ from and are on a much larger scale than other wars on land in consequence of the vast spaces. Areas as large as European States were often conquered in a few weeks. And yet such an area is only a battlefield. There grew up a new relation between space and mechanism. This does not mean that space has been conquered by mechanism but thanks to mechanization it has lost its terrors for the soldier.

← **A base is attacked.** *Like ships ploughing the sea, the tanks advance across the plain. The tactics of the tank attack are clearly visible from the perspective of the photograph and the tracks on the ground PK. Photograph: Front Correspondent E. Borchert †*

→ **The comrade of the tanks.** *A German tank grenadier on the Eastern Front. He has already two burning summers, two bitter winters and dozens of battles behind him PK. Photograph: Front Correspondent Jäger*

The Soviets came . . .

taken of the stocks of all factories and of all large business houses. These stocks were expropriated without compensation and the bank accounts of these firms were blocked. But the former owners are compelled to pay all debts and all taxes immediately. A second fear now comes for the moneyed classes in the Baltic countries. A wave of auctions at which, under the compulsion of the commissars, furniture and personal belongings are sold for a song in order to squeeze out money for the payment of taxes.

But the Soviets had prepared the way well. It is only the rich who have been expropriated, it is declared, only the large concerns. And as a lively unrest is making itself felt in the agricultural areas among the peasants who are used to owning their own property, a great flaming proclamation of extreme urgency is brought out just before the winter sowing: To till the soil is more important than ever before! Till the soil according to the official cultivation plan! Those who sow will harvest! Those who cultivate their fields well will themselves derive the benefit from them!

Fourth stage:
"The land belongs to the State"

The winter seed is in the ground, the winter has begun. The next step can now be taken.

A decree promulgating the expropriation of the land: All privately owned land is expropriated. All land belongs to the State. But every land-owner receives seventy-five acres of the land he previously owned and is responsible for its cultivation and administration. The remainder of the expropriated land will be distributed among those who owned none. Agricultural labourers without implements, and young farmers receive ten or twelve acres for cultivation and are given a cow and a horse. Hateful spectacles can be seen in the small Lithuanian villages where they are photographed for the propaganda of Moscow newspapers. A statue of Stalin is erected on the village square. Those who receive land are obliged to parade in a long procession. On their knees in front of the statue of Stalin they have to express their gratitude to the Soviet Union and to their "beloved chief Stalin."

It was at this time also that private ownership of shops, house ownership, and carrying on a trade as an independent craftsman were abolished.

The second wave of "nationalization" occurs during the winter. All businesses are expropriated down to the smallest grocers' shops. The owners? Some are installed as the administrators of their former concerns and others are allotted to other places of work.

The houses? That can easily be regulated by decree. Any house the floor area of which exceeds 215 square yards —that is about the size of a normal house for one family—is expropriated and becomes the property of the State. Without compensation, of course. The domiciliary rights of the individual? Every Soviet citizen in the newly acquired countries has a right to a living area of 10½ square yards. In the case of married couples the first two children have no extra claim to dwelling space. But the houses and rooms in only very few cases are built in conformity with this 10½ square yards limit. The solution is simple: if the distribution of the rooms is not in accordance with the decree, the tenant has to pay 50 % more rent for the space in excess of the regulation amount.

Crafts play an important part in these Baltic countries where industry has been built up only during the last 20 years. But independent workshops run by individual craftsmen are impossible for Bolshevism. Community workshops for craftsmen are installed which it is possible to join voluntarily. Working communities to which the instruments of one's craft, one's sewing-machine, for example, are handed over so that in future the worker receives a wage from the working community and uses his own tools of which he is no longer the owner.

Here and there voices are raised in criticism. Conversations are carried on in an undertone in offices and shops.

"Have you heard the latest? Wood is being sent here from the Ural Mountains for the saw-mills! Haven't we enough wood in our own country? And our own wood is being sent to Siberia!"

"That merely shows that you don't understand. That is plan economy."

"Have you seen the Moscow 'Pravda'? I mean the edition which is forbidden in Latvia. Our Latvian furniture is the latest attraction at the Moscow trade exhibition. Our furniture is being used as the latest models in the Soviet furniture industry."

The Soviets are already sufficiently firmly established to be able to combat these whispered conversations energetically. The transportation period begins. Lists have been drawn up during the first few months, lists of intellectuals, lists of people with property, lists of all those who have played a part in public life. For Latvia alone, a programme of transportation has been drawn up which includes 80,000 men. Lorries draw up in front of houses. Cheka officials appear in the apartments. At the stations, trucks are loaded with prisoners. Trains full of people being transported roll towards the east.

Fifth stage:
Compulsion to do things voluntarily

Everything has been prepared for the final introduction of the Soviet system. But there are still craftsmen who had not yet joined the work communities. There are still peasants who strive to farm what remains to them of their former land. For the Soviets it is time to end such independence. It is time to destroy the remnant of independence still remaining after the first months of the Soviet rule.

Craftsmen working on their own can do so only if material and machinery are available. And so material and machinery must be taken away from them. The State has all materials at its disposal. It is obvious that the available material is first allotted to the work communities. Independent craftsmen will be supplied if there is surplus material. The workshop must wait three or four months? Very regrettable —but why doesn't this craftsman's workshop join the work community? It would then receive material and regular wages. The master craftsman has no

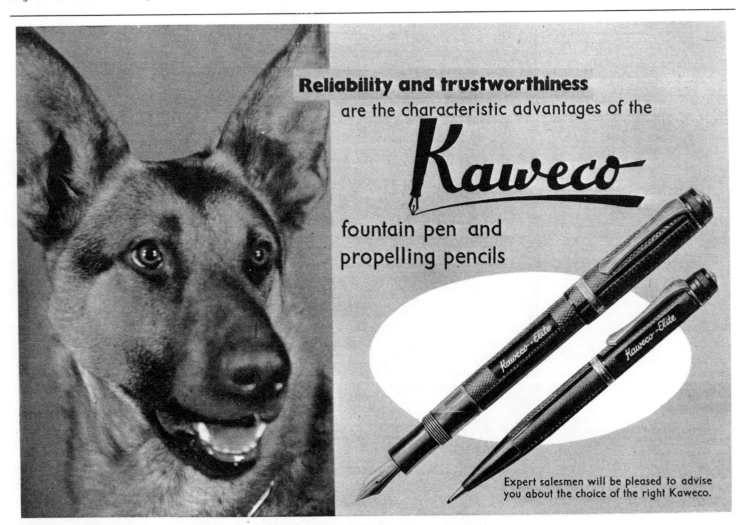

desire to become a workman paid by others for his work? Well then, he must just wait and pay taxes.

Taxation is one of the most important means of forcing the independent craftsmen into the work communities. People with an annual income of 2,000 roubles pay only 80 roubles in tax, that is to say, only 4 %. But people with an annual income of 24,000 roubles pay one third of their income in taxes, that is to say, 8,000 roubles and, beside that, 60 % of the remaining sum. Anybody with an income of 24,000 roubles therefore has practically nothing over for himself and his concern. What dressmaker under these conditions would not decide to hand over her own sewing-machine to the work community and then continue to work at this machine for wages?

In the country there are still farmsteads which have not joined the Kolchoze voluntarily, the farming communities to which all the land and farming equipment are given and for which the peasants then work for wages. But steps have already been taken to insure that these farmers will one day be compelled to give up their independence voluntarily. The people who have been given land have received lots of ten, twelve, fifteen or at most twenty-five acres. In order to be able to live, between 50 and 75 acres are required in the Baltic countries.

The soil does not produce sufficient to feed the family? Quite simple, you merely have to join the Kolchoze and surrender the land you own. Then you receive wages and are looked after, even if it is only badly.

But there are still those farmers who have been left 75 acres to farm. Can they be forced into the Kolchozes? Of course! It is forbidden to employ farm workers and also to leave land lying fallow. What are the unfortunate farmers of 75 acres to do? Their only way out leads them to the Kolchoze.

But there still are obstinate people who continue to resist. When they have experienced for a time what taxation and the surrender of a part of their produce is like, they too will yield. The taxes? The value of the land, cattle and implements is added together and the resulting figures showing the value of the property and the taxes to be paid make the brain swim. The compulsory surrender of produce? The State demands tributes in produce, in wool and in butter. The amount to be surrendered is calculated according to the size of the farm. The peasant has not sufficient cows and sufficient sheep in order to be able to supply the prescribed amount of butter and wool? Then he has to buy the butter and wool in the open market, for the State tributes must be paid.

That is the stage of compulsion to do things voluntarily. All the restaurants, all the cafés and all the places of entertainment were nationalized a long time ago. In the class-rooms of the schools notices hang on the walls. They are large sheets of paper covered with type which state that a certain pupil has behaved in a non-Communist manner, that he has neglected his duty towards the Youth Organization, and his parents tremble lest they should consequently be accused of insufficient Communist convictions. In the offices of the authorities and business houses even whispered conversation ceased a long time ago, and when two people now converse in the street, they are silent when a third person passes, for they cannot know whether he is not a spy.

The balance

The Soviet rule in the Baltic countries lasted almost exactly one year. What is the result for the population, for trade, for daily life, for the administration of the State? Look at the shop windows in the State-owned shops in Vilna. A suit costs 1,200 or 1,500 roubles? That is 120 or 150 marks. Ladies' stockings 30 roubles. That is to say 3 marks? Those prices cannot be regarded as too high.

But what do these prices mean for the population? As the national currency and the rouble had automatically been equalized, a trained workman in Vilna earns 350 roubles, that is to say only 35 marks. And a shorthand-typist had a monthly income of 400 roubles, that is to say 40 marks. When these facts are taken into consideration, the prices in the State-owned shops appear in a different light. Of what use was it to increase wages by 75 % as far as the figures went when, in consequence of the equalization of the rouble and the national currency, the workman and the employee were actually receiving only a fifth or a sixth of their income?

The people in these countries realized their impotence against the Soviet rule. But their despair made them seek remedies. In Lithuania, death battalions were formed of former soldiers, men of the Lithuanian National Defence, officers, non-commissioned-officers, workers and peasants who combined together in these death battalions in order to fight against the Soviet rule at the first sign of weakness. In Latvia young officers, students and workmen formed a partisan movement which equipped itself with rifles which were kept carefully hidden.

One year of Soviet rule. When it began there were people here and there in the Baltic countries who expected miracles, people who greeted the first Soviet troops on the march through the Street of Liberty in Kaunas or at the National Monument in Riga with great expectations. But after one year of Soviet rule, hatred, bitterness and the atmosphere of conspiracy filled the Baltic countries. There was not a workman who had not been hurt by criticism of his work. There was not a peasant who had not been robbed of his hopes of possessing the soil he tilled. There was not a family which was not full of anxiety for one of its members who had laid himself open to suspicion as the result of an incautious word.

And it was only the small band of those who had bound themselves to the Soviet system, who had succumbed to it and now had no way of escape, who fought with hopeless determination for the maintenance of Moscow's rule. Despised by their own countrymen, and isolated on the soil of their native country, they were lost, no longer even believing in what they had formerly imagined.

That is the balance after one year of bolshevization. But what is the balance like there where Bolshevism has spread and entrenched itself for twenty years, where people live cut off from the rest of the world and are not familiar with anything but a life of fear, misery and poverty and where they are in continual danger of losing their existence, their homes and their families.

Under the

Every movement in the open shows the enemy where to aim, and is at the same time intelligence for him. In modern war-fare good camouflage is a matter of life and death, for the rank and file, and half the way to victory for those leading them.

What is behind this mat,
the enemy will know soon enough, but then it is too late

Day and night
sharp eyes are watching everything that is going on in the enemy lines. Good camouflage, well adapted both in shape and colour to the country and the changes in the weather, renders it both possible and easier to carry out this task successfully

Well camouflaged himself the reconnaissance airman raises his camouflage cap a little

The sharp eye of his aerial camera renders the camouflage and dummies of the enemy useless. Flying with his camouflaged machine at a very great height, he brings back aerial photographs revealing the intentions and positions of the enemy

Relief of troops camouflaged

The actual moment when troops are being relieved is always accompanied by particular danger for them. There must then be particular care with the camouflage

A record in camouflage

The observer has crept up to within a stone's throw of the enemy position and is observing it. The photographer is as well camouflaged as the observer himself, and taking photographs at his side

German storm artillery has just forded the Bug and is climbing up the bank of the river held by the enemy. This new weapon, which is the result of the experien gained in the preceding campaigns, is especially suited for fighting against the Soviet armies. Moving on caterpillar tracks, it can cope w every type of terrain and can travel where even cyclists or infantry would sink. The modern quick firing gun of this accompanying a

s with direct fire, the "gun carriage" is so mobile that enemy artillery is not given the opportunity of finding the range. Dug-outs, field positions, and fortified houses are the chief targets selected by this itinerant gun which is rendered completely immune to infantry fire by its armour plate. When crossing rivers this weapon demonstrates an extraordinary "wading" capacity: the logs behind the turret are used as a kind of "wooden carpet" for the caterpillar tracks when they "churn" in the mud and slime

Photograph: PK. Huschke

The romance of war as in bygone days...

When we think of the up-to-date German machines of war, the endless columns of tanks and all the mechanized arms, it seems as though the spirit of the old troopers and the colourful life of the soldier have entirely ceased to exist. But life in the German

army is infinitely varied, and the magic, which it formerly possessed, still exists today in the stamping and neighing of horses, in the wild forward rush of a baggage column, where everything depends upon the efforts of man and beast. It is found in the hands and muscles of the soldiers who put their weight behind the wheels when the going is heavy, and also in the machine of the dispatch riders as they scorch along—and with it goes the varied and multi-coloured romance not only of the campfire but of the superhuman exertions of the advance. And it is also found in the external experiences which cause the heart of every soldier to beat faster, in the roll of the drum and the screeching of the wheels, the cold nights and the pale light of dawn. Photograph: PK. Bauer

A rubber boat with six men

They are in distress. Before baling out of their pla
taining a bright green solution, and with this liquid

was beyond help, they got their rubber lifeboat ready and threw it out. They carried with them a bottle con-
the water round their boat. It is visible to their comrades high up in the air who immediately send for help

Horses and tractors before shooting practice at the artillery training centre. The campaign on the Eastern Front has given the well-bred, well-treated horse an honourable position beside the well-constructed, well-treated engine

THE ISLAND

The story of an interrupted revolution

Since the outbreak of war, or at least since the summer of 1940, the British have been almost completely isolated on their island. Scarcely anybody can leave the country with the exception of the soldiers. Only few travellers arrive from abroad. Britain has lost contact with Europe. She finds herself abandoned to increasingly superior forces in the shape of her Ally. We in Europe can, therefore, ask what internal effects the war has had on the island. Are the British being influenced by new ideas? Are they pursuing a fresh path? SIGNAL does not give a premature answer to these questions. We describe the state of affairs as it really is

A few years after the first World War, a witty Dutchman published a book on England with the strange title: The English: are they human?" In it he describes the strange fact that there are two completely different kinds of Englishmen. In the opinion of this Dutchman, who has lived in England for many years, these two kinds of Englishmen have only very little to do with one another. It is quite easy to distinguish between them. The one kind, he says, pronounce the "h" at the beginning of words whilst the others leave it out. This external difference is far more than a question of dialect. Whether an Englishman says "home" or "'ome" is, on the contrary, a sure sign of caste comparable, shall we say, with an Indian's tattoo marks. What is known abroad about England, apart perhaps from the ports between Lisbon and Shanghai, concerns for the most part only those people who can say "home". Compared with the total number of Britishers, however, this. the author continues, is an astonishingly small class. It alone is of any account. The millions, on the other hand, who persist in saying "'ome" and "'unger" are the silent, the unknown and even the unexplored England. More unknown perhaps than any of the tribes in Darkest Africa. It is possible to have lived for decades in England, even in the very heart of London, and yet have learnt very little of the actual people who go to make up the British nation.

"Bomb socialism" of 1940

Let us concede that our Dutch authority exaggerates a little. In 1940 in any case the British themselves felt that a revolution was quietly taking place in their country. The people who say "home," "hunger" and "Hun" were suddenly facing the same dangers in the cellars together with those whose lips never uttered the treacherous "h". The United States observers in London were very enthusiastic at the time. They wired home in articles columns long that nothing short of a social revolution was taking place in England now that ladies in ermine coats had had longer conversations with the Cockneys in the East End than they had ever before had in their lives with taxi-drivers and railway porters. For the first time in history there existed something which might be called a British democracy. It was in the months following Dunkirk that "Punch" published a cartoon showing an English gentleman in evening dress with cape and tophat together with a transport worker in the crow's nest of a sinking ship. Both were doing their best not to make a mistake between the life-saving belt marked "For Gentlemen" and the other belt which was just marked "For Men."

It was the time when the first Churchill Cabinet including the Labour Party leaders had just been formed and a cartoon was published showing Ernest Bevin hurrying with rolled-up shirt-sleeves and grim, determined face from Transport House, where the offices of the trade unions are, to Whitehall, the seat of the Government. It was the time when everywhere in the British press and particularly in the periodicals with a large circulation, it was proclaimed that a new England was now being born. The symbolic "h", which invisibly but inexorably had divided the English into two very distinct classes, was to be abolished. The day seemed to have come when the upper classes, which had ruled England alone for so many centuries, were to retire and be replaced by new men, new ideas and a new social order. Churchill, who belongs to the family of the Dukes of Marlborough, the man who as an arch-Tory and the incorporation of the extreme Right Wing of the Conservative Party, had until then been the most insistent representative of the traditional British social structure based on classes, announced that he had now changed and intended to place himself at the head of this new England. The wealthy City, the financial centre of London with its ancient office buildings with creaking floors and soot-covered roofs, had been burnt down following a German air raid. Large numbers of Britishers said at that time: "Let us not grieve about it. This conflagration on the holy site of British plutocracy is the auto da fé in which the old England is being reduced to ashes."

The crisis of British self-confidence

A considerable time has passed since then The crisis of British self-confidence began during the months following Dunkirk. It was linked up with the general feeling that not only clear class distinctions were now intolerable but also above all the tradition which had placed all political power in England for centuries in the hands of just a few families. Nobody knew what was now to happen. All, however, seemed to know that something new, another England, was to come. It has not come. The pall of smoke over the City has dispersed. The ruins have remained. The new England, however, has not appeared.

This is the result at home of nearly four years of war which in consequence of the threat first from Germany, then from Japan and, finally from the United States has driven Britain's power to the verge of disaster—the inarticulate mass of the British people has no leaders who were capable of seizing the reins when they seemed to fall into their hands. The old class, however, from which the leaders used to come is spent. It has no new ideas and spiritually it belongs only to the past. That is England's tragedy. That is why England has not been able to seize the chance of an internal regeneration through this war. That is why the young people of Britain have continued to be excluded from the leading positions or at least from participation in the country's political and spiritual leadership.

Why do the young people stand aside?

On the outbreak of war, the present House of Commons had been in office for three years. Nearly four years have passed since then. Last year already, a man described as an active officer and former Labour Party candidate wrote in the "New Statesman" that the vast majority of young men and women had never taken part in an election. In 1943, he continued, there would scarcely be anybody under thirty years of age having even the loose connexion with a party consisting of having once voted for it. In two years' time the Labour Party would no longer mean anything for anybody under forty years of age and its leaders, even Morrison and Bevin, would then be cast by popular opinion into the same pot as the people going by the name of the "Government" or the "old clique."

These lines were written before the old tactician Churchill completely revealed his Janus head. It has meanwhile become clear that the descendant of the Dukes of Marlborough by no means intends to become the leader of a new England but that he made concessions in 1940 only in order to be able to defend the position of the old leading class more grimly and more skilfully. The Labour Party has no leaders but only tacticians of mediocrity. Even in England nobody any longer places his hopes on names such as Attlee, Morrison or Bevin. Cripps, who himself belongs to the plutocratic class but might have been dangerous for Churchill as he is a radical outsider, has finally faded into oblivion because he appealed to the deep Puritan instincts of the British. In home politics, Churchill immediately reversed his course as soon as his prosecution of the war had for the first time met with a certain success in the shape of the American landing in Africa and the Soviet Russian offensive. Fourteen days after the North African enterprise, Churchill re-formed his Cabinet, dismissed Cripps from the War Cabinet in a sarcastic letter and replaced him by Oliver Stanley, Lord Derby's son, a typical member of the old British plutocracy who had been appointed Minister of the Colonies. As soon as the first glimmer of hope appeared on the war horizon, the British reactionaries immediately resumed their old positions on the bridge of the British State vessel.

The "Spectator" wrote last year that somehow or other their internal strength had deserted the British. The national substance was undoubtedly different from that in 1940 when the Prime Minister spoke of Britain's best hour in words which accorded with the general feelings of conviction. Nobody could then assert that the British were then experiencing their best hour. The morbid cynicism of youth, the indolent indifference and selfishness of middle-age were a fatal clog on Britain's efforts for victory. Did the British only need to sit in armchairs, the periodical continued, and demand a concentrated air offensive against Germany in letters to the papers? It might be achieved, but it would be carried out by the flower of Britain's youth. What were they to expect when they flew through rain and snow into the cone of searchlights and the hail from the flak and were liable at any moment to be attacked by a Messerschmitt? The knowledge perhaps that they were guarding the lives of the masses packing the Albert Hall at a boxing contest whilst outside a thousand cars were parked whose owners laughed the petrol restrictions to scorn? Or for the extortioners who filled their bags with purchases on the black market and when condemned to prison had the option of a fine which they could pay ten times over? Did England want them, the periodical concluded, to fight for this?

Where are the ideas, where are the new men?

We have here quoted not one of the extreme views but a typical expression of the feeling of uncertainty and uneasiness prevailing in England since the élan of 1940 has passed away without any fundamental changes having taken place, without that new England having been born on which the masses placed their hopes. England is ripe for the revolution but has no revolutionaries.

The objection might be made that England perhaps does not want this revolution, perhaps she feels quite secure with this ruling upper class which holds not only the political power but also has control over two thirds of the British nation's capital as well as over nearly all the foreign investments made by England in the Empire and overseas. But there is no question of that. This upper class has allowed the British workman to live under the worst social conditions—with the possible exception of the South African mining areas—in the whole world. It has not even established a system of social insurance but—a cause for just indignation—has abandoned the sick and widows of the working class to private philanthropy. This naturally never sufficed although large donations oc-

German grenadiers ... their N.C.O. is a holder of the Knight's Cross PK. Photograph: Front Correspondent Knödler

The first man in the rank and file to be awarded the Knight's Cross

Hubert Brinkforth, a German lance-corporal, the son of a Wesphalian peasant, has been awarded the Knight's Cross to the Iron Cross by the Führer. On 27th May 1940, during the defensive fighting round Abbeville, Brinkforth, serving as No. 1 on an anti-tank gun in an advanced position, smashed the attack of a powerful British tank unit. He destroyed eleven tanks in 20 minutes, which, in spite of heavy firing, he allowed to approach within 100 yards before opening fire.

Photograph: Umbo

casionally made by individuals shed glory on the benefactor's name.

Not only the masses in England have again become dumb but also the young people. Their discontent goes far beyond the criticism always levelled by the young generation against the older generation in office. These young men are fighting just like their fathers fought during the first World War. They do not lack courage and they put forth every effort. But what for? They do not know. In any case, they cannot express it. At best they have a vague general feeling. At best they are the raw materials of a revolution which, however, does not take place for the very good reason that fertile ideas are lacking.

The substance of the nation has become hollow. Anybody who has come into contact with the young people of Oxford and Cambridge during the last decade before this war knows the symptoms of this process. The profound pessimism which has filled the young people of England since the end of the first World War is intimately connected with the wavering Puritanism of the English middle class. Business and superficial religion were the only interests of this middle class. It rejected both philosophical problems and artistic enjoyment. Even a profound thinker like Dean Inge pointed out long ago that not only thought but artistic feelings, two strong features of every human soul, did not exist for the middle class Englishman. Together with those bearing the great names of the aristocracy and controlling its vast wealth, this Puritan middle class carried England's imperialistic and capitalist rapacity over the whole world during the 19th century. The young people of England increasingly turned their backs upon this Puritan spirit, but there was nobody to give them new ideals and open new prospects for the fultilment of the human existence. When the "Spectator" expresses regret at the "morbid cynicism" of these young people, it is only criticizing the general state of affairs which has arisen in consequence of the paralysis which has seized upon the ruling class in Britain.

What fascination has Moscow for the British?

We can now understand why Bolshevist propaganda has penetrated into England almost unchecked to the horror of the ruling hundred families. It did actually advance into an empty space which the political leading classes in Britain were no longer able to fill. This is true of the young people of all classes as well as for the workers who, as is shown by a letter to the "Spectator," are working harder for supplies to Soviet Russia than for the defence of their own country. The writer of the letter to which we refer says that the working class in England feel themselves to be slaves and outcasts and consequently place more belief in remote Moscow than in their own leaders. Now, the British worker certainly has no leaning towards radicalism. He feels himself, however, to be in a political vacuum. That is why the proofs of the steadily increasing wartiredness are becoming more abundant.

There are many signs that the secret anxiety felt in England at this develop-

ment is growing. On that memorable Sunday, 22nd June 1941, Churchill expressly stated that he, formerly the bitterest hater of Bolshevism, would not unsay what he had formerly said about it. These words indicate the dilemma in which the upper class in Britain now finds itself. It sees that a war of ideas is raging with unimagined intensity over the whole world, but that it is unable to occupy any convincing position in this struggle. It is obliged to yield more and more ground to Bolshevist propaganda in Britain although at the same time it is defending its position of plutocratic power in which the people, whom it must, in spite of everything, win over for its own aims, in no way participates. It is to the young people, however, that it consequently has nothing to say and nothing to offer. England is isolated from Europe and its problems. England does not see that ideas are developing further among the peoples of Europe, that something completely new is growing up in Europe.

Compromises are not sufficient

British plutocracy has almost entirely reconquered its old position of power since the autumn of 1942. This is merely the consequence of the fact that the weak attempt of the Labour Party to bring about a social revolution in England by means of decrees and ordinances was doomed to failure. The plutocrats were skilful enough to avoid it. It is impossible to lay hands on them—they are like a chameleon. Their womenfolk are now wearing the uniform of some auxiliary corps or other. That is all. As far as the external aspect of society is concerned, the England of 1943 is no different from that of 1938 or that of 1902. The new social structure on which the Labourites had placed so many hopes got no further than half-way. It ended in a compromise. The art of compromise has been a feature of British statesmanship for centuries. Those times, however, are past. It is that very fact which is felt by Englishmen of all classes. They realize that things are going wrong, but they have only the old recipes at their disposal and they are no longer effective.

We now understand the deeper reasons why even the harmless plan proposed by Sir William Beveridge of a large-scale scheme of social insurance could be sabotaged. Beveridge's document containing 165,000 words was stifled at birth by a few transparent Parliamentary tricks employed by Kingsley Wood, the Chancellor of the Exchequer, and Sir John Anderson, Churchill's confidential adviser on questions of home policy in the War Cabinet. The reasons are more than obvious when the fact is recalled that 43 Members of the present House of Commons are directors and members of the boards of the big insurance companies and when the further fact is called to mind that about 50 peers sitting in the House of Lords are also members of the boards of these insurance companies. These English insurance companies have vast reserves of capital at their disposal because, as a state insurance does not exist, all the insurance transactions of a large and prosperous nation are in their hands. Like a second Don Quixote, Beveridge, riding in the saddle of his verbose reform plan, charged the impregnable walls of this stronghold of British finance. There was not even a fight. Be-

fore the white-haired and blameless knight knew what was happening, the drawbridge across which he had intended to enter the sanctuary of British plutocracy at a gallop, had already been raised. A solemn proclamation was made from the battlements that in principle everything desired by Sir William would be carried out. Only not now. Later on, later on. An unpleasant debate took place which the Prime Minister avoided by being ill. The victory of insurance capital, whose big shareholders are so powerful in the Government and the House of Commons, was already assured. All that has remained of the Beveridge Plan will result in a small and insignificant reform of British social legislation which will not in any way affect the power of the insurance companies capital. Bevin and Morrison provided the Parliamentary tactics of the Government with full cover much to the annoyance of the radical wing in the Labour Party. By so doing they have proved that they, too, long ago joined the ranks of those who pronounce "home" and "hunger" correctly.

The lack of a rising generation

That is why the British feel so uneasy. They see no way out. After the terrible failure of the government of old gentlemen surrounding Neville Chamberlain, Samuel Hoare and Sir John Simon, the members of the big family clan at England's head realized that in all probability the hour had come when they would have to retire. At this unique hour in England's history, however, no other leaders were available. The inarticulate mass, which cannot pronounce its "h's," moved stolidly like a gigantic and clumsy animal. The young people, however, succumbed to a hectic merriness, they not only affected no concern with the dark crisis through which their country was passing, but they also said so quite openly. The members of the wealthy aristocracy, which controls the House of Commons through the Conservative Party, gradually reoccupied their old posts because actually there was nobody to compete against them. They rubbed their eyes after the darkness of 1940 and to their astonishment they saw that nothing had altered. But they had not learnt anything in the meantime as is clearly proved by the strangulation of the Beveridge Plan. The British are placed in an equally difficult position by the phenomena of Bolshevism and Americanism. They feel both to be a menace and they are allied to both. They want to sacrifice Europe but save their own skins. In their heart of hearts they realize that the victory of their Allies would only set the seal on their own defeat and sow the seeds of a third World War. We are consequently right in regarding all these phenomena as a crisis of British self-confidence with which this country, which lives only on tradition, can no longer cope.

Have the British so far not had the advantage of being unproblematic? The result is today that they are incapable of spiritual rejuvenation. Was not the British self-irony an inestimable advantage giving them superiority? Today it undermines and disintegrates anything in the nature of constructive thought. That is why the masses are no longer under control as they used to be. That is the reason for the disinterestedness of the young people, who wish to live only in the present, and for the lack of flexibility among the old people,

who wish to live only in the past. That is the reason for the lack of confidence in the future which has become the chief characteristic of England in this war.

"When we return from our work with the Women's Auxiliary Corps, we slip into an evening gown and go to a dance," a young Englishwoman recently told a neutral acquaintance who spent a few days on the island. "We dance until we are exhausted," she said, "for that is the best way to avoid speaking and thinking. We don't want to think! What would be the use of it?" We would not dare to assert that the young people of England all share this young girl's opinion. There are certainly others. But her words reflect the abysmal hopelessness resulting from the lack of a great idea in England which would survive the war.

We, the Europeans, who are no less directly affected by the sufferings of this war than the British, sense a deeper meaning in this war which is our war of unification. We can already see our multifarious Continent advancing towards a social future as a community. That is our advantage over the people of the British Isles. They are remaining behind whilst we are striding forward.

Quick to help. *The engine had "coughed" during the night attack. Men belonging to the company of mechanics change it* PK.Photograph: War Correspondent Bülow

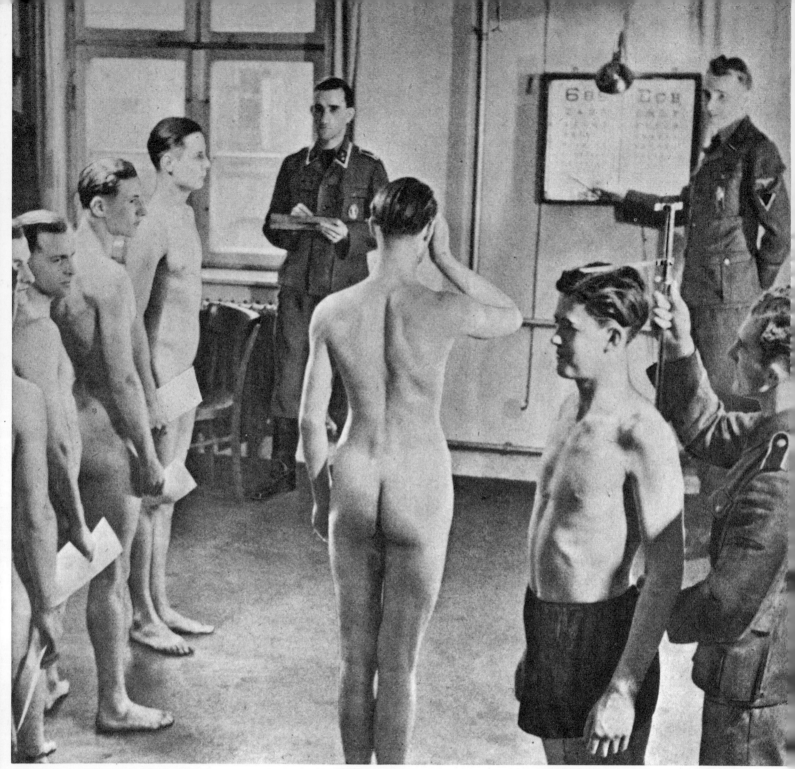

Fresh from the Labour Service and therefore physically fit and trained in the elements of soldiering, the soldiers of tomorrow present themselves for medical examination. "All these young fellows are physically fitter and mentally more alert than their counterparts in the first World War," is what an experienced old M. O. said to us   PK. Photograph: War Correspondent Huhmann

SOLDIERS OF TOMORROW...

In spring, summer, autumn and winter hundreds of thousands of recruits pour into the German Army training centres. In the following pages SIGNAL publishes a pictorial report on what they learn there and with what thoroughness they prepare themselves in a few months for the hard battles to come

Men of tomorrow

The pedagogical aim of the Adolf Hitler Schools

The new Germany has also created a new kind of school—the Adolf Hitler Schools. As is always the case with an innovation, wrong conceptions became current concerning this kind of school. During the last few decades quite a number of new educational methods and scholastic systems have made their appearance in various parts of the world. National Socialism naturally refuses to have anything to do more especially with those founded on a Marxist or Communist principle. The aim of the Adolf Hitler Schools is actually very simple. In contrast to the schools where only knowledge is taught, they aim at training high-grade individuals and characters from all classes of society. In the education and training of youth they strive towards a new creative balance between the individual as a personality and as a member of the national community. The age-old hostility between the generations is also by this means to find a new and fertile solution.

The Adolf Hitler Schools accept only pupils who are chosen according to the qualities of their physique, intelligence and character. Many a father able to send his son to one of these institutions perhaps had doubts beforehand whether the boy might not receive a one-sided training for definite professions such as a military career or one in the service of the State. His son, however, will himself be able to reassure his father on that account during his first holiday at home. For if a pupil has any particular talents, he encounters in these institutions the greatest willingness to foster them and do everything for their development. The instructors and teachers in the Adolf Hitler Schools have received special instructions to help their pupils most carefully in their search for the profession best suited to them. Particular gifts in all the spheres of human activity are too rare for the nation to lose any one of them. But how many clever people have not first reached their real calling in life after a long period of groping? Such unnecessary detours in the careers of talented young people, which constitute a loss for the nation as a whole, are avoided as far as possible when the school is enabled by the way in which it is organized and the wide variety of its activities to observe every germ of individual talent and carefully foster it.

A people needs gifted men, pioneers and people above the average in all the walks of life. In most cases, young people do not realize until relatively late the aptitudes they have for a particular profession. In the Adolf Hitler

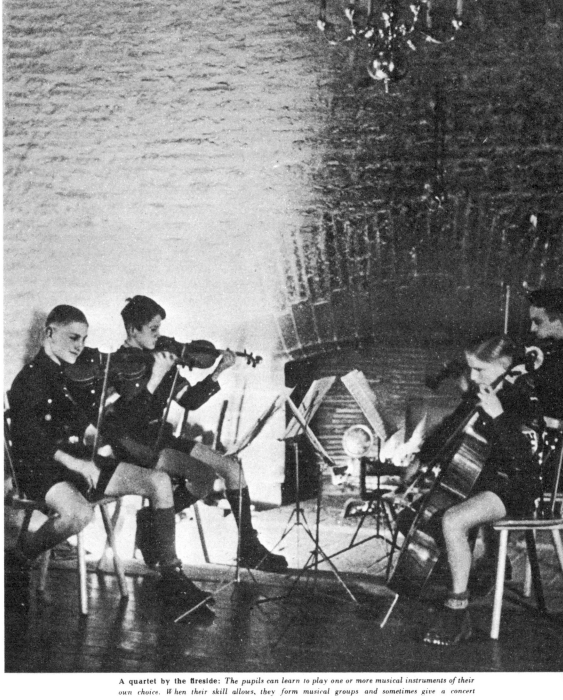

A quartet by the fireside: *The pupils can learn to play one or more musical instruments of their own choice. When their skill allows, they form musical groups and sometimes give a concert*

Schools, which not only have laboratories but also sport grounds at their disposal, everything is done in order to avoid the possibility of making mistakes later in the choice of a career. It is the aim of the Adolf Hitler Schools with the help of a determined and creative view of life to develop what is strongest and best in the hereditary character and personality of each individual to full maturity — for the benefit of the whole nation.

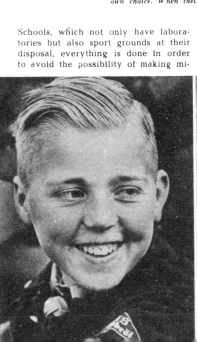

Three among many

ALMOST RAMMED! *A Hurricane has been attacked by a Messerschmitt. White smoke from the fuselage shows that the petrol tank has been hit. The Hurricane tries by curving obliquely to the right to escape from the enemy's field of fire. The manoeuvre brings it so close to the Messerschmitt that it is almost rammed. In the film the Hurricane appears so large that only a part of the wings is visible*

I FILM MY AIR VICTORIES

In most German fighters there is a built-in miniature camera which is coupled by electricity with the guns and works automatically. The film the pilot brings back with him provides documentary proof of the victories which can be recognized as such. SIGNAL here shows a few of the photographs taken during air combats over the Channel

← **How the miniature camera is built in.** *A window behind which the lens is situated has been fitted into the wing. The camera is introduced through a large aperture in the lower side of the wing and fixed in place. It is so built that it can photograph everything that comes within the range of fire of the weapons on board. The mechanism is set in motion simultaneously with the guns*

THE LEFT WING *has been hit. The photograph has recorded the moment of the impact and the detonation of the shell*

... and a second later. *Only the smoke of the explosion can be seen. Parts of the wing begin to trundle through the air*

1 **The fatal shell.** *Light specks under the fuselage show the path of two shells the upper one of which will hit the fuselage*

2 **Hit!** *The shell has hit the lower part of the Hurricane's fuselage. The petrol tank is on fire*

3 **The fire spreads.** *The fuselage is already enveloped in a sheet of flame*

4 **Another hit!** *The white streak on the right indicates the path of another shell which is destined to be another hit*

5 **The end.** *The fire has become so big that the entire middle section of the Hurricane is obscured by flames. In a few seconds the plane crashes* Photographs: Luftwaffe

A FALLACY

By Giselher Wirsing

In Britain they are talking about the division of Europe into "spheres of influence." What does this mean in reality? It is time people realized once and for all what these misleading slogans signify

In summer the British periodical "The New Statesman and Nation" published a letter written by a Czech emigrant living in London, which is so typical of the disillusion penetrating all circles, that it is worth while to quote it.

"You state plainly, that the 'murder of thousands of Polish officers' has not been the sole reason for the Polish-Soviet break; the matter going back to 1939. That means that the policy of the Polish Government has been antagonistic to the wishes of the Russian Government for two to three years. I refuse to believe that the Polish Government in London would have pursued such a policy without the knowledge, or assistance, if not connivance or encouragement by the British and American Governments. So the Polish-Russian break is in reality a British-Russian and American-Russian conflict.

This is the first conclusion. The second conclusion touches the fundamental point: Is Europe to be governed after this war by power-politics or the 'Atlantic Charter'? Your answer—referring to spheres of influence—is, by implication, power-politics. If so, then let the British, American and Russian Governments state it plainly in their broadcasts to the occupied countries. In tortured Europe men, women and children are fighting hard; harder—I think—than the British and Russian soldiers, because they fight under worse conditions. They fight bravely for freedom. The freedom they envisage is—to be free to choose their own Government. When they will be told that the only alternative is German or Russian, German or British-American domination, they will think twice before risking their lives daily.

To give an example: I am opposed to Communism, but if my people at home would choose to introduce a Communist system in Czechoslovakia, I would bow to their decision and accept it. But I would never accept a Communist system dominated by Russia, or under Russian pressure, or imposed by a Government under Russian control."

This Czech is speaking for hundreds of Europeans who have either become the vassals of the anti-European Powers, or have hoped for some form of "liberation." It is by no means the case that the leading political questions merely turn round in a circle. From month to month they become clearer and clearer. The current year that is drawing to its close has brought forward an exceptional justification for the European idea championed by Germany since the western campaign, which has been confirmed more emphatically than would have been possible for Germany alone by the discussions which arose between the British, Americans and Soviets in spring.

War for idylls

From the French Armistice until Katyn the war aims proclaimed by the British and the Americans were founded on the strange slogan, to which the intellectual situation in Europe gave much force, that war was being waged by the two oceanic powers for the re-establishment of the status quo. The people's right to self-government was to be the last word spoken on war aims by the Anglo-Americans. Numerous powers in Europe actually believed that a restoration of the conditions prior to 1939 or even prior to 1919 was possible and that the Anglo-Americans had entered the war for the sole purpose of executing such a re-establishment. In the background was the wish of many French, Italian, Greek, Swiss or Swedish citizens that the end of this war would mean a long, idyllic siesta for them. The Germans, however, repeated over and over again that such a wish to return to a status quo and the longing for idyllic oblivion was nothing but harmless provincialism when compared with the great revolutionary forces which had come forward. It was a pure illusion to imagine that open or secret wishes could be realized without taking into consideration the concrete factors ruling our age. In Germany it was said that this war demanded that the European Continent would have to agree to surrender many of the special rights grown dear to the heart of individual nations to the world powers harassing them from abroad if it wished to have the prospect of surviving this world struggle both as a whole and as separate nations. This was frequently described as nothing better than veiled imperialism. On one occasion, a neutral paper quoted Bismarck's words "Qui parle Europe a tort" without reflecting that words which were entirely justified in Bismarck's time have become meaningless today.

Power-politics or the Atlantic Charter

The Czech quoted in the opening paragraph is typical for the extent of the confusion and despair bound to overcome those Europeans who have thrown in their lot with the anti-European powers against Germany. They must recognize that in this gigantic conflict, the European powers are not aiming at just any old principles of self-government or the Atlantic Charter. They must recognize, on the contrary, that it is a question of pure power-politics, which neither now nor in the future will concern themselves with the fate of the small and smallest nations of Europe, which has revealed itself as the Anglo-American-Soviet war aim.

This has been made still clearer since the open conflict broke out between the Poles and the Soviets during 1943 after the Katyn affair. In Moscow Stalin has founded his own periodical—"War and the Working Class"—whose task it is to represent the power-political and world revolutionary claims of Sovietism to the Anglo-American allies. For the time being it demands the greater part of pre-war Poland, the Baltic States, considerable areas of Rumania as well as unlimited Soviet influence in Bulgaria and the other Slav States in the south. Simultaneously, it violently attacks Turkey and her Government, declaring that Turkish neutrality is advantageous to Germany alone and asks insidious questions which reveal clearly that the Soviet aspirations in the Dardanelles, expressed by Molotov in Berlin in November 1941, still hold good today.

Castles in the air

By now, the danger these Soviet power-politics would mean for the whole of Europe is comparatively clear to all the nations of Europe with the exception of the avowed hirelings of Moscow in certain neutral countries. Nevertheless, the illusions have not faded. People hoped that Britain and America would see to it that the Soviet claims would be duly restricted should the German opposition to this perpetual offensive from the east weaken. It is apparent that certain European circles still cherish this opinion and that the analysis of the situation formulated by the Czech emigrant quoted above is only slowly spreading. The reason is that these circles have not and never will have any deeper insight into the possibilities open to the British and Americans.

"Spheres of influence"

On the British side, the "Times" became the champion of a return to power-politics in 1943. We must recall that already in March 1943 it declared that the Soviets would have to be granted extensive spheres of influence in Europe. This thought was discussed in detail in the "Times" towards the end of August 1943. It would be useful to study these sentences once more. The "Times" wrote:

"There are, at any rate in theory, two alternative bases on which this collaboration might rest. The first would be an arrangement by which Russia and the Western Powers concert together broad measures of policy applicable in consultation with the smaller countries concerned, to Europe as a whole: such an arrangement would imply joint concern and joint responsibility, though not necessarily always joint execution of measures decided on. The second would be an arrangement by which Britain, or Britain and the U.S.A. accepted the main responsibility for the organisation of security in Western Europe, and Russia in Eastern Europe, each co-operating with the countries in its own sphere. but each renouncing any responsibility in the appointed sphere of the other. The arguments in favour of the first solution are exceedingly strong. Yet, by a baffling paradox, British and American action in the past few weeks has, perhaps unconsciously but not less decisively, pointed towards the second solution."

What the harmless expression "spheres of influence" means under these circumstances, was demonstrated by the Soviets in the Baltic countries in 1940. In Esthonia the major part of the intellectuals was either liquidated or deported to Siberia. Since Katyn we know what happened to the Poles. And all this happened at a time when the Soviet Union was at war with neither Esthonia, nor Latvia nor Poland. It is inconceivable what would happen now that, all passions have been stirred to their depths.

The Soviets will never be able to set up a "sphere of influence" in the countries of Eastern Europe as long as they are protected by German soldiers and German arms. If this were no longer the case, Sovietism would immediately spread over Central Europe and so render untenable both politically and above all militarily the West European sphere of influence claimed by the British. This is true for France, for the Iberian Peninsula and for the Scandinavian countries. How could the western sea powers hold their own against a Soviet land power stretching unopposed from Archangel to Central Europe and restrain the expansion of Soviet power in the remaining territories of Western Europe? British and American politicians have not yet been able to answer this question. They are not able to. And here is the fallacy which is still deluding many circles in Europa. Germany is continuing unwaveringly her gigantic battle of defence to prevent the appalling consequences that would be unavoidable should one become a victim to this fallacy.

REICHS-RUNDFUNK

European Service

To hear your Continental Programme in English from the European Service of the Reichsrundfunk, tune in to:

Calais I   on   582 kilocycles (514 metres)
Calais II   and on   995 kilocycles (301.6 metres)

In addition, after 8 p. m. German Summer Time (or British Extra Summer Time) the following shortwave station can be heard:

DXM   on 7270 kilocycles (41.27 metres)

News bulletins are broadcast at the following times (all German Summer Time or British Extra Summer Time):

6:30 a. m., 1:30 p. m., 2:30 p. m., 5:30 p. m., 6:30 p. m.
8:30 p. m., 9:30 p. m., 10:30 p. m., 11:30 p. m., 12:15 a. m.

William Joyce (otherwise known as Lord Haw-Haw) broadcasts daily following the news at 10:30 p. m. and 1:30 p. m.

In addition to the standard stations and wavelengths given above, the following stations are employed at various times of the day:

Deutschlandsender	on 191 kilocycles (1571 metres) at 6:30 a. m.
Luxemburg	on 232 kilocycles (1293 metres) at 6:30 a. m. 1:30 p. m., 2:30 p. m., 5:30 p. m., 8:30 p. m., 9:30 p. m. and 10:30 p. m.
Friesland	on 160 kilocycles (1875 metres) at 6:30 a. m. 7:30 a. m., 1:30 p. m., 2:30 p. m., 5:30 p. m., 6:30 p. m., 7:30 p. m., 8:30 p. m., 9:30 p. m.
Bremen	on 758 kilocycles (396 metres) at 6:30 a. m. 7:30 a. m., 1:30 p. m., 2:30 p. m., 5:30 p. m., 6:30 p. m., 7:30 p. m., 8:30 p. m., 9:30 p. m.
Breslau	on 950 kilocycles (316 metres) and
Cologne	on 658 kilocycles (456 metres) at 10:30 p. m. 11:30 p. m., and 12:15 a. m.

Finally the following shortwave stations are employed in addition:

DXJ	on 7240 kilocycles (41.44 metres) at 5:30 p. m. and 6:30 p. m.
DXZ	on 9570 kilocycles (31.35 metres) at 7:30 p. m. and 8:30 p. m.
DXT	on 15230 kilocycles (19.70 metres) at 1:30 p. m.
DJL	on 15110 kilocycles (19.85 metres) at 2:30 p. m.

Special feature programmes are broadcast at 7:30 a. m., 3:30 p. m., 4:30 p. m., 7:30 p. m. and 8:30 p. m.

The German War Communiqué is regularly read at dictation speed every day at 5:45 p. m.

Deutschlandsender

on 1571 metres or 191 kilocycles

Daily (with the exception of Sundays)

	17.15—18.30	Late afternoon concert with concert music of four centuries.
Sunday:	20.15—21.00	Musical treasures.
Monday:	20.15—21.00	Concert with well-known soloists arranged by Professor Michael Raucheisen, who also takes part.
Wednesday:	20.15—21.00	Contemporary music.
Thursday:	20.15—21.00	Open-air music.
Friday:	21.00—22.00	Musical plays or short histories of music with musical illustrations.

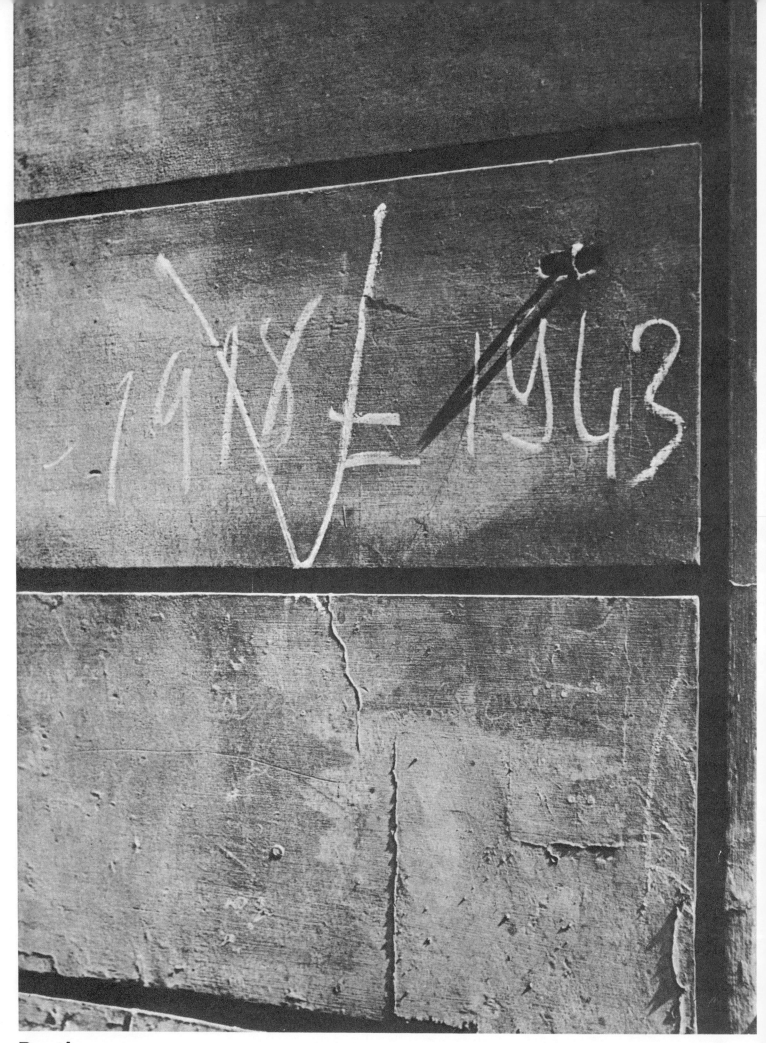

By the way . . .

18 = 43 was the catchword with which the Anglo-Americans prophesied the collapse of Germany and the end of Europe in 1943. The year 1943 is over and the slogan has lost its magic: 43 did not equal 18. Europe is now expectantly awaiting the magic word for the year 1944

HEIMKEHR

PAULA WESSELY · PETER PETERSEN · ATTILA HÖRBIGER

Ruth Hellberg, Berta Drews, Elsa Wagner, Gerhild Weber
Carl Raddatz, Werner Fütterer, Otto Wernicke

Scenario: Gerhard Menzel · Music: Willy Schmidt-Gentner

Producer: Erich von Neusser
Director: Gustav Ucicky

A Gustav Ucicky film — the Vienna film — a Ufa production

Deported and banished? According to Stalin, Germany has carried off millions of former Soviet citizens into slavery. Here are three of the "slaves!" They are working girls from the east visiting the Potsdam palace on a Sunday outing. They have already adopted European fashions and have quickly learnt the West European style of hairdressing

IN GERMANY...

They experience
Germany...

On principle, the eastern workers in Germany receive exactly the same rations as the German workers who share with them like brothers. The German wartime rations, especially when they are tastefully cooked in community canteens, are more plentiful than what many of them. ever received at home. Of course, all the girls do not look as smart as the three girls on the last page. The badge they wear has already become a badge of honour, for the workers from the east have proved how careful and willing they are under proper leadership

This canteen dining-room in which the eastern workers take their midday and evening meals corresponds to an ideal perhaps propagated by the Soviets but never realized

During a break in their work, these girls from the east were photographed in the yard belonging to a big munition factory. The anxiety customary in the faces of the Soviets in the east has given place to carefree gaiety. When busy in the big workshops the girls like to sing their native songs

TUNIS: PERSONAGES AND COMBATS

By the mere invasion of French Morocco and Algeria the United Nations had expected to gain control over North Africa and thus secure a convenient base for an incursion into the European defensive front. They had counted upon the fact that France and her colonies were weakened and disrupted by incapable politicians and treasonable generals, calculating that victories and conquests, of which they were so urgently in need, could easily be obtained. The Axis Powers, however, succeeded by their resolute counter-action in establishing a bridgehead in Tunis. Thereby they not only brought confusion into General Eisenhower's plans of advance and operation, but at the same time they formed an advance bastion for the protection of the entire northern coast of the Mediterranean. It is of great importance that all of Europe should recognize the significance of the fierce combats raging in the North African desert under a blazing sun or in the inaccessible mountains of Western Tunis. PK. War Correspondent B. Wundshammer, who spent several weeks on the Tunisian front, relates his impressions at this newest theatre of war in a series of articles

The officer commanding the Axis forces in Tunisia, Colonel General von Arnim (on the left) at the officers' observation post of a German division in Central Tunisia. On the right the division commander

The Leadership

When in the middle of November 1942 German parachutists and airborne troops occupied the harbours and bays of Bizerta, Tunis, Sousse, Sfax and Gabès, the Anglo-American tank forces were almost at the gates of those towns. Masterly leadership most effectively employed the small but powerfully equipped Axis units and within a few days shattered the enemy's hopes. At Tebourba, a few miles west of Tunis, an attack carried out by a few German tanks under the personal command of General Fischer, a wearer of the Oak Leaves, who was killed on the Tunisian front on 1st February 1943, placed the initiative to a considerable extent in the hands of the Germans. Dive-bomber units, fast bombers and dashing fighter squadrons effectively supported the operations of the ground troops. Reinforcements flowed into the country across the Straits of Tunis. The system of employing small units with high firing power distributed apparently at random, which the enemy did not discover until too late, successfully made up for the enemy's superiority in numbers and material.

The armoured wireless car of Colonel General von Arnim during a operations

In front of the palace of the Bey of Tunis: The representatives of the Axis Powers are received with cheers and clapping of hands in front of the palace in Hammam-Lif

His Royal Highness Sidi Mohammed El Moncef Pasha, Bey of Tunis, thanks the people from the window of his palace for their ovations upon the occasion of the festival Aid el Kebir

↑ *The French Resident-General, Admiral Estava, extends to His Royal Highness the sincere wishes of Marshal Pétain for the welfare of the Tunisian people*

Colonel General von Arnim, Commander-in-Chief of the Axis forces in Tunisia, is most heartily welcomed ↓ *by His Royal Highness, the Bey*

Reception in the Palace of His Royal Highness

Upon the occasion of the great Arab Festival Aid el Kebir, His Royal Highness Sidi Mohammed El Moncef Pasha, Bey of Tunis, gave a reception to the representatives of the Axis Powers in his winter palace at Hamman Lif. The Commander-in-Chief of the Axis forces in Tunis, Colonel General von Arnim, was welcomed upon his arrival by the Arab population with cheers. The Bey of Tunis as well as the Commander-in-Chief manifested most heartily their determination to intensify the collaboration of the Axis Powers and the Tunisian population. We quote from the speech of His Royal Highness the following sentences: "... I express my gratitude for the protection extended by Germany and Italy to the population of Tunisia against the Anglo-American aggression. All Tunisia is firmly convinced that the Axis Powers will soon succeed in restoring order and peace throughout the country. I gratefully acknowledge the exemplary and disciplined conduct of the German-Italian troops who have won the full sympathy and admiration of the Tunisian people. Our hearts, as well as the hearts of the entire Arab world are with your brave soldiers in this struggle."

Steel-Cylinder Valves

Straight-way valves and angle valves

for all kinds of compressed and liquefied gases

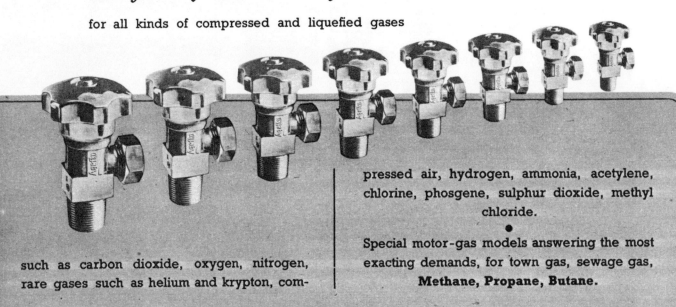

One of the scenes of terror during the 30 minute air-raid on the open town of Tunis described in the following pages: buried alive! *This woman was buried under the ruins of her house during a bomb attack and was only set free, half demented, after hours of hard work by members of the "Défense Passive" who are here seen taking her to the nearest first aid station*

↑ **Handkerchiefs as a protection against smoke.** *The bomb set fire to the ruins of the house. There was no time to give proper gas masks to the members of the air raid precautions unit who had hurried to the scene. The victims required immediate help*

Destroyed homes. *Shrill cries of terror and the half smothered sobbing of children make themselves heard among the ruins and spur* ↓ *the helpers on to the greatest speed*

TUNIS: II.

"FLYING FORTRESSES"
OVER THE OPEN TOWN

SIGNAL's collaborator, War Correspondent Benno Wundshammer, was in Tunis during an American air-raid. We here publish his illustrated report on the scenes of terror he witnessed in the course of half an hour

The plates and glasses on the table shake and rattle, fluttering candles throw a flickering light on pale faces. The tiny "boîte" trembles as though an earthquake were taking place—it is the thunder of the guns throwing an anti-aircraft barrage round the bombed town of Tunis. The people scarcely speak and continually suppressing the fear stupefying them, they eat their thin soup. The 'patronne' in the background carefully wraps her baby up in silk quilts and places the whimpering bundle on the counter among piles of plates and apéritif bottles. Now and again a dull explosion shakes the earth and while all the spoons, apparently petrified, stand in the air, we listen to the rumbling cascade of falling ruins.

Tunis is being bombed! They are bombing the residential quarters of a town whose population scarcely realizes as yet that there is a war. For the most part the young couples here are of modest circumstances. They are eating their usual supper of hors d'oeuvres and white bread and trying to make out that everything is the same as it used to be. The double-breasted,

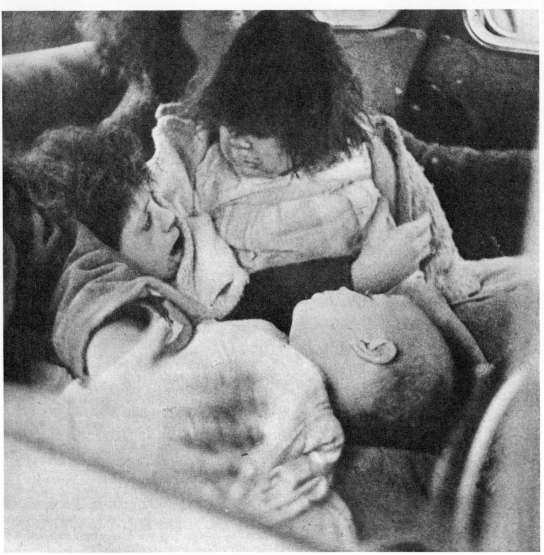
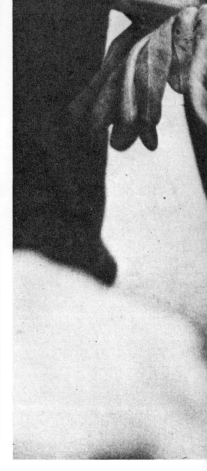

Military targets for "Flying Fortresses." Three injured children being taken to hospital. The one-year-old boy in the foreground has Arab parents. the girl on the left is the daughter of Italian settlers. the third is the child of a French widow

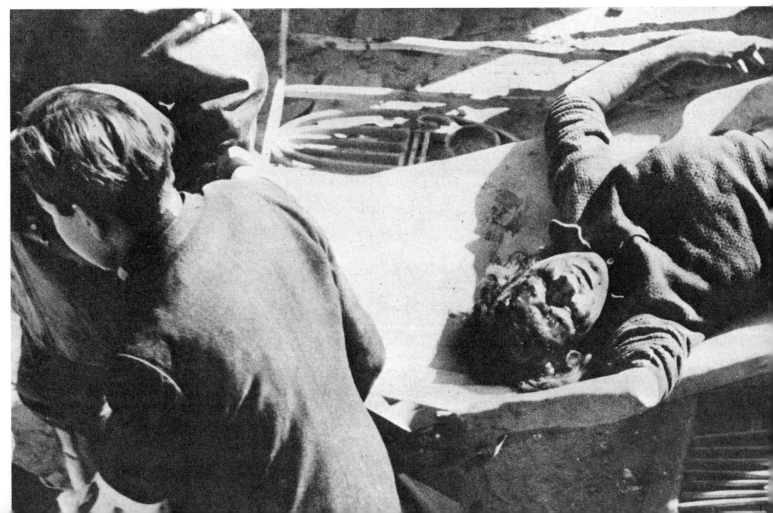

"Je les ai vues tomber!" Stammering and half mad with terror, the rescued woman tries to relate her experiences to her helpers: "I saw them clearly . . . the whistle of the bombs was horrible . . . the cupboard fell on top of me . . . help, help! . . . the women and children are being bombed! It's unheard of . . . Where is my daughter? . . . I want my daughter! Drive them away, ces salauds!"

broad-shouldered suits of the young men and the expectant lipstick on quivering mouths make me feel strangely sad. These pale faces, the steadfastness of these eyes and this attitude in face of death, which is raging outside the rattling windows, is a moving accusation harder to endure than the sight of dismembered soldiers on the battlefield.

The sirens begin their customary wailing at 5 a. m. I jump into my clothes and whilst I am tying up my shoes, the house becomes full of noise as the people living in it crowd on to the landing. The air is icy as it comes in from the street. The pale moonlight illuminates the muffled figures hurrying to take cover. Scarcely a word is spoken. Like a silent procession of strange nocturnal spectres, the terrified people stream to the old Jewish cemetery the only open space in this part of the town. Most of them have thrown blankets and cloths over their head. In this light they almost look like the Arabs who come galloping up out of their parts of the town in dazzling white burnouses and disappear among the groves of cactuses in the direction of the trench shelters.

The wide expanse of the cemetery is full of excited voices which penetrate

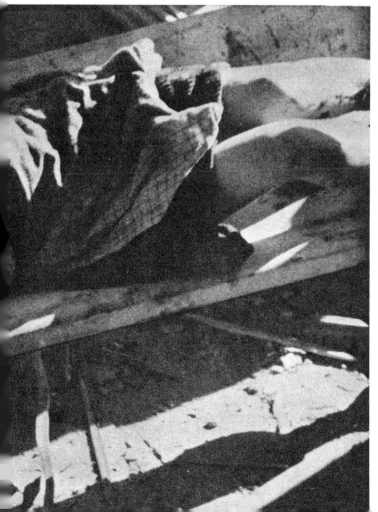

Killed in her kitchen! *The heavy bombs fell shortly before midday when most of the women were at home. This housewife was killed by bomb splinters in her kitchen just as she was about to serve her husband's soup*

the air as though all taking part in the same conversation. In the narrow streets behind us echoes the long drawn out call of the anti-aircraft wardens: "La lumière! La lumière!" A thin drone causes every noise to die down the darkness is shattered by the reverberating explosions of the heavy flak and the booming detonations of big calibre bombs. Flashes of fire quiver in the sky; a blood-red rain of sparks rises from the chalky freestone houses. The wind forces the glow down and its reflection changes the tops of the palms into jagged, coppery dusting whisks.

This time we are not hit by the bombs. When an hour later we return home tired in the dim light of dawn, a little girl tells us amidst her tears that her little kitten has been killed by a splinter from a bomb. ". . . He had yellow patches and a white one on his chest.". . . The losses in the Arab quarters of the town were heavy and far into the morning the ambulances were driving through the terrified city.

Towards midday I sauntered across the Avenue de France, one of the main streets in the European part of the town, in order to make a few small purchases. The bright sunshine lit up the coloured clothing of the native population. The violet blossoms of the bougainvillea hedges awakened in me a longing for spring, the sea and a

➡

swim. Queues of waiting people stand outside the tobacconists' and bakers shops. The trams are crammed full and people are standing on the footboards. It is the time when people do their shopping and the stream of the customers in the shops is unbroken. The hum of the streets is suddenly shattered by the roar of a heavy battery. Just for a few moments the flood of life seems to stand still. The increasing fire of the flak guns breaks the momentary silence. I look upwards and high in the silky blue sky I see a shimmering white path marked by exploding shells which is drawing near to us and running exactly parallel to the avenue.

Fourteen Flying Fortresses are approaching! It isn't possible! Everything happens very quickly. Panic-stricken, the people rush across the street and the houses swallow up the yelling masses. Driverless donkey-carts zigzag and sway between parked motor vehicles and out of an overturned cart a bright-red stream of oranges flows across the causeway. The droning of the engines has become stronger, the thunder of the artillery has increased to a hurricane And then the horrible fluttering of falling bombs begins. They are coming down with a hollow wail. Suddenly —I don't know how—I am lying in the shallow gutter between the causeway and the pavement and press my head down against the hard stone as closely as I can. The bombs are still howling, they take an eternity to drop and every one of them seems to strike you in your very heart The overwhelming primeval force of the detonations then wipes out all feeling. The skyscrapers shiver and shake under the concussion, a tinkling rain of splintered glass smothers us. The façades of houses collapse with a dull crash. There is a moment's pause.

As I get up in order to look for better cover, I catch sight of five young soldiers next to me who have all taken cover precisely as they learnt in their period of training—the barrel of their rifle is resting on the lower part of their bent left arm. I make a short dash forward followed by the clatter of the young soldiers hobnailed boots.

Again there comes the whine of a bomb! I just have time to make a dash for the corner of a house so that I have two ways of escape at the last moment. I choose the right side and as I leap, I still hear the hobnailed boots of the soldiers behind me. Then the bomb explodes. About 50 yards behind us an apartment house has collapsed like a castle of sand. A chalky cloud of dust billows towards us whilst the moaning of many people and the suppressed crying of children cut us to the heart. We race to the ruins As the bombers fly westwards and the guns become silent, we begin the sad work of rescue. It is only women and children that we dig out of the débris with our bare hands. Escaping gas threatens to suffocate us. Most of the victims are dead and on the chalk-covered faces of the children the red gashes of their wounds utter a bloody protest.

Refugees! Endless streams of the inhabitants of Tunis now without a roof over their heads leave their ruined homes in order to seek shelter in the country

Supplies for Tunis. *Assault guns and tanks, ammunition and rations are taken on board and disappear into the vast hold of the Italian freighter. Several Mediterranean harbours serve as Axis supply bases for North Africa* PK. *Photographs : Front Correspondent Feuchtne*

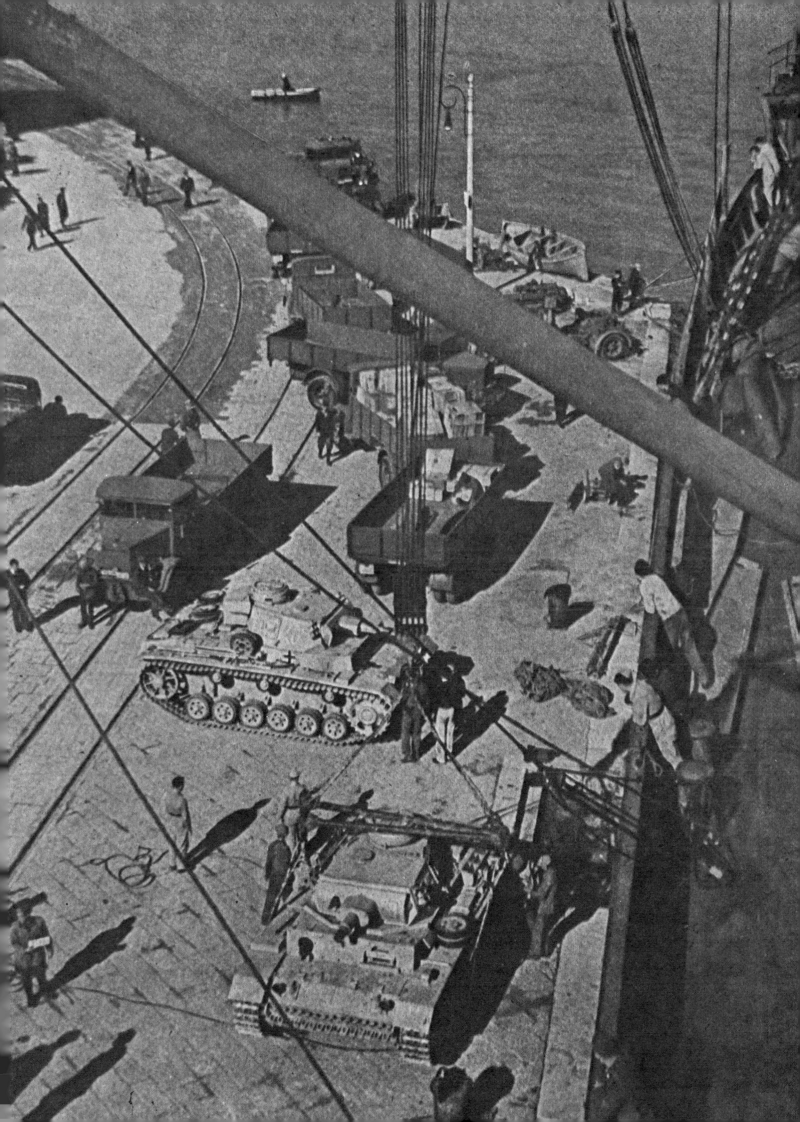

Through clouds of water and sand

Through the foaming spray of the wave breaking over the bows of the troopships, through the dust of the African desert sand rising round the armoured reconnaissance car ... two photographs of the way which lead General Rommel's mobile troops to victory in Africa. Photographs : Mahlo and Schultz

His first flight in Africa

An American airman tells his story

PK. Photographs: War Correspondens Friedrich, Wagner

Dragging his parachute along behind him, the shot down American flying officer approaches with his hands raised in surrender. He is eager to talk, a natural reaction after the mental strain of the air engagement and being shot down. The American lieutenant says that he is 24 years of age, a native of Philadelphia and had volunteered for service in Africa. The journey had been deuced unpleasant. His ship had made long detours and had finally sailed close in along the coast of Africa being menaced all the time by U-boats. At long last he had reached the front but had been brought down on his very first flight . . .

A German war correspondent in Africa photographs an American bomber as it crashes some distance away on the horizon. The cloud caused by the impact becomes visible first and then . . .

. . . there is an explosion followed by a dense black cloud which rises steeply into the air and—picture below— slowly disperses. Another front correspondent, however. spots the American pilot descending by parachute

A little later the American met his vanquisher, a sergeant-major who has been awarded the Knight's Insignia to the Iron Cross. Their encounter took place at an altitude of 18,000 feet. The American lieutenant admits that he was extremely surprised to find himself suddenly attacked by a German machine in spite of the security provided him by the large bomber unit in which he was flying. He had then tried all the usual tricks in order to shake of his antagonist who had nevertheless forced him to go down to 3,000 feet and scored many direct hits on his plane so that finally he had no other alternative but to bale out . . . The American was quite obviously pleased to have escaped so lightly. His machine (picture below) is a complete wreck

THE LAST LANDING

A number of Bristol-Beauforts were brought down during a combined American and British night air-raid on the open city of Tunis. Flak gunners rescued the crew of a plane which crashed near them and gave the wounded first aid. The observer of the crew was killed. In his pocket was a letter from his mother wishing him "happy landings." The survivors made the following statements.

→

The Beaufort crashed into the water in the immediate vicinity of this light flak position. The men. who only just before had been operating the gun, rescued the enemy they had brought down

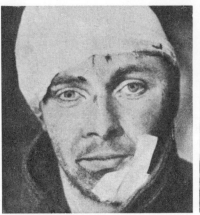

Pilot John Tayler Seddon, 36 Darley Grove, Farnworth, Lancashire: "The first shells from the flak set the left engine on fire, a splinter had killed the observer next to me. The plane came down on to the water in a glide. We were near the shore. German soldiers came in answer to my shouts for help"

Aeroplane mechanic John Cheeseman, Abchaster, Durham: "I was seated in the rear turret and when the plane hit the water, I broke my collar bone. I immediately lost consciousness. My pilot held me above water until the Germans rescued us. When I came to, I found myself in a room where two German flak soldiers were covering me up with blankets"

Fighter Lieutenant Harry Joseph Murphy. Deroit, Michigan, U.S.A.: "German Messerschmitt planes brought me down at Shousse. My twinbodied "Lightning" burned out. What has made the deepest impression on me? I experienced my first attack by Focke-Wulff 190's over St Omer in France on 2nd June 1942. Nine machines in my squadron were brought down"

Augus Davar Henderson, 63 Clifton Road, Toronto, Canada, fighter pilot: "I was escorting British bombers. Whilst I was sweeping the domeshaped roofs of the Arab village with my guns, a bullet hit my radiator. I made a forced landing and crawled into a water hole. When the Germans came, I said: "Kamerad." They only answered: "Come."

←

Frank Carbert, Grime Torpe, England, wireless operator of the brought down Beaufort plane: "When our plane came down, it remained afloat for a short time. The inflatable boat was not air-tight. We swam to shore. Our wounds were dressed in a flak dugout. The German soldiers lent us training suits and blankets. A lance corporal offered me some wine. We chatted together and when I told him I had been over Cologne, he answered: "My house was destroyed during an English air-raid"

The crumpled inflatable boat on the shore at Tunis, where attacking enemy bombers meet their end every day

"Flame throwers advance"

An enemy dug-out attempts to hold up the German advance by offering desperate resistance. But taking advantage of every undulation the flame thrower immediately stalks forward in the direction of the enemy. One jet of flame follows the other, black clouds of smoke obscure the view. The dug-out's battery has been silenced, the German advance can continue

Photograph F.K. Weber

An American Boston destroyer has crashed in flames, its engines roaring, after being hit

THE AMERICANS IN TUNISIA

American prisoners are assembled after an engagement
PK. Photographs:
Front Correspondent Dr Feitl

1. **Where they are needed:** *Soldiers, weapons and munitions hurtle down. Their work is to disorganize, to reconnoitre and to take prisoners*

ASSAULT TROOPS FROM THE AIR

The fighting in Sicily had brought both friend and foe face to face with new situations demanding fresh tactics to meet them. The German parachutists, for example, who have proved their worth on many theatres of war, thus carried out tasks previously reserved for the infantry such as assault troop engagements and offensive reconnaissance

2. **Landing under the enemy's nose:** *The parachutists land as thick as on the drill-ground. They must be ready to fire quicker than the watchful enemy*

3. **On the enemy reinforcement route:** *Parachutists attack. All according to the nature of the resistance, they can draw important conclusions as to the plans of the enemy*

4. **For their own air force:** *Points reached and made free are marked. When this is done, the shock-troops dropped down from the air must fight their way back on foot*

5. **After breaking through to their own lines:** *Parachutists return. They have succeeded in carrying out their orders and have brought in Americans as prisoners*

Shock-troops descend from the air: *A beautiful jump. The parachutes glide down like a huge bunch of balloons*

1 *The crew of the submarine have left the storms and dangers of the Atlantic behind them after weeks of successful hunting; witness the 9 victory pennons. Almost every man is on deck waving to comrades attached to the coastal defence while the signaller replies to the welcome from the signal station. A big protecting craft (right) took the U-boat under its wing far out at sea and is now escorting it into port*

AT A SUBMARINE
base on the Atlantic

In the following eight chapters of his pictorial report PK. War Correspondent Hanns Hubmann describes the return of a German submarine to its base on the Atlantic, the short weeks of relaxation for the crew and of repairs for the vessel and the new departure for active service

← **Active service in the latitude of Cape Town**

PK. Photograph: War Correspondent Lieutenant Weiss

2 *The crew has come up on deck and is touching itself up for the return to civilization. Caps are set as smartly as possible on the wild manes of hair—the cocade exactly in line with the nose—and the beards, the pride of the homecomers, are given a last twirl*

3 *Slowly the U-boat moves up to its mooring place; the first mate is in charge of the manœuvre, the men have fallen into line and hundreds of spectators have come to welcome them. The band is playing: "Denn wir fahren gegen Engeland..." In another second the mooring ropes will be heaved across...*

4 *The boat is lashed securely and after many weeks at sea—though land was often in sight they never went on shore—the first bit of the home country comes on board, a narrow plank*

5 *The moment they had longed for has come at last: on shore again! They are presented with flowers by young girls*

The immediate effects of the war on shipping

... not what was expected

SIGNAL here publishes an account of extremely important repercussions of the war on shipping which have so far not received much attention

BY VICE-ADMIRAL LÜTZOW

Since the outbreak of hostilities there have naturally been so many opportunities of speaking about the efficiency of our war on shipping that there would be no necessity to refer to it again had not various facts and trains of thought from the enemy camp recently become known, which throw light more particularly on its immediate effects. In order to understand their full significance, however, we must give a short survey of the events during the first years of the war. Even the attack on Scandinavia planned by the enemy for April 1940 was connected with our counterblow against the British hunger blockade. As is proved by captured enemy memoranda, this attack did not merely aim at counterbalancing the German successes by seizing the iron mines in North Sweden, thus cutting Germany off from that source of raw material. A further object was to establish complete control to be exercised from the northern blockade line between Scotland and Norway, over the eastern limit, that is to say, the Norwegian coast, with the object of making it impossible for our naval units to reach the Atlantic Ocean. The failure of the operations rendered it necessary to withdraw the blockade westwards to the line Scotland—Iceland—Greenland. The islands of Iceland and Greenland, which are connected with Denmark by personal union, were occupied by force in spite of protests. Great Britain was nevertheless obliged to suffer the dispatch of a contingent of the United States Army to Iceland. The British Government could naturally do nothing but welcome this American intrusion as a sign that the U.S.A. was willing to continue to afford help in the prosecution of the war in violation of neutrality. But it is just as obvious that far-seeing Englishmen acquainted with the discord which has always existed between the United States and Great Britain and which at various times during the last twenty years has become very serious, regarded the extension of the U.S.A.'s power to the vicinity of home waters with the greatest anxiety. For it was perfectly clear to all concerned that the Americans would not leave the new base in Iceland voluntarily any more than Great Britain would ever get back her West Atlantic colonies from Newfoundland via the West Indies to Guiana once she had ceded her territorial and other rights over them in exchange for fifty out-of-date United States destroyers. Already by the end of the first year of the war, the difficulties had increased to such an extent in consequence of our war on merchant shipping that it had become necessary to conclude that bad piece of political business.

Unexploited tonnage

The employment of harbours on the west coast of France, the adoption of new types of U-boats and the support given to them by submarine tankers made it possible to extend the sphere of operations of German and Italian U-boats in action in the Atlantic Ocean. The enemy was thereby compelled to adopt a corresponding extension of the convoy system in spite of the resulting dispersal of the protection given to merchant shipping by warships and the less efficient exploitation of the cargo tonnage. A merchant ship ready to set sail, for example, could not do so immediately, but was compelled first of all to proceed to the spot where its convoy was to assemble and wait there until all the ships had arrived. During the passage, all the ships forming the convoy had to adapt their speed to that of the slowest. In areas where danger from U-Boats threatened, the convoy was obliged to steer a zigzag course. It was necessary to guide it to its destination by devious routes as soon as there was any danger of attack. The speed of the journey was considerably reduced by all these factors. When the convoy at last arrived safely at its destination, a number of the ships had to wait for shorter or longer periods before having their cargoes discharged, because the harbour installations could not cope with the rapidly advancing demands placed upon them. Travelling together in the convoy put a greater strain on the engines and boilers than the normal passages where ships sailed alone and also led to collisions resulting in damage which had to be repaired in dock. The need for ship repairing yards and the work they had to cope with rose rapidly. About two dozen repair yards in Great Britain, which had been closed down some years before as being out-of-date, had to be reopened. New shipping yards had to transfer specialist workers to them with the result that their own standard of performance decreased. Taken altogether, these difficulties experienced by enemy merchant shipping reduced the degree to which it could be exploited by about one third.

Problems connected with the building of new ships

The war in the Pacific, which had been so frivolously precipitated by the President of the United States, made the American people, against its will, the ally of Great Britain on the Atlantic, it is true, but the value of that help was affected in an unforeseen manner, more particularly by the victories of the Japanese Fleet which tied up the major part of the American Fleet in the Pacific. Another factor was the unexpected appearance of German U-boats off North and Central America. The successes they scored resulted in a considerable aggravation of the shortage of shipping. Discussions then took place in the United States whether cargo boats or transport planes should be constructed in order to make up for the losses. A decision was eventually reached in favour of the cargo boats. Fresh differences of opinion occured on the question whether the solidity and speed of the new ships should be given precedence over numbers or whether as many makeshift cargo boats as possible should be built in as short a time as possible without regard to their solidity and speed. The latter course was adopted. The result was not only that complaints were very soon made regarding the insufficient speed of the ships, but also that the amount of cargo they could load did not equal that of a normal ship built in peacetime. The reason for this was that the rapid construction of the new vessels could only be attained by a simplification of the shipbuilding methods which prevented the full exploitation of the cargo space.

According to an official statement made by Admiral Vickery at the beginning of June 1943, the heavy losses in tankers inflicted on the enemy particularly in the early part of 1942 made it necessary to convert a hundred cargo boats into tankers. Other ships had to be converted into auxilliary aircraft carriers in order to afford the convoys better protection. The United States Admiralty has stated that the shipyard installations appear not to meet the increased requirements for the repairs to damaged ships so that new floating docks have to be constructed. British shipyards complain of a shortage of skilled workers. Not even the minimum numbers, it is said, can be maintained. This shortage has been considerably aggravated as the result of the extension of the maritime war to all the world's seas, for it is no longer possible, as is usual in peacetime, to bring the warships and cargo boats, which have suffered damage in foreign waters, back to harbours at home. New repair yards for them have to be built in oversea harbours and skilled workers have to be sent out from home to run them.

Lord Woolton's anxieties

The continual pressure exerted by these circumstance has caused the Americans to reproach the British on a number of occasions with using too much tonnage for purposes not directly serving the prosecution of the war. This reproach, however, is in contrast to a spreech made a few weeks ago by Lord Woolton, the British Minister for Supplies. He stated that he did not think it would be possible to increase the meat ration before the end of the war, in spite of the fact that it was very small. He merely hoped that it would not be necessary to reduce it even further. He realized that all the present rations were extremely low and bordered on the minimum essential for life, but there was very little prospect of improvement. Some people, he continued, were inclined to say that everything was going smoothly in Britain's food supplies. He, the Minister, however, could not share that view. We need not inquire whether Lord Woolton's last remark referred to the complaints made by the London newspapers concerning the discrepancies in the distribution of the new food and clothing cards. The "Daily Mail" reported on 18th May 1943 that agricultural workers were demanding special food allowances and were threatening to adopt drastic measures if their claims did not meet with a sympathetic hearing. The British Minister of Agriculture, Hudson, said at the end of May that the home supply of food was so strained that it was necessary to begin immediately with the cultivation of grasslands lying idle. The area affected amounted, according to his statement, to eleven million acres.

All this results from the shortage of shipping which Great Britain provoked by instituting the hunger blockade in 1939. Quite apart from the fluctuations in the amount of tonnage sunk, the fact asserts itself in the above-mentioned effects of the war on merchant shipping that since the outbreak of the war, Germany's enemies have lost 31 million tons of shipping and that it will be impossible to make good the loss.

British shipbuilders outstripped

The further consequences, however, arising for Great Britain from the war on merchant shipping are extremely serious. Until 1939 Britain used to possess the biggest merchant fleet in the world. Twenty-five years ago, it carried one half of the world's entire oversea trade, and in 1938 we may estimate that it carried two-fifths. It was two and a

Mountain riflemen enjoying a short rest
PK. Photograph: Front Correspondent Rieder

half times as large as the United States merchant fleet and was also capable of considerably better performances as most of the ships were newer than the American ones. This state of affairs has undergone a great change, however, in consequence of the present war. From the outbreak of hostilities until the end of April 1940, the United States sold 188 old cargo boats with a total tonnage of 713,000 tons. They were no longer profitable to run according to peacetime standards, but 75 of them were disposed of to Britain and Canada. The severe losses inflicted on the British merchant fleet could not be made good merely by new ships built in the British shipyards. The United States merchant fleet increased at the cost of the British. Since 1942 American shipyards have been able to build five times as many ships as the yards in Britain. The time is approaching, therefore, when the relative strength of the British merchant fleet as compared with that of the American will be the reverse of what it was in 1939, that is to say, the United States will possess two and a half times as much merchant tonnage as Great Britain and the ships will not be out-of-date but new. Of the once vast British merchant fleet plying to India, only a fraction, therefore, now remains and in the harbours of South America, too, the British colours are only poorly represented. To this must be added the fact that, in consequence of the shortage of shipping, Great Britain had encouraged the Dominions to build ships and to establish industries of their own for that purpose. The consequence was fresh competition. This outstripping of the British merchant fleet by other Powers represents a serious menace to Great Britain. Politically, because the safety of the Empire depends upon the strength of the Navy and the merchant fleet. Furthermore, the shrinking of the merchant fleet represents an economic danger for Britain; for many years she has been importing more goods than she has exported. The consequence was that a foreign debt accumulated each year which amounted in 1937, for example, to 432 millions. About one-third of the debt was covered by the profits made on shipping which in 1937 amounted to 130 millions. It can be estimated that during the course of the present war, these profits have shrunk to little more than a third of what they used to be. This decline is all the more serious as another source of income, the most important, used for paying this import surplus has decreased by 60%. This source of income consisted of the interest on British capital invested abroad from which it was possible to pay approximately half of the import surplus. As we have already stated,

sources of income have decreased by about three-fifthes, because it has been necessary to relinquish these capital investments, to the Dominions more particularly, in return for help in the war.

Competition instead of help

Political and economic reasons are thus forcing Britain to continue to attach great value in the future to the maintenance of a strong and up-to-date merchant fleet. In striving to achieve this object, however, she is finding herself more and more hampered by the United States, who quite openly has several times claimed to possess the world's biggest merchant fleet. The opinion might perhaps be held that in the interests of Anglo-American trade co-operation, this claim could be reduced to a degree tolerable for Britain. The anxieties of the United States, however, stand in the way of such a solution. During the years of peace, the U.S.A. failed to get rid of her workless whose numbers sometimes reached as many as 17 millions, or even to reduce unemployment to any considerable degree. The lack of success in this sphere was one of the reasons why the Government in Washington worked for war. In future the U.S.A. intends, therefore, to double or even treble her exports as compared with the pre-war period and also to build a correspondingly large merchant fleet. For it is an undisputed fact that "a merchant fleet sailing under the flag of the exporting country is one of the main weapons in extending oversea trade." Britain's example, in particular, has continually proved that doctrine in the past. The consequence is that in the long run the efforts being made by the U.S.A. and Great Britain to develop their merchant fleets are directly opposed to one another. Leading periodicals in both countries also admit that no solution of the problem has yet been found. The seriousness of the rivalry in the shipbuilding competition naturally results in discord regarding the replacement by newly built ships of ships already sunk. The loss of 31 million tons of shipping as the result of the war against tonnage waged by the Powers of the Tripartite Pact has led to the decision being taken to build as many ships as possible in as short a time as possible without regard to solidity and speed. The increasing competition between Britain and the United States of America, however, has caused the experts to demand fast ships built on rational lines.

When Great Britain instituted her long-distance blockade of Germany in 1939, British statesmen spoke of an easy war. Thanks to the successes gained by Germany's war on merchant shipping, Britain has instead become dependent upon the United States, which means that the existence of the Empire is threatened. This success, the consequences of which are inestimable, is due to Germany's counter-blockade of Britain.

Darkened daylight-illuminated darkness

The columm of smoke from the burning tanker rises, dark and sinister, many hundreds of yards into the air

The flames leaping from the ammunition supply ship illuminate the tall fountain of water caused by the second torpedo hit

Seven pioneers and their company commander

A day on the Eastern Front like many that have preceded it. One huge offensive gives place to the next. The series of tremendous battles is unending. The battalion had been encircled in a village by a numerically superior enemy. A force was rapidly gathered together with the object of relieving the surrounded unit. Its backbone consisted of a tank pioneer company.

The first attack failed. The second attack was successful in forcing a breach in the ring round the battalion. Almost simultaneously, the encircled men dashed through the opening with their wounded, weapons and equipment. The tank pioneer company was also able to withdraw from the enemy who was putting up a desperate fight. Not until he had reached an undulation in the countryside did the commander of No. 1 Company, Lieutenant R., notice that one of his armoured cars with its crew of seven men was missing. It had not lasted more than a minute, nobody had noticed anything owing to the speed at which they were travelling. What could be done? To ask for fresh artillery support was impossible because it would take too much time to provide information about the targets and range. Simply to return was still more impossible. Yet that is what they did. It seemed scarcely feasible, tactically out of the question. The terrible tension of what the men had just gone through was beginning to relax.

The men were suddenly roused by the order given to No. 1 platoon to turn about and make their way back. Lieutenant R.'s armoured car was already rumbling up the slope, the much practised order of march was found automatically, the men gripped their steel helmets, their machine-guns and peered over the protective plating of steel. They rapidly retraced their tracks, their thoughts flying to the men ahead of them. In their imaginations they saw their comrades engaged in a desperate fight. Everything else appeared non-existent. The fate of their comrades had become their own. When the Reich War Colours appeared from the Lieutenant's car, they thought they were dreaming although the first bullets fired by the enemy soon brought them back to reality.

They could now see their comrades some distance off. Their armoured car was standing tipped up over the front wheels. Rifle fire was flashing all around, black clouds of smoke rose from exploding hand grenades and was then wafted away, a number of brown figures ran towards them from the right flank. The platoon of tank pioneers described a wide circle round the armoured car which had got stuck. The foremost car laid a smoke screen. Bolshevists loomed up like spectres and disappeared again outside the ring. The first cable, with which they tried to move the armoured car, broke. At the second attempt it twisted. Two vehicles were finally attached to it, they gave it a jerk backwards and the car stood level on the ground. The axle, however, was very much bent. As chance would have it, one of the tractors which had pulled out the damaged car now rammed it in the artificial smoke screen with the result that the axle was more or less put straight again.

They had managed it. Two of the seven men had been wounded and two of those who had relieved them were also hit. A day on the Eastern Front like many that had preceded it.

The men jump on at full speed. They have been guarding the action on the flanks and are now helped by their comrades. Seven men have been relieved

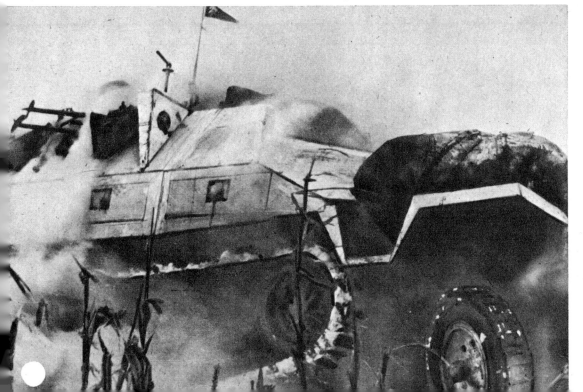

▌**The caterpillar tracks** crunch their way through snow and sand back towards the line. Once again an artificial smoke screen is laid. The enemy's fire dies away

Admiral of the Fleet Raeder
Commander-in-Chief of the German Navy

The big and the small
submarine man

After a long and particularly successful trip in enemy waters Commander Schepke, decorated with the "Ritterkreuz", and the whole of his crew were invited to a ski - ing party at the winter resort of Ruhpolding in upper Bavaria, where they were able to enjoy themselves on the slopes of the mountains to their heart's content. The ski - ing equipment was lent by the Reichenhall Alpine Corps. Commander Schepke was the guest of the well known long distance ski - er Toni Plenk. — Here he is explaining a model submarine, which he has given as a present to youngster Horst Plenk

REICHS-RUNDFUNK

European Service

William Joyce, otherwise known as "Lord Haw Haw" at the microphone, while reading his "Views on the News"

To hear the News in English from the European Service of the Reichsrundfunk, tune in to the following stations and frequencies:

6.30 a. m. German Summer Time (or British Extra Summer Time)

Deutschlandsender	on 191	kilocycles (1571 metres)
Calais		
Bremen	on 785	kilocycles (396 metres)
Friesland	on 160	kilocycles (1875 metres)
Luxemburg	on 232	kilocycles (1293 metres)

2.30 p. m. German Summer Time (or British Extra Summer Time)

Calais		
Bremen	on 785	kilocycles (396 metres)
Friesland	on 160	kilocycles (1875 metres)
Luxemburg	on 232	kilocycles (1293 metres)
short-wave-transmitter DJL	on 15110	kilocycles (19.85 metres)

5.30 p. m. German Summer Time (or British Extra Summer Time)

Calais		
Bremen	on 785	kilocycles (396 metres)
Friesland	on 160	kilocycles (1875 metres)
Luxemburg	on 232	kilocycles (1293 metres)
short-wave-transmitter DXJ	on 7240	kilocycles (41.44 metres)

9.30 p. m. German Summer Time (or British Extra Summer Time)

Calais		
Luxemburg	on 232	kilocycles (1293 metres)
short-wave-transmitter DXM	on 6200	kilocycles (48.39 metres)
short-wave-transmitter DXJ	on 7240	kilocycles (41.44 metres)

6.30 p. m. German Summer Time (or British Extra Summer Time)

Calais		
Bremen	on 785	kilocycles (396 metres)
Friesland	on 160	kilocycles (1875 metres)
short-wave-transmitter DXJ	on 7240	kilocycles (41.44 metres)

11.30 p. m. German Summer Time (or British Extra Summer Time) and

12.15 p. m. German Summer Time (or British Extra Summer Time)

Calais		
Breslau	on 950	kilocycles (306 metres)
Cologne	on 658	kilocycles (456 metres)
short-wave-transmitter DXM	on 6200	kilocycles (48.39 metres)

"Views on the News" by William Joyce (otherwise known as Lord Haw-Haw) are broadcast daily

at 10.30 p.m. German Summer Time (or British Extra Summer Time)
via:

Calais		
Breslau	on 950	kilocycles (316 metres)
Cologne	on 658	kiiocycles (456 metres)
Luxemburg	on 232	kilocycles (1293 metres)
short-wave-transmitter DXM	on 6200	kilocycles (48.39 metres)

Fish in the Northern Pacific

The Japanese-Finnish-Russian Fish Convention, for the last seven years temporary arrangement renewabl e ev 12 months, applies to the especia rich fishing grounds between Sacha and Alaska. In 1943 the contract betw Tokyo and Moscow was prolonged another year. The American press rega this new extension by Moscow with o dissatisfaction

←

Not torpedoed this time

When dining with Wendell Willkie Moscow on one occasion Stalin prope a toast in which he accused England having seized in Scotland 150 Ameri planes from a convoy bound for Archan It is a fact that the ships with these plo intended for the Soviets were held in Scotland and sent to Africa ins of to the east. By order of Eisenho

Parliamentary elections in warti

Denmark is the only country in Eu that has been able to elect new mem of Parliament in a normal, peaceful fas despite the war. The polling was g 93% as compared wi h 82% previou The result showed distinct approval o Danish Government policy up to the pre

Two pictures of the reception given by Reich Minister Dr Goebbels and his wife to a delegation of the S. S. tank grenadier divisions which played an outstanding part in the recapture of Kharkov and of an afternoon in the Minister's family circle. With a wealth of details the soldiers, who are holders of all including the highest decorations, present a living picture of the spirit of the troops and the character of the fighting in the fourth year of the war

Reich Minister Dr Goebbels has once more assembled round him holders of the Knight's Cross who have come from the centres of fighting at the front

ye-witness reports

nt soldiers visit Reich Minister Dr Goebbels

General Field Marshal Rommel photographed with the children of the Reich Minister on the occasion of a visit to Dr Goebbels

Western Germany: Four-engined American bomber brought down with crew of 10, 8 being killed

71 from 91
in two days

The Anglo-American Air Forces lost 207 bombing planes in four days in terror raids on Reich territory between the 25th and the 28th July, according to the German High Command Communiqué. Of this number, 91 bombers were lost in the attacks on Hamburg and Hanover and in flights on the 27th and 28th July. SIGNAL shows the wreckage of 71 out of these 91 planes. They were all four-engined bombers of the Halifax, Lancaster, Liberator, Wellington, Stirling and other types. During June, the Anglo-American Air Forces lost 614 planes, including 408 bombers, in attacks on the Reich and the occupied western territories

Hanover: Halifax bombers, 4 out of 5 dead

Hamburg: American bomber, 8 out of 10 killed

Western Germany: Halifax bomber, 5 dead

Hamburg: British plane, all 7 men killed

Western Germany: Remains of a British bomber

Hamburg: British bomber, 4 out of 5 dead

A new fighter squadron
eady to take off for its base. In
he background, Ju transporters
aking spare parts from the
epair airfield to the front
K. Photograph: War Coresp. Berger

Hamburg: Halifax bomber, 5 men, 1 killed

Hamburg: British bomber, 8 men, all dead

Hanover: Wellington bomber, 6 men, 1 dead

Hanover: British bomber, 5 men, 1 dead

Hamburg: The remains of a British bomber

Northern France: American bomber, 10 men, 8 dead

Holland: Lancaster bomber, 8 men, 3 dead

Western Germany: British bomber, 7 men, 5 dead

Channel Coast: Four-engined British bomber, 10 dead

Hamburg: Four-engined British bomber, 7 dead

Hamburg: Halifax bomber, 5 men, all dead

Hamburg: Lancaster bomber, 8 men, 8 dead

Western Germany: Halifax bomber, 7 men, 4 dead

Hamburg: Lancaster bomber exploded in the air

Hanover: British bomber, 7 men, 6 dead

Hamburg: British bomber shot down by anti-aircraft

On the Channel: British bomber, 4 parts, the remnants

Northern France: Stirling bomber, 5 dead

Hamburg: Four-engined British bomber, 7 men dead

Channel Coast: Lancaster bomber, 8 men, 7 dead

Western Germany: British bomber after being brought down

Hamburg: All that remained of a British bomber

Hamburg: Wellington bomber, 6 men, 3 dead

Western Germany: Halifax bomber, 5 men, 4 dead

Holland: Hampden bomber, 7 men, all dead

Hanover: The wreck of a "Flying Fortress"

Western Germany: Halifax bomber, 5 dead

Hamburg: American bomber, 10 men, 9 dead

Channel Coast: Spitfire, brought down by fighters

Hanover: British bomber, 5 men, 4 dead

Western Germany: British bomber, all 10 men dead

Western Germany: American bomber, 10 men, 8 dead

Hamburg: Halifax bomber, 7 men, 6 dead

Western Germany: British bomber, 3 men burned

Hamburg: Lancaster bomber, 8 men, 8 dead

Holland: Lancaster bomber, 8 Australians dead

Holland: Lancaster bomber, 8 Australians dead

Channel Coast: Lancaster bomber, 8 men, 5 dead

On the Channel: Liberator bomber (U.S.A.), all dead

Hamburg: British bomber, none saved

Dutch coast: Liberator bomber, 10 men dead

Hamburg: Wellington bomber, 6 men, 1 dead

Northern France: American bomber, all men killed

Hamburg: The remains of a "Flying Fortress"

Hamburg: American bomber, 10 men, 9 dead

Hamburg: British bomber, exploded in the air

Channel Coast: American fighter none saved

Holland: Lancaster bomber, 8 men, 6 dead

Hanover: British bomber, 7 men, 6 dead

Northern France: British bomber, 7 men, 7 dead

Channel Coast: All that remained of a British bomber

Channel: A Wellington bomber being taken to pieces

Hanover: Halifax bomber, 7 men, 6 dead

Channel Coast: Stirling bomber, wrecked in crashing

Northern France: British bomber, all killed

Holland: Lancaster bomber, 8 men, 4 dead

Hamburg: Wellington bomber, 6 men, 4 dead

Hamburg: Lancaster bomber, 8 men, 3 dead

Hamburg: what remained of a British bomber

Hanover: the wreck of a Wellington bomber

Western Germany: British bomber, 8 men, 4 dead

Holland: Liberator bomber, 10 men, 9 dead

Atlantic Coast: British bomber, 5 men, 1 dead

Channel: 3 men rescued in an inflatable boat

The dawn after the night of terror. *Smoke is still rising from the burnt-out opera house (on the right) and a large hotel; it hangs over the square where men belonging to a salvage corps are seeking a few minutes' rest on mattresses which have been saved*

The dawn after the night of terror. *"I put out three incendiaries," says Gardener Thiessen who looks after the swans in the city park. A few weeks ago his home in the old part of the town was destroyed by an explosive bomb. His face tells the story of the night of devastation*

A NIGHT OF TERROR...

War Correspondent Hanns Hubmann experienced one of the heavy night raids on a town in the west of Germany. Ten days later, he revisited the same town and its inhabitants. SIGNAL here publishes his report

This town in western Germany has already been the object of a hundred night air raids. Of more than a hundred, but this one was one of the worst. War Correspondent Hanns Hubmann was there and saw the innumerable conflagrations. The opera house and many of the large hotels were destroyed. Reich Minister Speer, with whom Signal's War Correspondent was travelling, helped to salvage mattresses and other things. Hundreds and thousands of people lost their homes. Everybody helped in saving what could be saved. On the morning after the raid, the smoke was still hanging like a pall in the streets, but the people were already hastening to their work again. Yet their faces reflected the terrors of the night. Ten days after this night raid, Hubmann returned to the town. The marks of destruction on the housefronts were naturally still unchanged. But the faces of the people and their whole life clearly showed that they are overcoming the hardships of the nights of terror. How they are doing so is shown by Signal's photographs. Men who take home a bunch of flowers to their wives ten days after such an air raid and women who cannot hide their so disarming anxieties about hats and handbags, people who stream to their work in the early morning after the night of devastation as though nothing had occurred—such people are stronger than their fate.

The dawn after the night of terror. *On their way to work already, they pass ruins and wounded people. They have had no time to shave, because they all want to be at their machines at 6 a.m. as usual. The trams are not running and at most they have a bicycle at their disposal for getting to the factories*

← **Under the glass roof of his cockpit.** *The wireless operator at the M. G.*
PK. Photograph: War Correspondent Speck

The dawn after the night of terror. *Their appearance still bears marks of the night of devastation. They have taken off their collars to be able to fight the flames and do salvage work. The alert had brought them together by chance in an air-raid shelter—Schäfer, the municipal inspector, Strathmann, the grocer and Arenswald, the master basket-maker. They had done good work. Ten days later? (See below)*

They have recovered their good spirits . . .

. . . for they still have their Rhineland humour. These three men are a municipal inspector, a grocer and a master basket-maker. Ten days after the heavy air raid things are taking their normal course again—the one is selling sausage, the second is carrying on his office work between makeshift walls and the third is again making neat baskets.

"This is my office now. Don't you agree, cupboards take the place of a wall nicely?"

"Would you like some real Brunswick tongue sausage again? It has just come in fresh!"

"I've just finished making these baskets. And there is a new pane in my shop window, too"

The waitress Kate

The morning after the night of terror, *Signal came across her sitting with a colleague on a few stools she had saved together with a number of other things including the cash register from her café (on the left of the picture)*

↓ **Ten days later,** *the reporter happened to see her working as a National Socialist People's Welfare helper distributing food (on the right of the picture)*

Architect and photographer...

"Hallo, where are you taking that pail?" "Up the ladder to the staircase and then to my atelier!" Mrs Hehmke-Winterer, a photographer, lives on the 5th floor. The atelier was not wrecked. Her husband, the architect Konrad Wagner, has built a makeshift hearth out of a few bricks. They fetch water from a pump in the yard. She has a smile on her face for life is still going on as usual.

The dawn after the night of terror. *Wagner and his wife, in front of their house*

Ten days later *the architect Wagner is again at work with his women assistants in a makeshift office in the heavily damaged house*

She wanted to buy a pair of stockings ...

"What a lovely dress!" Two friends strolling past the glittering show-cases in Kurfürstendamm in Berlin stop to admire the pretty things displayed (below). "Do look at these adorable undies!" — "Darling," sighs her friend, "I only want to buy stockings. Besides think of the clothes card! But maybe it would do no harm just to ask in the shop . . ."

Horseshoes bring good fortune

according to a super-stition know all over the world. But to the army blacksmith they bring work, the careful execution of which exercises a particular influence of its own on the "fortune of war"

PK. Henisch

"I'll have the second from the right" says Hilde as she admires the new handbags which have just been placed in the repaired shop window. A notice says that business will begin again in a few days time

"We're getting brandy," the boy says as he registers customers for spirits to help his mother. There are special rations for the population of the bombed cities

Ten days later . . .

"Yes, we begin business again tomorrow the girls in a stocking shop say with a sm But it will be in a shop being shared w three other firms. Now they are busy fetch stocks from a warehouse which was not

ow good the army bread tastes!" Par-
arly is this the case when Rhineland
help to distribute the bread from the
y bakeries at food centres for people
se homes have suffered damage from bombs

Roses and marguerites. Flower-sellers have
set up their gay stalls again in front of the
burnt out façade of a departamental store. Husbands come and buy bunches of flowers for their
wives. Ten days after the night of terror . . .

...And the main thing:
The work goes on

NAZALIA

The girl from the Ukraine

Nazalia is one of the many girls from the east who left their homes when the country became part of the war zone and are now working in Germany. She acknowledges the confidence placed in her with industry and loyalty. Here, too, we have evidence of the change in the attitude to Western Europe of the peoples of the east who have been exposed to western influences by the war

When they told her that the French eat snails, she said: "Oooooh!" Her voice rose in astonishment just like a child's when it sees a conjuring trick. Nazalia, whom we are going to call Natasha here, and who is so amazed at the refinements of the western art of cooking, is no longer a child. She has a robust, full figure like the farmers' wives in rich agricultural districts in Germany and her face is a womanly oval. It is difficult to say what is in her dark eyes. She seldom opens them wide and her glance is veiled with gentle melancholy. She often thinks of her native country. The clay hut in which she helped to rear her brother's children, a cottage surrounded by a garden full of sunflowers, stood in a village near Isjum that was destroyed in the course of the fighting. The house was burnt, her brother disappeared and she has heard nothing of her sister-in-law and the children since the night when a German soldier found her unconscious in a crater behind the burnt-out house. All that she can remember is that there were many fires in the village and that she made a long, long journey.

Sometimes, when cheerful, peaceful pictures of home rise up in her mind, Natasha sings or hums. It is always the same melody with a few unchanging slurred phrases rising sharply to the top notes which she then sustains for some time. She sings it every day and even in the early morning although it is a melody more suited for the evening when the day is drawing to a close and all work is done. But she works while she sings. She sweeps out the rooms of a beautiful, rather old-fashioned but comfortable flat in the heart of the city. It contains many things Natasha had never seen before, such as finely carved furniture, crystal and porcelain. In the beginning, she handled it reluctantly and distrustfully and broke much of it. In front of the clock, however, she stood respectfully with her head on one side as she listened enchanted by the silvery tone when it struck the half and the quarter hours. For the sake of this enchantment her mistress forgave her the breakages, scolded her and showed her how delicate china should be handled. Since then Natasha is much more careful with the cups, for she loves her mistress. She does not kiss the hem of her skirt or her hands, but when food is scarce Natasha does without her share, and when the family met with sorrow, for three days she neither ate nor drank. Then, because her mistress often sits looking at the flowers in the window-boxes, Natasha never forgets to water them although no one ever spoke to her about it.

Her life is the same daily round of washing, cleaning and darning. Now and then she writes a letter to her sister who has remained in Kiev or she reads the Russian newspaper in the kitchen of the big house. Since she bears this life and her home-sickness cheerfully and patiently, her mistress lets her go early on Sundays. She puts on the flowered dress that was given her and instead of the usual middle parting, she wears her hair in a plait twisted like a wreath round her head. She makes up, too, but clumsily, and dabs round, red blobs on her cheeks. When people told her she looked like a clown, she opened her eyes wide in astonishment and did not understand; so they left her alone. Then she goes for a walk with other girls from her village, with Lisa, Maria, Anna and Katja. Sometimes her friends, who work in a factory and live in a camp or in huts, call for her. Arm in arm, they stroll singing through the park. And when they are not singing, they are chattering like a class of schoolgirls. They read each other's letters and when they contain something funny, Natasha laughs so that her whole body shakes. Her laughter can resound strangely. It comes from the depths like her astonishment and she makes no attempt to try and look pretty. From the same depths as her laughter and her astonishment comes something else which frightened her mistress in the beginning. Once, half the night long, she was sitting alone in her room and heard from Natasha's room low groans followed by half-stifled screams. She thought fearfully that someone might have come up the back stairs to assault the girl. At that moment Natasha rushed out with dishevelled hair and black, glittering eyes, speaking Russian at a terrific speed. It was some time before she recognized her mistress and then she stammered something about fire. Shaking her head with astonishment, she went back to bed. She had been dreaming and recollections of her shattered home that had sunk deep in the well of her sub-conscious mind to slumber beneath a surface of patient indifference, drove her from her bed.

Clever people had advised the housewife to be strict with the foreign maid and sometimes even hard. But the mistress of the house is from the Rhineland and it is not in her nature to be strict. She is kind to Natasha and very just, for she has felt that the young Ukrainian, like all simple and natural people, is very sensitive to injustice. She strokes her hair when the wild dreams torment her. Since then, Natasha has become more calm and is very docile. Her confidence in her master and mistress is great and wondering like that of a child. She will be sad when the wife one day returns home with her husband and daughter and cannot take Natasha with her.

To this family it appeared that humanity is the best teacher for unspoilt children of nature.

TERROR

Signal

pictures of the terror attacks made by the Americans and the British on Antwerp and Paris. Thousands of men and women, old people and children were crushed, torn to pieces and burnt to death. Europe will not forget it

Silent accusation

A church: it is part of the system of the terror raids to destroy centres of religion and art

A school: 300 children failed to return home

ANTWERP

Like thousands of others: a married couple viewing the ruins of their existence

One of the places where the victims were collected: the last medical examination...

... and then the last charitable service: a nurse fills in the names for the coffins

American and British airmen attack "military objectives"

PARIS

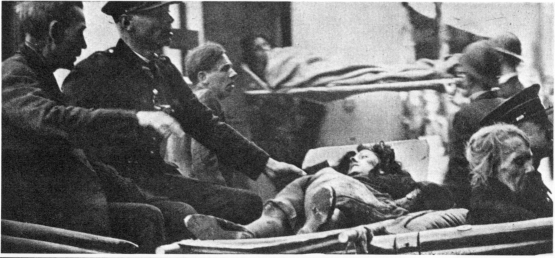

A quarter of an hour later : innocent victims

A member of the Spanish Volunteer Division, one of those young people who know what is at stake in this war — the political, economic and cultural liberty of Europe's future and consequently, therefore, of their own future

PK. Photograph : War Correspondent Hans Sönnke

Where does Europe's rising generation stand?

AIR BASES AND WORLD HEGEMONY

The United States know perfectly well what they are after in this war. They pretend they are fighting for democratic liberty, but in actual fact they are systematically extending their power. An example of this is the way they are ruthlessly building up by every means an air transport system spanning the world

The United States are making plans for after the war. They realize that a world merchant fleet decimated by the U-boat warfare will be faced by the accumulated requirements of transport and they believe that air traffic will be destined to satisfy them to a large extent. They look upon it not only as a profitable business but primarily as a means for putting into practice the dream of the American century.

The birth of air imperialism

It is nothing new for American air transport to strive to establish a monopoly. It began with the secret opposition to the interests of European air companies in South America. The open struggle began when during the years just before this war, Germany after a long period of pioneer work had created the technical foundations and the organization for air traffic across the North Atlantic. Permission for a regular service between Europa and North America was refused as was also the supply of helium for zeppelins for air traffic. The United States did not want any European air traffic across the Atlantic.

The outbreak of war provided a welcome opportunity of destroying the traffic net built up by European companies in South America. Pan American Airways, which had been called into existence for American air traffic abroad, systematically forced its way into South America and took over the national traffic companies there to the exclusion of all European influence.

Air supremacy over the Western Hemisphere had been established and was immediately followed by a thrust into the Eastern Hemisphere. A beginning was made with the air service established before the war across the North Atlantic to Ireland and Portugal. In 1941 came the leap from South America to Africa and the breach made in the British interests. Being incapable of herself establishing an air transport organization to satisfy the military requirements in the Near East, Britain was obliged to yield to the United States. American transport routes were developed from the west coast of Africa to Egypt, the Persian Gulf and as far as India.

Bases in the service of air supremacy

When Churchill made that bad barter transaction "American destroyers against bases," he certainly did not suspect the U. S. A.'s ulterior motives in gaining possession of them. Even the first of these bases formed ideal junctions for the projected world air traffic network. These "leased" bases in the Western Hemisphere were followed by others, some of which were obtained by treaty and some taken by force; Iceland was occupied and American airfields were established in Belgian Congo, French Equatorial Africa and the Persian Gulf. The first chain for air transport to the Soviet Union had been forged. The construction of air bases in the British Empire, in some cases without consulting the mother land, was a further step; India Australia and New Zealand ceded bases to the United States. The second and third aims, connexion with Chungking China and an air route to Australia had thereby been achieved. The mesh of the net was drawn even closer by the occupation of Liberia, Dakar and Tunisia.

Without being a colonial empire in the real sense of the word, the U. S. A had achieved that which had taken great colonial empires of the past a whole century. U. S. bases are now strewn all over the world. They are not naval bases in the old style, it is true, but just because they are planned and developed as air bases, their importance is all the greater.

The U. S. A. have not hesitated to begin the practical exploitation of their air bases within the framework of war requirements. Pan American Airways and the military air transport organization immediately began flying regular passenger and courier routes Apart from the well-known and frequented routes from New York to Ireland and Lisbon, the Americans today fly via Natal at the eastern extremity of South America to Africa, from there via Khartum and Cairo to Karachi and thence on to Chungking. The route to Australia runs from the west coast of North America via Hawaii, the Samoa and Fiji Islands, and New Zealand. All these routes, which at present are being used more or less for military purposes, are at the same time the chief routes of an air traffic system after the war. Trade is to follow the flag.

Britain cannot fly British

The British public was at first indifferent to the symptoms of U. S. air imperialism. Not until British statesmen with Churchill at their head continually used American planes for their trips to Moscow, the U. S. A., etc., was it suddenly discovered that Britain could no longer "fly British." The British Overseas Airways today actually possesses scarcely one modern air traffic type of its own and is obliged

fly its routes—in so far as it does so at all—with the help of American planes.

London gradually began to see through American intentions. The bartering of the bases now appeared under another light as well as the arrangement concerning the sharing of work in airplane construction according to which Great Britain was for the most part to restrict herself to the construction of small fighters whilst the U.S.A. were to develop long-range bombers and large transport planes.

The U.S.A. speak plainly

The American Ally now suddenly revealed itself as a dangerous competitor in postwar air traffic.

The champions of American air imperialism declared that in future there was to be only one air traffic system under the Stars and Stripes. The demand was made to Congress that after this war, foreign planes should not be allowed to fly to and across United States territory, whilst American planes should enjoy the right of transit all over the world.

Pan American airways circles expressed opinions like the following concerning the rôle of air bases: 'The United States have spent milliards of dollars in developing their bases and in wireless and meteorological installations. All these things are essential for world air traffic. If six months after the end of the war these installations have not been transferred to the possession of that nation which built them, then . . .'

The United States did not even hesitate to remind their Ally that the consignments of planes sent during the war have been supplied according to the Lease and Lend Act and that Great Britain must not think, for example, that she can use them after the war for the purposes of civilian air traffic.

Great Britain is out-manoeuvred

There are some Britishers, it is true, who realize the whole danger of the ruthless game being played by their American Ally, but they console themselves with the thought that Britain will succeed after the war in retrieving the U.S.A.'s booty. The prospects of doing so, however, are very small. Whilst British airplane engineering during the past few years has been engaged almost exclusively on the development of war planes to meet the requirements of the war and has almost completely ceased to construct passenger planes, the United States have done very much, particularly in this sphere. The American airplane works have not only built a series of big transporters which are at present being used for military purposes, but numerous plans for big flying boats and land planes have been made in anticipation of their employment in the postwar passenger service.

If the war ended as the United States desire, this lead in aeronautics, together with the network of bases already obtained, would suffocate British air traffic and deprive it of all possibility of competition. Whether the American plans of world hegemony in the air will ever be realized is another question. The war is not yet over. Britain, however, is out-manoeuvred in any case.

On the Red Square in Kharkov. *This shock troop leader was one of the first Germans to clear the Red Square, the centre of the re-captured city, of the enemy. He is one of the innumerable soldiers who frustrated the winter attempt made by the Soviets to break through to Europe*

After a winter of severe defensive fighting: KHARKOV

Kharkov, which in 1910 had a population of only 200,000, was developed by the Soviets as an armament centre. The entire mineral riches of the Donets Basin were made available for this purpose. The necessary people were taken from the land. Nowhere was there a bigger lack of living accommodation and nowhere was there more misery among the workers than in this town which before the be-

ginning of the campaign on the Eastern Front had a population of nearly a million. The Soviet love of experimenting found a vent in building skyscraper-like edifices to which the Intourist omnibuses drove the occupants straight from the station. This town, as the eastern pillar of the Ukraine, has formed the objective of the fighting on more than one occasion. The German troops occupied Kharkov four

months after the commencement of the Eastern Campaign. Sixteen months later they evacuated the town and considerable areas of the neighbouring region according to plan. The Bolshevists walked into the trap laid for them which snapped to three weeks later. The photographs on this and the following page show aspects of the five-day battle for the recapture of Kharkov.

The corner pillar of the Ukraine. *View from a range of hills across the centre and southern part of Kharkov*

How they recaptured Kharkov

Tanks engaged in street fighting. *The tanks convert into a heap of ruins a skyscraper which had been strongly fortified. They thus open the way for the shock troops who capture house by house and street by street. The shock troops, who bear the main burden of the fighting, are supported from the air by dive-bombers*

Shock troops advancing. *Bolshevist snipers, who fire at the advancing grenadiers from roofs, windows and cellars, are posted in the houses of Kharkov. Whilst the shock troops comb the houses, they are slowly followed by the tanks. Columns of armoured transport lorries (picture below) soon rattle through the streets, which have been cleared of the enemy, and take reinforcements up to the front line* PK Photographs : S. S. War Correspondents King, Adendorf

"AMERICANA"

Concerning the "Victory Girl" and what "Collier's Magazine" has to say about her

How to become a "Victory Girl." *American newspapers, periodicals and magazines have published innumerable pictures of this kind by which the young girls of America are made into the "Victory Girls" discussed in this article*

It would sometimes be a very good thing if the people of Europe were able to form their own judgement on that very same United States of America which asserts that it is the most progressive country in the world. Far be it from us to ridicule American conditions. After reading a large number of American newspapers and periodicals published in 1943, however, even the most impartial observer must obtain a nothing less than shocking impression of the moral degradation of a certain part of the people of the United States. The war has completely destroyed what few personal and moral ties existed. This is all the more

"Collier's Magazine," one of the biggest American family periodicals with a circulation of a million, for example, on 13th March 1943 published an article on the deterioration in morals of American youth.

Ever since 1941, when conscription was introduced in the United States, there have been many pictures in all the magazines of the new type of "Victory Girl" who confers her friendship and other favours of various kinds on American soldiers and sailors. In the magazines, of course, it was usually film stars who were shown together with half a dozen enthusiastic soldiers. Sometimes photographs were published

> play out on the streets at night, and go along with a truck driver for a nickel or a dime. That is the sum.
> Now, since the war, many girls go out with soldiers and sailors, partly for the fun and the proud display of their "feller" in uniform, partly because the servicemen are lonely in a big, strange town and the kids feel they are doing something patriotic. They want to give something, so they give themselves. They're called "Victory Girls." Many are between twelve and fifteen; most have no idea of the consequences. Venereal diseases have risen alarmingly. Some girls, of course, have no objection to the money in it. One child of sixteen came to Juvenile Court with thirty offenses in one night to her credit, at $1.00 each. I asked if they ever went after the man.
> "We can't do much about them," the judge said. "The men all give the girls the same name—Tex—or Boston."

A few lines quoted from "Collier's Magazine" of 13th March 1943

remarkable because the United States is not suffering any direct effects from the war. It is, nevertheless, the case.

We do not wish to make vague assertions and will consequently quote what has been said in America itself.

depicting one of these "Victory Girls" during an afternoon visit to an American military camp where she distributed several hundred kisses to the boys. Such a thing may lack taste and is perhaps unhygienic too, but the reader

One of the pictures about which the article in "Collier's Magazine" says: "…in girls of thirteen to fifteen, delinquency rose by 35%, in Detroit by 43%…"

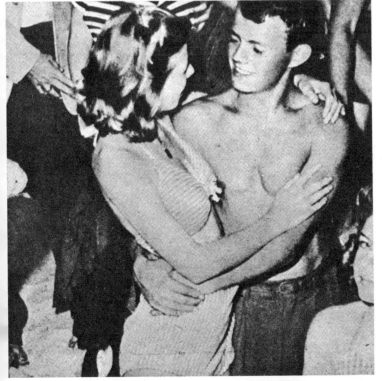

will not be unduly perturbed. We will now let "Collier's" inform us of what the consequences of the propaganda for the "Victory Girl" really are and the terrible conditions in the U.S.A. resulting from it. "Collier's" writes: "Since the war, many girls go out with soldiers and sailors, partly for the fun and the proud display of their 'feller' in uniform, partly because the servicemen are lonely in a big, strange town and the kids feel they are doing something patriotic. They want to give something, so they give themselves. They are called 'Victory Girls.' Many are between twelve and fifteen; most have no idea of the consequences. Venereal diseases have risen alarmingly. Some girls, of course, have no objection to the money in it."

"Collier's" then gives particulars of some of these "Victory Girls" which we cannot reproduce because they would be too offensive for any European. "Collier's" asserts that during the first six months of 1942 there was a 14% increase in juvenile delinquency in New York and that the most spectacular rise was in youngsters between ten and thirteen. In girls of thirteen to fifteen, delinquency (which also includes the above mentioned excesses of the "Victory Girls") rose by 35%, in Detroit by 43% and in the Niagara Falls area by 58%. J. Edgar Hoover, head of the F.B.I., has said that all juvenile delinquency has increased at least 20% all over the United States and that it will continue to rise unless something is done.

Murder gang of thirteen-year-olds

"In Los Angeles, a Mexican boy was shot and killed," Collier's goes on. "Police investigated and came upon a huge, organized gang of boys and girls involved in every kind of crime—holdups, robberies, shootings, murder, attempted kidnapping. None could join the gang who hadn't committed robbery or seduced a girl. All smoked marijuana. (Marijuana is a dangerous narcotic.) By August last, 400 boys were in custody, 28 were indicted for murder, and their "girl friends" were held as accomplices. In Detroit, a juvenile mob of over 400 boys and girls invaded night clubs, theater lobbies, movies, bars, smashed windows and furniture, tore down dis-

plays and terrorized patrons and passers-by. In New York City schools, the subject has become a grotesque nightmare. Two Brooklyn boys of 16 and 19 shot and killed their mathematics teacher. The papers were full of their brazenness, their zoot suits, their cold-blooded unconcern for any human values. The boys had objected to being reprimanded by the teacher...

... A 'reign of terror' has actually grown up in the city schools. Teachers are beaten by their students; students are beaten by their teachers. The teachers, through their guild, have appealed to the city police to protect them from bodily harm.

People blame Negro children; others blame foreign races. Most recent investigators say the picture includes all races, all religions, colors and creeds, and is worse only in the most overcrowded districts and in the underprivileged areas."

It is not uninteresting to note "Collier's" assertion that the Russian girl sniper, who is reported to have killed 309 Germans, has become a heroine. This woman has become just as famous as the gangsters like Al Capone used to be. These, then, are the consequences. Let us not forget that in Henry Luce's magazine, in which he proclaimed that the 20th century was the American century, recently published a series of pictures showing how a man could best be killed by being stealthily approached from the rear. This series was intended to be of help to American soldiers in Africa. In the article where Henry Luce claimed that our century was the American century, he wrote that the U.S.A. already led in all the trivial things of life. If we are to believe "Collier's," the U.S.A. leads not only in trivial things but also in crime. We may certainly regard all this as proof of what we will have to expect if these Americans were to "civilize" Europe. Of course, even today there is another America for which morals and decency still exist—but it is condemned to silence and patience. Most of the young people, however, are following the path described by "Collier's." This problem is one which concerns the whole of humanity—these are the first signs of the internal decay of a people which was once great.

Vol. 4, No. 16, Second August Number 1943 / SIGNAL / A bi-weekly publication / Editor: Wilhelm Reetz, Deputy Editor: Hugo Mößlang / Signal is published and printed by Deutscher Verlag, Berlin SW 68, Kochstrasse 22-26 / Copyright under international Copyright Convention / All rights reserved

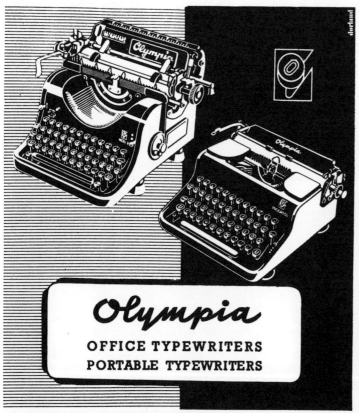
AMERICANA:

Between favour
and hatred

Racial problems have existed ever since human being
have been aware of their various races. The follow
ing report shows how the United States deal
with them. The reader may draw his own conclusion

At the Presidential elections in 1940, it was the negro votes in the Northern States of the U.S.A. which tipped the balance in favour of Roosevelt's re-election. Little has been said about this fact in the United States—for obvious reasons. It nevertheless has had extremely important consequences. Both Roosevelt and Willkie, too, who has already announced his candidature for 1944, have been engaged for months past in keen competition for the favour of the negroes. Not a month passes without one of the two rivals expressing his particular sympathy for the American negroes by some symbolic gesture or other. On a number of occasions, Willkie, in particular, has recently demanded complete equality of rights for the negroes in the U.S.A. and above all in the army.

Mrs. Pearl S. Buck, for example, the celebrated authoress of Chinese novels, has championed equality of races in the U.S.A. in numerous articles. She has declared that the most important argument for keeping the negroes down was fear of intermarriage between whites and blacks. This, however, was not an adequate reason for the bad treatment meted out to the 12 million negroes in the United States. The danger of intermarriage should be faced boldly. American democracy would be able to weather it. So much for the speeches and gestures.

At the same time, however, the most violent colour riots since 1919 have taken place this summer. Fighting, in which hundreds of blacks and whites have lost their lives, has occurred i places as far apart as Los Angeles o the Pacific coast, Florida in the south Newark and New York in the east an the most violent fighting of all was i Detroit, Henry Ford's town.

The police were unable to quell th colour riots which raged all over th whole of Detroit for a day and a nigh at the end of June. In Paradise Alley the negro quarter of Detroit, th rumour spread that a negress and he child had been drowned in Lake Eri by a mob of whites. It spread lik wildfire. Within half an hour, negroe had stormed and plundered all th shops whose owners were whites. Car were held up and set on fire. A docto who by chance had been called to Pa radise Alley at that very time, wa discovered by a mob of negroe Trampled to death by dozens of black he died to the accompaniment of th frenzied howling of the African bus The following day, white armame workers dressed only in trousers an shirts marched through the streets Detroit with their sleeves rolled u and armed with sticks. They beat u every black they could lay the hands on. Many were killed. The com motion was so great that in numerou armament factories 90 % of the em ployees did not appear that day. Sim lar occurrences took place a few wee later in Harlem, the negro quarter New York.

The reasons for the flaring up of th racial hatred are obvious. Since 194 hundreds of thousands of negroes, wh

A scene from the race riots in Detroit, *which animated this big American city during the latter part of June of this year. Mobs seethed on the streets, blacks against whites, whites against blacks. Many deaths occured. In numerous munition factories 90% of the workers failed to show up*

...d so far been working on the land ...the Southern States, have migrated ...rthwards to the industrial towns. ...ere they live in wretched barracks ...d huts made of tin cans on the ...tskirts of the towns. Nobody pays ...y attention to them. According to ...merican reports, the hygienic and ...cial conditions in these new slums ...e indescribable. At the same time, ...wever, the white workers are afraid ...at the blacks work for lower wages, ...though, as the big coal strikes have ...own, even present wages do not ...ffice for the white workers in view ...the inflation in the United States. These factors have all served to raise the colour hatred in the U.S.A. to the highest pitch. The official statements made by politicians concerning equality of rights for negroes have had exactly the opposite effect.

The white workers only feel the consequent pressure being exerted on their own social level by the restive masses of negroes. Nothing was more typical than that 20,000 of the workers in the Packard car factory at Detroit should strike because a few negroes had been appointed foremen. The directors of the Packard concern had only attempted in a very modest way to apply the principles advocated by Roosevelt, Willkie and Mrs. Buck. The result was a catastrophe. It was necessary to dismiss the negroes who had been appointed foremen before the 20,000 white workers would go back again.

In the Western States, the racial conflicts have already spread to the large Mexican minority living in California. During the colour riots in Texas and California, no distinction was made between Mexicans and negroes. The problem is most difficult, however, in the armament industry in the north and east. There the negro question has become an insoluble dilemma, because the Yankees in the north have not had the same experience in dealing with negroes as the white upper classes and the white workers in the south. It is there, in consequence, that the greatest danger threatens.

The official statements made by prominent people in the U.S.A. are thus of no importance where the real course of events is concerned. The chasm yawning between whites and blacks has been made wider than ever. Washington can find no way out of the dilemma. The unsolved colour problem is gnawing deeper and deeper like a slow venom into the unstable, social structure of the U.S.A. The colour riots this summer are in all probability only the forerunners of even more serious disturbances.

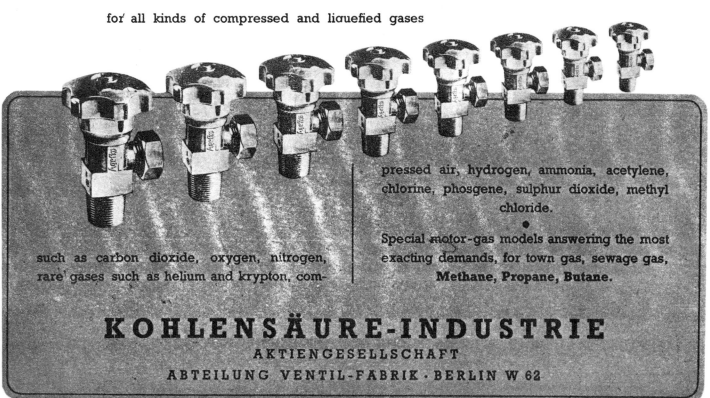

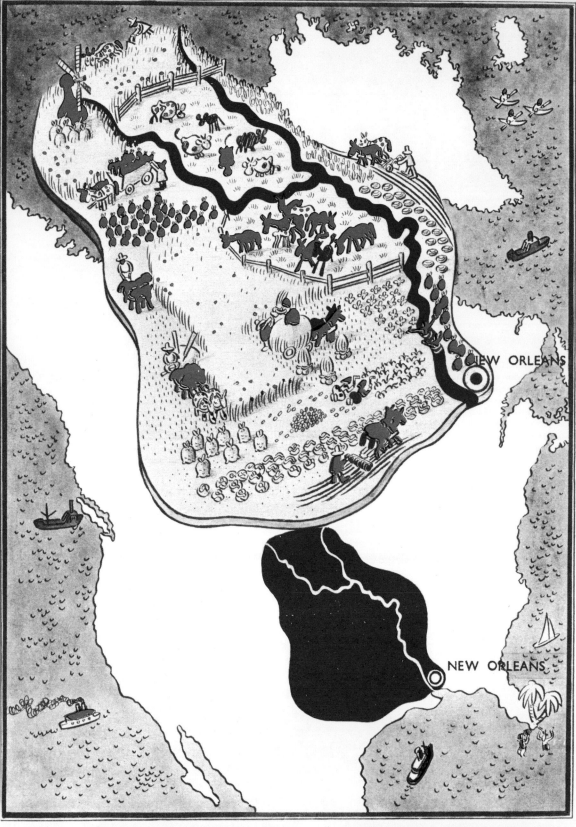

In the article "Europe's climate wi[ll]
improve when..." in Number [?]
SIGNAL referred to the destructio[n]
of American agriculture. Toda[y]
read about the reasons and con[-]
sequences of this developmen[t]

The burning sun beats down on th[e] reservations of the Cheyenne I[n-]dians in the state of Dakota. The lan[d] is parched by the scorching heat. Th[e] air is full of fine dust and the land[-]scape lies bathed in a dull sulphu[r] yellow light. The dust has been raise[d] by the herds of cattle that have to [be] moved from Dakota to other parts [of] the United States to save them fro[m] starvation. What has happened to D[a-]kota, the cattle paradise, to make th[e] exodus of a million head of cattle n[e-]cessary? Drought more serious fro[m] year to year has burnt the last cr[op] of summer grass.

A cow for ten marks

The herds are rounded up in th[e] Missouri plains. Every blade of gra[ss] has disappeared; the earth is bare. [In] the distance the green vegetation alo[ng] the river banks can be seen as su[r-]prising as an oasis in the middle [of] the desert. But the green is not gra[ss.] It is stinking, poisonous marsh veg[e-]tation. Slowly the cowboys urge [on] through the meagre bushes by the [ri-]verside the herds that are bellowi[ng] with hunger. The men are weari[ng] handkerchiefs over their mouths a[nd] goggles to protect themselves from t[he] dust that penetrates everywhere.

Scenes take place at the statio[ns] which mean the end of many a catt[le] farmer's career. Hundreds of anima[ls] already loaded on to the trucks a[nd] apparently healthy suddenly collaps[e.] On slitting open their bellies, the[ir] stomachs are found full of earth. Th[ey] had eaten the grass and the roots [as] well with the earth adhering to the[m.] Only the wealthy ranchers with her[ds] of over ten thousand head are in a p[o-]sition to pay for the transport of t[he] cattle. The small farmers, with only [a] few hundred animals cannot afford [it.] Near the station shots are heard. T[he] Government is buying cows for 16 d[ol-]lars a head and has them shot imm[e-]diately. Of the 16 dollars the farm[er] has to give 12 to his mortgagees. The[re] is not a single farm in Dakota whi[ch] is not in debt.

Black snow

A visit to such a farm reveals [a] ghastly picture. Before the farmho[use] snow" through which the farmer had [?] is a horseshoe—shaped heap of "bla[ck] dig his way out of his house one mo[rn-]ing. The agricultural implements sta[nd] out above the black heaps like [the] spars of a wreck buried in the sand. [In] the orchard the "snow" stands th[ree] yards high, the pond nearby is alrea[dy] too small for even four ducks, for it [is] completely choked up. These drifts [of] "black snow" are "gumbo" or go[od] black soil. As long as this humus [is] moist, it is one of the most fertile s[oils] in the world. But for several years th[ere] has been scarcely any rainfall. N[ow] the wind has distributed the dried s[oil] from the agricultural states over [the] eastern states.

There is a story going round in [the] United States: During one of the d[?]

The area the U.S.A. lost through erosion *is greater than France. The wind from the northwest, from the Rocky Mountains, sweeps over the States tearing up the soil which has been cleared of woods and grass. Today 78,150 square miles of once fertile land are lying waste and 156,000 square miles are seriously affected*

The man-made desert *in the agricultural districts in the Middle West. What were once immense fields of wheat, maize, cotton and tobacco are now a vast desert. Extensive tracts in North and South Dakota, Nebraska, Colorado, Kansas, Missouri, Oklahoma, Arkansas, Virginia — nine of the 48 states — will bear no crops for many a long year*

NEW ORLEANS

NEW ORLEANS

The green heart of America

American reality — gone with the wind

The people have become degenerate too. *Technical progress, the work of the European, is a blessing as long as mankind does not make it one of its idols as in America where people now live on tinned food, wear standardized shirts standardized hats and standardized suits. Thinking has been standardized too and in American civilization there is no place for culture. Today the standardized American is opposing Europe and her century-old cultural traditions*

storms which have been becoming more and more frequent in the lands east of the Rocky Mountains a farmer was sitting meditating in front of his door. With wrinkled forehead he contemplated the storm that had darkened the sky and driven the people indoors. "For God's sake, come in," calls his anxious wife. "What are you looking for outside?" "I'm counting the fields blowing by," was the reply. A grim joke but not at all exaggerated. In her book "Gone with the wind" the authoress represented the fate of countless fields in North-America as the symbol of the decline of the Southern States during the Civil War. The property of the Middle West farmer is literally carried off by the wind.

Fields washed away

But the wind is not entirely responsible for the destruction of the humus. Erosion by water is even more catastrophic. The farmer scarcely notices the first furrows the rain washes in his field. The furrows become broader and deeper and the soil is carried away by the floods. As time goes on the channels become still broader and still deeper. It is impossible to fill them up and the field is lost. In the cotton belt one single rainstorm can wash away a 2,5 cm layer of humus. At least 78,150 square miles of once fertile land have been destroyed by wind and water erosion and over an area of 156,000 square miles the humus has been gravely damaged. In the middle of the affected areas there is now desert land. The clods of earth, torn by deep broad cracks, lie there naked, parched and barren.

In the U.S.A. an area of arable land that would correspond to 200 farms of 84 acres each disappears daily. Year after year three million tons of soil are destroyed by erosion, enough earth to erect 600 Cheops pyramids every year. When the storms sweep over the land east of the Rocky Mountains they tear up the earth and carry it off. It penetrates as fine dust into the towns and on days when a dust storm is blowing the cars have to drive with their headlights on. Grains of soil from the farms in Kansas or Colorado fall in the streets of New York after being carried more than 1,250 miles from the fields where they belonged. The rivers are silted up by water erosion and inestimably valuable minerals are washed into the sea.

A United States committee entrusted with the task of prospecting for and reserving the national mineral wealth reports that the greater part of the area of the U.S.A. is unsuitable for permanent settlement. It is a rich country in which a culture can spring up in a very short time only to disappear in the course of a few generations. Without fruitful soil and without forest land which is perpetually renewed the splendour of the cities will become a ghostly shadow. Oceans and fleets are powerless to defend a country against hurricanes and floods and such calamities. A people whose land has a natural tendency to degenerate into

desert must take measures to preserve it or it is destined to certain ruin.

50 years "prosperity"

This seemingly honest report conceals, however, important facts. For 200 years North America has been exploiting her natural wealth in a most unprovidential fashion. During the last 50 years the system was carried out at a real American pace. The forests were ruthlessly cleared. Formerly one of the most densely wooded countries in the world, today America has scarcely enough wood for her own needs, for it goes without saying that no one thought of forest culture. Woods were treated like mines from which as much was to be got as possible. This system resulted, however, in a remarkable modification of the American climate. The city of New York which lies on the same latitude as Naples has an almost Siberian climate with extreme heat in summer and extreme cold in winter. Since the forests have been cut down, dust storms can rage unhindered in summer, and in winter come snowstorms which fill the streets with drifts several yards high. This state of affairs began to prevail after the forests in the hinterland had been cut down and the protective forest belt which moderated the extremes and held off the storms had disappeared. This modification in the climate can be observed in all the deforested land east of the Rocky Mountains. The forests which tend to retain moisture had been done away with and dry summers result in destructive drought. Vegetation that had once been able to subsist on dew and mist was parched as a result of the disappearance of the moisture reservoirs of the forests. Where there is no forest there is no dew and mist in the interior of a continent. In addition, the American farmer always looked upon his land as something to be exploited.

When in **Europe** the farmers planted hedges or left groups of trees standing in the middle of their fields perhaps they did not always know why. In addition to embellishing the landscape these hedges have a very practical purpose for they protect the fields and help them to retain their moisture. Without trees and hedges our fields, too, would become steppes.

The end of the prairie

The industrialization of agriculture in the U.S.A. made possible the "better" exploitation of the broad prairie land in the heart of America. In olden days the prairies were the ideal country for cattle ranching. But wheat is more profitable and so the prairies became wheatland and were condemned to ruin. The thick roots of the prairie grass which knitted the soil together and helped it to store up water were replaced by delicate cultivated plants. They were incapable of maintaining the necessary degree of moisture in the treeless and bushless steppeland. And so began the wind and water erosion on the prairies. Today

the prairie is nothing better than a desert.

That is what the inexhaustible American paradise looks like in reality. What a lack of appreciation of his own soil is revealed in the average American by his pride in eating canned vegetables! Tinned goods instead of fresh vegetables and fresh meat: artificiality at all costs! That is the essence of Americanism. Surely it is the hand of fate that so many inhabitants of a

country in which abundance and want are so close together should suffer from gastric complaints. Today the Americans are busy introducing their economic system of careless and ruthless exploitation to other parts of the earth. If the U.S.A. attain their imperialistic aims, one day we shall be able to see the characteristics of Americanism in these areas too: lonely skyscrapers towering up uselessly above barren and exhausted desert land.

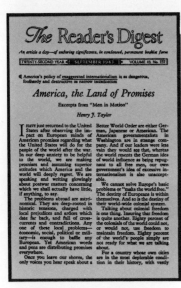

"The Reader's Digest," the American periodical which in its September number 1943 published the following as its leading article

AMERICA, THE LAND OF PROMISES

by Henry J. Taylor

"Reader's Digest" published excerpts from a book entitled "Men in Motion." The author, Henry J. Taylor, is presented to the periodical's readers as a war correspondent on United States newspapers for which he has worked in Africa, Palestine and Syria. His ideas are also of great interest for us Europeans. They confirm the extent to which the forecast of the development of American affairs continually provided by SIGNAL is in agreement with the opinion of clear-thinking Americans themselves. What this American has to say confirms more particularly how foolishly those people are acting who place their entire hopes on economic or political help from the United States. SIGNAL here reproduces the article from "The Reader's Digest"

I have just returned to the United States after observing the impact on European minds of American promises regarding what the United States will do for the people of the world after the war. In our deep anxiety to be helpful to the world, we are making promises and assuming superior attitudes which America and the world will deeply regret. We are speaking and writing glowingly about postwar matters concerning which we shall actually have little, if anything, to say.

The problems abroad are astronomical. They are deep-rooted in historic tensions, charged with local prejudices and ardors which date far back, and full of cross-currents and contradictions. Any one of these local problems —economic, social, political or military—is enough to baffle any European. Yet American words and pens are distributing promises everywhere.

We cannot solve Europe's basic problem or "make the world free." The destiny of Europeans is within themselves. And so is the destiny of their world-wide colonial system.

Talking about colonial freedom is one thing. Insuring that freedom is quite another. Eighty percent of the colonials of the world could not, or would not, use freedom to maintain freedom. Eighty percent of the world's people simply are not ready for what we are talking about.

The reverse of the "American world order"

For a country whose own cities are in the most deplorable condition in their history, with vastly rich areas like Boston, Detroit and Philadelphia facing financial crises in spite of maximum employment and maximum taxes, our government planners go far afield in trying to solve the colonial problems for the world.

The attitude of some of our politicians and speechmakers concerning our allies' colonies, mandates and dominions is already building up vast problems in these places. America's social theorists, tying themselves to our war effort in the colonies of our allies, are creating vast confusion and disturbance abroad. Their folly is working against every solution which our allies may find for their own problems in their own lands.

In support of stubborn schemes for America's Better World Order, the

The Eskimos and Americanism

We set wage scales for labor abroad which make it impossible for anyone else to hire a native man or woman wherever the American Boondoggling Corps operates—*and they are everywhere*. Authorities in these distant communities, who have the long-term responsibility for peace and safety, are outraged. It is one of the most deepseated cleavages among the governments of the United Nations.

For example the Eskimos in Labrador have always lived by fishing, and trapping for furs. In this way an Eskimo family earns eight to ten dollars per week. The work is productive, and the community life has always been peaceful. In came the American Boondogglers. They paid such high wages for labor and so much for furs that overnight the income of the Eskimo family became 80 dollars per week. When an Eskimo got as much in a few days as he used to make in a month, he quit work. The supply of furs decreased at once, there was a famine of fish, and the willingness of the Eskimos to work on American air bases disappeared. In order to get the Eskimos to work the Boondogglers had an inspiration: they boosted their fur and fish prices and their wage scales still higher. They ran the Eskimos' income to 120 dollars per week!

That soon stopped all trapping, fish-

credit and substance of our citizens are being expended now and pledged for the future in the same irresponsible way which made a scandal of the WPA.

Having abused the sound principle of emergency public works at home by using public monies to buy votes and political power and to stimulate political machines throughout the country, these same determined men have now put boondoggling on a global basis. Nothing restrains them.

ing and work for sure. So next they put the price down. And when they did that the Eskimos couldn't understand it. Serious dissatisfaction and unrest spread in Labrador. And then the American Boondogglers turned to the local Newfoundland authorities to put the Eskimos in their place.

"They're out of hand," they said. "Control them. We're spending a lot of money here."

Bureaucracy behind the lines

There is the same hodge-podge duplication of federal offices abroad as in our own country. Nobody can make sense out of the swarm of United States Government employes. They are mystery both to the natives and to each other. They conduct negotiations independently of our ambassadors or ministers. They pay American cash to local politicians who are in opposition to the governments of countries friendly to the United States.

Anything may happen when the representatives of our various and sundry government agencies show up. Take Bolivia. One fourth of the world's tin is produced there. Tin is sorely needed in the United States now. The Bolivian contingent of the American Boondoggling Corps has a program in Bolivia which has so much politics and so little economics that it is doubtful

whether Bolivia's tin will not stay in Bolivia for the balance of this war.

Coffee bulges all Latin-American warehouses. We have allotted to each coffee-producing country a quota for export to the United States. The reason we do not get more coffee is not because there are not enough ships. It is because no one in the Board of Economic Warfare has had gumption enough to authorize lifting the quota whenever an empty ship was in any port where the quota had been filled.

Meat abounds in Australia, for the shipping lane to England—formerly the market for Australia's mutton and beef—has been struck by the Pacific war. Because of this, American meat is sent to England. A constant flow of American vessels transports men and equipment to Australia, but for the most part these ships come back empty when they could bring Australian meat.

The government's policies abroad are undermining the morale of our troops. This is not the time to pay an American workman 1,000 dollars a month to fix electric wires on the airfield at Accra while privates in the United States Army, working on the same field, are paid 50 dollars a month. This is not the time to build immense bases such as we are building in Eritrea with an understanding that only union labor be sent abroad. This is not the time to play into the hands of labor racketeers who require that any skilled American civilian electrician working overtime in Algeria be paid more per month than General Eisenhower is paid. This is not the time for anything but victory.

A shrill whistle on deck. The boatswain summons the watch off duty to parade on the quarterdeck.   PK. Photograph: War Correspondent Pietzu

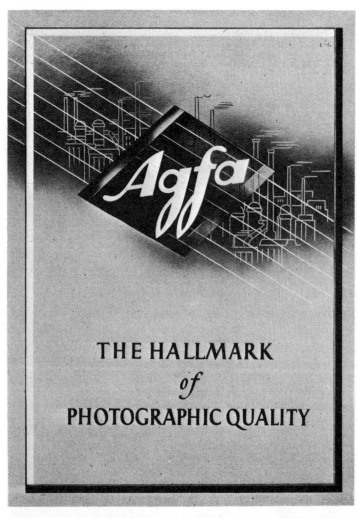

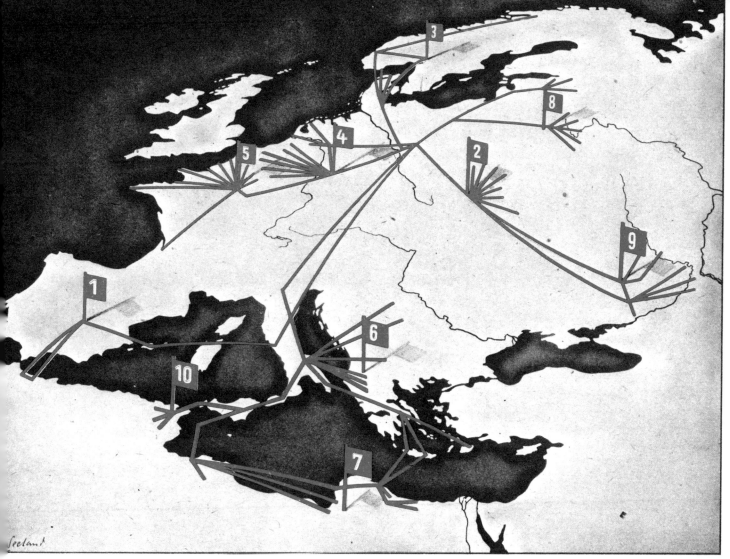

750,000 miles

From the earth to the moon and back and another ten times round the globe is the distance flown by "Berta Dora" during the war. This amounts to . . .

The area in which "Berta Dora" has been employed during the war comprises almost the whole of Europe and a part of North Africa. She has taken part in nearly all the campaigns. The little red flags on the map show the areas where this plane has been employed in chronological order. Without any alterations or replacements being made in the engines or other installations in the plane, it has flown both in the heat of Africa and in the winter cold of Russia. In its often very dramatic flights, this plane has withstood temperatures ranging from 50° Centigrade to minus 50° Centigrade, a difference of 100° Centigrade

1

The first trial

The "Berta Dora" did her first war service during the Spanish War of 1936 to 1939 when she was chartered by General Franco. The pilot had volunteered for service. The transport by air from Morocco to Spain of large units of fighting troops enabled Franco to continue the struggle and gain the victory. Within a short space of time, the Ju transport unit conveyed 13,528 soldiers with full equipment and 265 tons of war material from one continent to another

→

On the two following picture pages:

Ju 52 in winter . . .

Filling the tanks of one of the famous transport planes camouflaged with white paint which carry out thousands of flights during the winter to supply the front with reinforcements

. . . under the African sun

German troops are landing on an aerodrome in Tunis. The grenadiers leap out of the faithful transporters

PK. Photograph: Front Correspondent H. Hubmann
Front Correspondent Lee

THE LOGBOOK OF A JU 52 (CONTINUED)

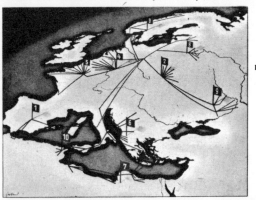

PK. Photographs:-
War Correspondents
Lysiak 20, Seeger,
Beissel, Gerlach, Hadel,
Dietrich, Horster,
Heidrich, Hans Speck

4 **Parachutists in action!** *The "Berta Dora" squadron is to drop the parachutists behind the Dutch ter line. They jump above Rotterdam, Waalhaven, Delft, the Hague, Leiden, Dordrecht and everyw wrest the aerodromes from the enemy. The second wave of transports lands in the midst of the enemy fire. borne troops leap out, bring their guns into position and take an active part in the fighting on the ground. In s of many hits."Berta Dora" takes off another five times on the first day of the fighting in the campaign in the*

2 **All railway lines smashed.** *For 18 days the German squadrons droned in the skies over Poland. The advanced units of the German troops were supplied by means of transport Ju's as the railway lines had been destroyed. Native vehicles were hired to help The squadron to which "Berta Dora" belongs transferred no less than 45,000 litres of petrol to the tanks in one day. On the 15th day of the war the laconic entry was made in the logbook: "Made a forced landing in the front lines as we had been hit. Observer killed, remainder of crew wounded"*

5 **Wounded soldiers fly to Germany.** *"Good old Mrs Ju," for such is the name now given to her b soldiers, has changed her garb. She is now snow-white with big red crosses on the fuselage and wings flies medical supplies, bandages and stretchers far into the heart of France and takes back wounded to Germ Eight severely wounded men or twenty-two light casualties as well as the crew and the medical orderlies all be accommodated in her huge fuselage. In 5 weeks 843 wounded had been flown by the "Berta D*

6 **Air borne troops join in the fighting.** *The Peninsula of Corinth is to be taken. It is one most difficult tasks during the Balkan campaign. Parachutists begin the enterprise. "Berta D with her squadron then lands air borne troops on small meadows and fields to support the parach During one of these landings, she is suddenly subjected to enemy machine-gun fire and the centre e is put out of action. The logbook recalls the episode in the terse sentence: "Take-off with two eng*

3 **Where is our base at Narvik?** *The fog in the fjords and off the rugged coast of Norway was dispelled by the Arctic storms. The transport squadrons seek their way across the glaciers and snow-covered peaks to the places occupied the previous day. The "Berta Dora" carried reinforcements for t e mounta n riflemen to Oslo, Stavanger and Narvik. "Two hits in the rudder" is the entry in the logbook.—The history of the bold Norwegian campaign will always praise the transport squadrons*

Change plugs! *When the prescribed number of flying hours has been reached. "Berta Dora" flies to an aeroplane overhauling station to have her "heart and kidneys" examined. She has already had new engines put in several times*

7 First Crete and then off to Africa . . .

There are certainly faster and more elegant planes than the faithful Ju's, but none which are more reliable. This was also proved during the capture of Crete where a whole attacking army was landed from the air. It was again proved in flying over reinforcements to Africa for Rommel. Parachutists were flown across the seas in the south (above), guns were landed in Crete (left), and ammunition on the coast of Africa (right)

Cleaning up! *Part of the day's duties consists of "cleaning up" which is carried out by the air mechanic after every flight. He is one of the most busy men in the crew of the four-engined Ju*

8 . . . and now on the front in North Russia

"Berta Dora" has to carry out very varied tasks in the hard winter on the Eastern Front, the supplying of encircled units, the transport of field post, fuel, ammunition, wounded, spare parts, clothing and food. She is everything in one, a real "flying furniture van." Above: The supply base. Left: Shells for the heavy flak. Right: Field post for the front line

Filling up! *The quantity of petrol consumed by this plane alone during the course of long years of service has not yet been calculated, but it would certainly fill quite a large tanker*

must be cared for

British anti-aircraft! *An anti-aircraft shell made this hole. The damage to the wing of the Ju is quickly and expertly repaired at an aeroplane overhauling station such as is to be found on every front*

African sand! *The fine desert sand in Africa easily penetrates into the undercarriage and the brakes. It is carefully removed with a brush by the air fitter*

Russian winter! *Special equipment is standing ready on all the aerodromes on the Russian front to warm up the engines with hot air. No Ju has ever failed to take off*

9 Summer and winter on the Don

The advanced tanks asked for petrol, (above) the dive-bombers asked for bombs (left), and in winter there was even on one occasion a rapid flight home to the great joy of a number of men going on leave (below). You can rely on "Berta Dora" for everything. To the great enthusiasm of the grenadiers she once even brought along a whole front theatre with first-class actresses

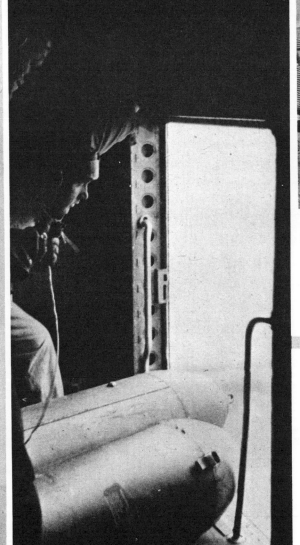

10 The last two flights in the logbook

Mail and beer for the Tunis front are taken on board (above) and "supply bombs" are dropped (left) over the foremost lines. The logbook closes, a new one begins. "Berta Dora" has become an old matron, yet she does not feel old yet and will keep many another logbook

The Ju 52, designed and built by the Junkers Works eleven years ago, was known all over the world before the war in its corrugated, all-metal dress as a passenger plane. Its construction initiated the serial production of big planes and even today it is still unsurpassed on account of its cheapness, reliability in flight and robust construction. It is exercising a decisive influence on the course of the war. This is a fact unique in the history of aviation and warfare. Tens of thousands of these planes have already left the Junkers Works and still are leaving them today.

Neditch visits the Führer

The Führer was paid a visit at his Headquarters by the Serbian Prime Minister, General Milan Neditch. This is the first Serbian State visit to the Führer since 1941

Eugene Lyon:

END OF THE COMINTERN

The following article by the editor of the New York "American Mercury," Eugene Lyon, was taken from the August number

"Persons afflicted with a good memory find it more difficult to work up enthusiasm for the recent dissolution of the Third or Communist International than commentators and editorial writers not thus handicapped. They recall that the "American" Communist Party, though it formally severed connections with the International in 1940, has followed zealously every turn and twist of the party line since then notwithstanding. They recall, too, that another Muscovite world organisation—the Profintern or Red Trade Union International—had been disbanded back in 1935. Far from ending party-line infiltration of American labor unions, that dissolution signalised a peculiarly energetic period of communist union-splitting and union capture tactics.

Most important of all, such people cannot help recalling that the Communist International in the last fifteen years had been increasingly the inert puppet of the Foreign Office, the GPU and other branches of the Soviet regime. It held only one world congress after 1938. It had ceased long ago to initiate anything, serving simply as a formal channel for conveying instructions of the dictatorship to its foreign legions. Unless more tangible proofs that the conspiratorial aspects of this world organisation have been abandoned are forthcoming, the liquidation, therefore, means only a change

in the messenger service the elimination of an intermediary who enjoyed no independent influence or conscience. It should be remembered that Moscow never had any physical or police control of its foreign parties. Obedience has been a voluntary discipline by job-holders and faithful believers. The erasure of the International does not in itself affect that discipline. There is as yet no reason for doubting that the party line will be followed with the same slavish and unthinking enthusiasm as in the past. The speed and unanimity with which some thirty national parties accepted and confirmed the order of dissolution in itself fortifies suspicions as to the genuineness of the gesture. Had the action meant any profound organisational or ideological revolution, at least one of the orphaned sections would have raised a howl of despair. The very act of relaxing centralized control of this world organisation has demon-

strated its amazing cohesion and the completeness of its subordination to the Soviet dictatorship."

Eugene Lyon goes on to say that it is not until the Communist Parties in the various countries together with their subsidized newspapers and the rest of their propaganda have been dissolved that the world will know that the Communist organizations controlled by Moscow and stretching all over the world have in truth been given up.

"The dissolution of the Comintern, in short, means nothing until we have positive answers to questions such as these:

Will the Imprecor and the Intercontinent News and other propaganda services for the Communist press out of Moscow be discontinued?

Will the Pan-Slav movement under Communist guidance here and in many other countries be liquidated?

Will the so-called Partisans, led by imported and local Communists, cease their private civil war against General Draja Mihailovich and his Chetniks in Yugoslavia?

Will the Chinese Communists, whose activities are tying up a large section of the Nationalist forces, merge themselves with the larger Chinese forces against Japan?

Will the special "Polish Army" recently set up in Russia without the consent of the Polish government-in-exile recognized by all the United Nations except Russia, be dispersed?

Will the Communist contingent in the De Gaulle movement break the pipelines to Moscow and follow a purely French policy unrelated to Russia's larger plans?

Will Communist infiltration of refugee groups—such as the Italian exiles in America and England—now cease, and one of the disruptive influences in the shaping of postwar plans thus be removed?

The mere formulation of such questions· indicates the nature of a true dissolution of the international Communist network. Only those willing to accept the word for the deed can overlook them. The word itself, the gesture of dissolution, may have certain propaganda values, but those who think or pretend that a genuine change has already taken place are helping to pile up dangerous illusions."

WE, THE EUROPEANS

BY GISELHER WIRSING

During the autumn of last year—I was attached at that time to the staff of a tank corps in the middle sector of the Eastern Front—I received orders to report to the German Agricultural Leader in a small Russian provincial town a few miles behind the front for the purpose of carrying out a special commission. Whilst engaged in carrying out my orders in the school building on the outskirts of the town where the Agricultural Leader had established the headquarters of the agricultural organization of a pretty large area as best he could, I noticed a young Bolshevist prisoner who obviously played a particular part in the self-administrating body of the newly formed agrarian unit. I learnt that the German Agricultural Leader had almost completely entrusted the difficult task of the organization of the dairy farming in this area to this young man. In spite of war conditions behind the front and by carrying out the instructions of the German expert, he had in the course of a year obtained better results than those of the Soviet system in the same region. I made inquiries regarding this man's personal fate. He told me that he had studied literature at a Soviet university but that he had soon come up against the restrictions placed upon all studies in the Soviet Union by the Marxist doctrine. He had then been mobilized and in August 1941 he had deserted to the Germans near Jelnia. He was not, however, the usual type of deserter. On the contrary, it had taken him several days and nights to reach his objective and he had had to walk thirteen miles before he finally found himself behind the German lines. During that time, he said, he had continually reconsidered his resolve but he had stuck to it because he had realized during his dangerous journey through no man's land that his road was leading him towards Europe. Vladimir—that was the young Russian student's name—is not a typical case. He was far above the average in intelligence. Yet he expressed exactly what tens of thousands and even hundreds of thousands of Ukrainians, Russians and Ruthenians felt vaguely when by one means or another they entered the areas which have recently come under Europe's sway in the east. Seldom have I felt Europe's particular qualities so plastically as when speaking with this lanky, pale, vivacious young Russian who in the depths of his heart had such a definite conception of what Europe is that he was prepared to risk everything for it. A proportion of the peoples inhabiting the eastern territories have nothing to do with Europe. Even the Russian, at any rate wherever he appears as the peculiar product of Soviet training, has nothing in common with the European. Vadimir, however, was a European. He wanted to think and feel like we do. He wanted to be one of us. He naturally did not wish to be a German, for example, but wanted to remain what he was by blood. He wanted to be it, however, as a European.

Europe is not a geographical but a spiritual conception

To begin with, all continents are only geographical conceptions. When we pronounce the names North America, South America Africa, Australia and Asia, a geographical unit with a definite outline appears before our mind's eye. Only Europe is an exception. We know, of course, where it begins—among those peninsulas and islands reaching far out into the Atlantic. When we proceed eastwards, however, our continent has no clearly defined frontiers. Does not Turkey quite rightly belong to Europe although it also includes a territory known as Asia Minor? Do not Reval's lofty towers form one of the symbols of the European character and European culture although only a little farther eastwards, along the marshy course of the Narova, there lives a Russian tribe still at the cultural level of lake dwellers? The geographers of all countries will never be able to define Europe. It is more than a continent. Europe is a spiritual conception. He who is a European, he who belongs to our unique cultural community, can always only be recognized by whether he adheres to it, draws his strength from it and has taken root in it. Were it not so, it would be impossible to speak geographically of "Europe" as a continent by itself. If we imagine its spiritual characteristics as having ceased to exist, it would only be the most westerly part of Asia comparable, shall we say, with India or the Malay Peninsula. But Europe is more than that. Europe definitely is a continent. Although geographically almost a product of the imagination, it is spiritually and politically a power, something real; even today it is still the heart of the modern world—as long as it does not abandon itself.

This merging, this geographical indefiniteness, which distinguishes Europe so remarkably from all the other continents, is, however, also the reason why the consciousness of European unity, at least since the collapse of the Holy Roman Empire, has existed only at certain rare intervals and why our view of history, as, too, our view of the present world conflict, is full of impressions and conceptions which long ago obliterated the feeling for the inescapably common destiny. The question has now arisen for us, the Europeans, whether we wish to continue to exist and can continue to exist as that fertile soil from which the modern world of today has grown up. The converse to it is as follows: Will this terrible storm raging over the whole earth and having our small European Continent as its centre destroy us and make us the impotent plaything of non-European powers? These powers are already employing a battering ram in order to smash down the solid gate to our continent which is guarded by Germany.

Hellas—an example and a warning

The dangers to which Europe is now exposed are plainly shown to us in the eternal example of ancient Greece more than 2,000 years ago. Europe originates from the Greece of classical antiquity. Greece produced the first myths which became the common property of all Europeans. Even our continent's very name originated there, the symbol in the shape of a woman borne on his strong back by the god himself—turned into a beautiful bull, the symbol of strength. The history of the Greeks, with which our European history also begins, is full not only of the veneration of beauty and the origins of our art and philosophy but also of an eternal civil war, of the struggle for supremacy between the Athenians, Spartans, Thebans and Macedonians. At various times they were all supreme in Greece. But the people's strength, the strength of the various States, was exhausted in this internal struggle. The Persians advancing from the east were successfully pushed back as the result of a tremendous effort, it is true, or otherwise Europe would have been reduced to the level of an appanage of Asia 2,000 years ago and have remained of no historical importance. But when we read today those speeches which Demosthenes the Athenian delivered against King Philip of Macedonia, those famous speeches which filled the whole of the ancient world with wonder, we are forced to regard them as the tragic error of a great spirit. It was the spirit of narrow-mindedness which was unable to see the unifying community of civilization and in consequence exhausted itself in civil wars. Greece was, therefore, doomed to decline. Her spirit, it is true, continued to extend for a few short centuries over the then known world. But her heart had ceased to beat from the effects of the civil wars. We, the Europeans living in the fifth decade of the 20th century now have to decide whether as a continent we are going to lose our strength, liberty and future just as tragically in consequence of the restriction of our spiritual horizon as was the case in the Greek tragedy at the commencement of our common history.

The European civil wars

Until the commencement of the second World War our European consciousness was determined by the European civil wars which devastated our continent from one end to the other for many centuries. During those wars the various European peoples, States and princes warred against one another although they knew perfectly well that they were all only members of one family. Even after the era of the discovery of the continents beyond the seas, the horizon remained restricted to Europe. It was here that the decisions were made. The rest of the world was of far less importance. The "grande politique" of the European cabinets consisted in the continual formation of new coalitions and alliances with the help of which the Great Powers of our Continent struggled against one another for supremacy. At times the Reich was opposed to France, at others France was opposed to Spain, at one time France, Sweden and Spain were allied against the Reich, at another time France and England against Holland, Prussia against Austria, France and Russia, Turkey against Russia and Austria until we come to the Napoleonic wars, the wars of German unification and finally the first World War. Even at the time of the great German historian Leopold von Ranke, this struggle of the European Powers for supremacy was regarded as the "grande politique" par excellence compared with which all extra-European questions were of little importance to our Continent. This was only possible because ever since the battle of Liegnitz, where the Mongolian onslaught was shattered by an army of European knights commanded by Germans, Europe had not been seriously threatened from outside. The Turkish danger during the 16th and 17th centuries—at that time Turkey did not yet belong to Europe—did unite all the peoples of Europe affected by it for a short space of time, it is true, but the two French kings Francis I and Louis XIV formed an alliance directed against Europe with this non-European Power. The feeling of unity had already died away. Considered from the point of view of European unity European policy was a succession of civil wars.

In spite of this, a tremendous flow of strength, which affected every part of the world, was poured forth by this disunited European Continent. North America and South America were the joint creations of the European Continent, the former the daughter of the North of our Continent and the latter the daughter of the South. The power of European nations extended across vast areas of Asia. The exploitation of Africa was one of our Continent's greatest achievements although it was carried out according to the ideas of a private capitalist imperialism which now appears strange and out of date to us. The whole of modern civilization, engineering and science originated simultaneously in our Continent and spread across the whole globe. Our European conceptions of international law acquired validity throughout the world. European spiritual movements such as the Reformation later played a decisive part in forming the history of whole continents as, for example, the Continent of North America. Italian, Spanish and Dutch art, French esprit, German music and philosophy climbed to great heights during these centuries of civil war and created a new world of free thought which to a greater extent than all the ancient civilizations of the Far East achieved recognition and validity all over the world.

We, the Europeans, thus built for ourselves an invisible empire extending infinitely beyond our visible power. In spite of all quarrels and disputes it remained unaffected by the European civil wars and gradually developed into a sublime unity.

WAR DOCUMENTS

Concerning war diaries

By Lieutenant Colonel George Soldan

THE STEEL STREAM FLOWS: CARTRIDGES...

TANK AMMUNITION...   ...AND SHELLS

When you entered what was then the General Staff building on the Moltke Ufer before the Great War, you came across a department called "War Archives" on the ground floor. It consisted of only a few rooms. It was in these and the adjacent rooms of the two departments dealing with the history of war that the great and immortal works of the German General Staff on the wars of Moltke and Frederick the Great had their origins. Those few rooms had sufficed to lodge the war diaries from the ages of Frederick the Great, Napoleon and Moltke.

In 1920 it was necessary to turn out of the large building of the former War Academy on the Brauhausberg in Potsdam in order to make room for the war diaries of Prussian units as well as for all the higher command staffs. The "Reich Archives" created at that time were fundamentally the successors of the "War Archives." They combined the Bavarian, Saxon, and Württemberg war archives, which as in the past continued to collect the diaries of their contingents, in its own organization as branches of the "Reich Archives." In Potsdam, as is well known, the official German work on the Great War was compiled, which had not been concluded at the commencement of the present war. This took the place of the work done previously by those departments of the General Staff concerned with war history, to which former officers were transferred as civil servants. Apart from this, the work also included the series of publications called "Battles of the Great War" which was published in millions of volumes. At the same time, the compilation of regimental histories was extensively encouraged.

*

If the war diary of a military staff under Frederick the Great were compared with that of the staff of a unit in Moltke's time, it would immediately be apparent that the increase in the volume of archives is not only due to the larger size of the armies but to the very much more thorough manner in which war diaries have been increasingly kept from war to war.

*

The further one rises from unit to unit, the more the operational aspect naturally comes to the foreground until finally, in the highest commands, the birth of the decisions becomes visible. It is here that the most important and most interesting sources for the subsequent writing of a war history are to be found, all that which after successful or unsuccessful wars is carefully reconstructed, often in order to demonstrate negligence or merits to succeeding generations, but always as an aid to experience for which the clearly presented historical development offers the best and most conclusive evidence. That, however, is assuming that the diary was written down whilst the events were taking place. Measures have today been adopted to ensure that in the higher staffs, particularly in the highest commands, nothing fails to come to the notice of the head of the War Diary Department. Day by day, it can even be said, hour by hour, he is told everything that occurs.

The situation map on which the units of the land forces, from armies down to divisions, are marked on the 650 miles long front provides him day by day with the basis for his work. It is essential for the heads of the War Diary Department in the highest commands to follow the origins of the orders issued to the troops and even a discussion between responsible executive officers, which might lead to the making of a new decision or which provides valuable indications in regard to the development of the situation, must not remain unknown to them. The abundance of the material received each day and the discussions at which he has personally been present and the conversations which he has heard have to be briefly and clearly summarized and this version has to be extensively supplemented and confirmed by the addition of all the original orders.

Innumerable occurrences from the time of the Great War show how essential it is for the higher commands to keep war diaries in order to obtain a subsequent historical representation of the facts at which no reproaches can be levelled. Often the responsible officers have had to be questioned afterwards concerning the making of extremely important decisions because the diaries did not provide an adequate explanation. It is obvious that such "recollections" can never have the same value as a documentary record made during the course of events. Reference need only be made to the mission of Lieutenant Colonel Hentsch which led to the breaking off of the Battle of the Marne. Neither the mission of this officer, the consequences of which were so vitally important, and which had been alloted to him by the Chief of the General Staff, nor his subsequent and no less important negotiations with the army commanders were recorded in sufficient detail, so that it has never been possible to reach a really reliable clarification of the whole matter.

*

The care with which war diaries are now kept ensures that as war documents they will one day provide exhaustive records for a completely reliable investigation into all the circumstances and phases of the development of this war.

Extract from a war diary:

O. B. / H. Gr. X: Is there still any purpose in advancing towards Krasnopole? Is there any more point in doing so?

O. B. / A. O. K. X: Is of the same opinion and requests instructions for further advance of the X. A. K.

O. B. / H. Gr. X: Then only a further advance towards Chechersk and Gomel is to be considered if it can still be carried out.

O. B. / A. O. K. X: Would order X. A. K. to advance to Chechersk and Gomel at once, but this line cannot be reached by tanks owing to lack of oil.

O. B. / H. Gr. X: Can you not attempt it with motorcyclists?

O. B. / A. O. K. X: I will try, but have enemy on my flank and must first beat him if he attacks.

"Take up arms!" They have received their orders. A party of parachutists prepares to set out to liberate the Duce. Laughing and full of confidence in their strength and striking power, they go into battle buoyed up by the spirit of Fort Eben Emael, Crete and Catania

Alert! Enemy bombers are attacking! Everything is set for the start, but the parachutists twice have to take shelter in old bomb craters

DOCUMENTS

PK. War Correspondent Lieutenant Bruno von Kayser recorded on colour film the achievement of the parachutists who liberated Mussolini

MARSEILLES

In Marseilles, ten thousand French policemen, both uniformed and in plain clothes, have just made the biggest raid in the history of crime. 40,000 people were examined and 1,200 houses in the old harbour district blown up. This vast crusade against crime in the ill-famed harbour quarter surpasses even the wildest flights of fancy of the criminal and those who celebrate him, the writers of detective novels. SIGNAL's reporter describes the raid and the motives behind it

Never before has any other writer seen the celebrated and notorious quarter of the old harbour in Marseilles looking so empty and desolate as it lies before me on this, the 1st February 1943. This evil-smelling block of 1,200 houses occupied a prominent place in literature. But it is going to be torn out now.

German soldiers are rolling heavy barrels across the quay in front of me. They leave a fine yellow trail of dust behind them—dynamite! It is between 11 and 12 in the morning and everything is quite quiet. All I can hear is the rolling of the barrels, a few commands and now and again the long drawn-out miaowing of cats.

A tall German policeman is climbing up the narrow façade of a house on the quay-side. The house is empty like all the other 1,200 houses surrounding it The shutters are swinging to and fro in the breeze, but the street door is firmly locked and barred. A kitten has got stuck between the bulging balcony railings on the first floor and is disturbing the peaceful morning with its cries of distress. Cats, of course, attach themselves not to people but to houses. When the people left the houses the day before, the cats remained—the cats and the rats, too. This cat has managed to get itself jammed in the railings. The policeman has reached it now and holding to the railing with his left hand, he sets it free with the other amid much miaowing. Then he climbs down again; but the kitten is frightened and, clinging to his uniform, refuses to touch the pavement. The policeman pleads with it, for he is on duty and must be moving on. Finally he takes it by the scruff of the neck and deposits it on the stones. The kitten, however, will not leave him and follows him as he walks along the quay. I have often seen the pair: wherever the policeman was, the kitten could not be far away. Maybe it will end up by joining the force. Sincere repentance often takes on this form.

Never has midday in Marseilles been ushered in as on that Monday. The noise of a siren wails across the quay. A German officer wearing a steel helmet comes running out of one of the narrow streets in the neighbourhood of the transbordeur and disappears through the door of a squat harbour building. For a few seconds the quay is completely deserted and then the air is suddenly rent by a tremendous explosion. When the noise has passed away, the bells within the ancient Gothic walls at the foot of Notre-Dame de la Garde over yonder begin to peal. The air pressure has set them swinging. A white cloud of smoke puffs out of the narrow street preceded by short black shadowy forms which scurry across the road and disappear over the bank. The rats are fleeing for their lives. Pieces of wood and stone rain down from the sky and a stream of water hisses in the cloud of smoke. The judgement on the criminal quarter in the old harbour of Marseilles has commenced. Six houses of sin and shame collapsed as the result of this first explosion. When I left the town five days later, five hundred of them already lay in ruins.

Every child in the world is familiar with the transbordeur in Marseilles. It is just as well known as the Eiffel Tower or Greta Garbo. The network of its iron wires and its thin silhouette have provided the background for the stories of so many exciting films. When it was built, it was regarded as one of the wonders of the world, a first-class technical achievement. Now they are ashamed of it and want to pull it down.

I climbed up to the top bridge of the transbordeur on foot, for the lift has been allowed to fall into disrepair. I am now sitting up here on a green garden seat looking down at the old harbour spread out below me where I can see the tongues of flame caused by the explosions leaping among the grey walls and can watch the houses crumbling to dust.

How strange people are. I have just paid a visit to the Préfet of Marseilles who resides in the beautiful old town-hall down on the quay. He spoke as

Narrow, evil-smelling and mysterious, the homes of disease, misery and adventure! That is what the old streets of the harbour district were like

She has permission to go and collect h furniture. When humanly possible the e cuees are allowed to salvage their furnit

The morning after the raid. *Criminals and suspects were arrested by the French criminal police during the night while the police barricaded the harbour area. The inhabitants, summoned from their houses by means of loudspeakers, collected with their hand luggage on the quayside and were transferred to camp. After a few days they returned and moved into new houses*

ench and German police protect the evaated quarter from marauders. A permit is uired by those visiting their abandoned homes

The youth of Marseilles gives a helping hand. *The Prefet of Marseilles collaborated with the Red Cross and the Women's and Youth Organizations to establish a large-scale relief service. They distributed food to the evacuees and helped them to move into their new homes*

a city father should. Monsieur Barraud, a slim gentleman with iron-grey hair, has not had a peaceful minute for several days past for on his shoulders rests the burden of seeing to the needs of the thousands of people evacuated out of the harbour quarters. He looks after their belongings and sees to their food and as he now watches their houses falling in ruins, the people also become transfigured in his eyes. The black sheep are becoming more and more white as he sees them.

Seated up here on the transbordeur, I glance through a newspaper published by the municipal authorities, by the Préfet himself. It is called "Marseilles' and the copy in my possession is number 21 of October 1942.

In it Louis Gillet, a member of the Académie Française, writes as follows: "On the hill Accoules between the Hotel-Dieu and La Major is one of the most obscene and putrid cesspools where the scum of the Mediterranean collects, of a foulness and depravity such as it is scarcely possible to imagine without having seen it. All but the stones seem to be consumed by foulness and pestilence. This worm-eaten hell, this kind of decomposing periosteum, is one of the places in the world most ravaged by tuberculosis. This is the empire of sin and death. How

The Poets' Porch is to be preserved. *The valuable cornices and stone garlands in the old city were carefully preserved from destruction*

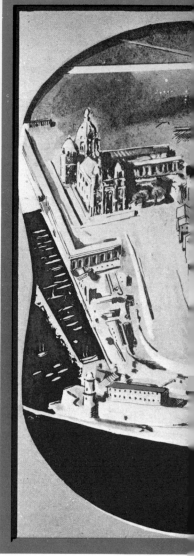

would it be possible to free these former patrician dwellings, which are abandoned to crime, misery and shame, from their putridity and regenerate them? The best that could be done would be to look in this sink of corruption for a few elements worth preserving, arrange for them to be saved and organize this part of Marseilles as a museum where people can stroll around and seek motives for daydreams . . ."

Is it possible that during the six months which have passed since this article was written, people have changed so much, has the quarter by any chance changed its character, or does the Préfet's opinion differ perhaps from that of the municipal editor? No, no, it is as I have said. Sympathy is to-day causing the Préfet to speak differently from the way in which Louis Gillet spoke six months ago when he received the Préfet's support.

If sympathy, however, so greatly changes the judgement on a thing worthy to be condemned to death, then I here beg mercy for the transbordeur. It is not only better but it is also more beautiful than the people down there in that stinking abyss. If it is taken down, it will soon be regretted. It is a monument to man's creative genius, a monument to the 19th century. He who now regards it as ugly will some day have to learn that in this steel skeleton, too, there is that sublime élan which rises in man's heart in his best moments. In thirty years' time people will consider the transbordeur beautiful, because our eyes will then have learnt to appreciate better the beauty of the age of technical pioneers. Mankind has not sinned so deeply against the transbordeur as against the old houses of the nobility in the harbour which have been so profoundly insulted and ravaged that it is better they should fall. War assumes a task an earthquake should have carried out.

What Louis Gillet desired and what the Préfet also desired at the time is now taking place in Marseilles. The cesspool is being drained and there remain only those elements capable of providing food for our better daydreams. It is very airy up here on the transbordeur. Yet I would not like everything that I have to say to be carried away by the wind. I have another copy of the periodical "Marseilles" in my pocket. The sub-title is: "Marseille sera demain . . . une ville moderne." This number was printed at the municipal press of Marseilles on 15th May 1942 and I find the following on the front page: "The Préfets of the Department Bouches du Rhône, who have succeeded one another in office since October 1940, André Viguié, Max Bonnafius and J. Rivalland, with the aid of the co-opted Préfet Pierre Barraud, have had a plan drawn up for the extension of Marseilles and the rebuilding of the over-populated parts of the town." The article then goes on to say that the carrying out of the project has been entrusted to Monsieur Eugène Beaudouin, the head architect of the state buildings (the first person

The future city—not a dream. *For years the municipal administration of Marseilles has been busy with the plan to demolish the old harbour quarter and build new hygienic dwellings surrounded by gardens. SIGNAL had this panorama drawn from the authentic plans of the French architects. In the future, too, the new arrival will be greeted by the classical old harbour front though all that remains standing is the first row of houses, the Town Hall, twelve ancient houses of artistic value, the churches and the old squares planted with plane-trees*

to be awarded the Grand Prix de Rome), that the official commencement of the work had taken place on 1st February 1942 in the presence of the then Secretary of State, Lehideux, and that this work was being carried out within the scope of the law concerning the rebuilding and extension of Marseilles which was sanctioned and financed on 30th May, 1941.

A rare thing has consequently occurred here. A war measure coincides with schemes planned long before and already begun by the municipal authorities and the Government.

When the German Army occupied that zone of France which until then had not been occupied, it also had to turn its attention to the defence of Marseilles. The town is beautifully situated but some parts of it have indisputably been regarded until now as a place of refuge for criminals. The houses and the life there were an inexhaustible source of themes for film and novel writers. The harbour quarter with the Rue Vivaud, "the street of secret murders," and the Rue de la Tour, the Rialto of procurers, is particularly notorious. A combination of stench and indecency made it impossible to penetrate into this labyrinth of streets. It is said that for more than thirty years the police have not carried out a single night raid in this part of the town. The authorities did not

know exactly how many people and what people lived in this quarter. It was consequently the ideal place of refuge for all who desired to establish themselves with hostile intentions behind the front. In view of this state of affairs, it was right to ask the German Police Force for advice. Their opinion was that the quarter should be done away with. The French Home Ministry agreed and it was arranged that the evacuation should be entrusted to the French police. After all, it was French people who had to be dealt with and evacuated although they were not all of them the best type of Frenchmen.

Thus it was that the biggest police raid in the world, the combing of all the criminal quarters in Marseilles, was carried out.

Eight thousand men belonging to the motorized police force were assembled from all parts of France. There were also more than 2,000 secret police in mufti. It was to be expected that incidents would occur with which the French police perhaps could not cope. A German police regiment was consequently held ready for safety's sake to give the action armed support.

The raid went off without incident. Not a shot was fired. The extent of the action probably paralysed all resistance. I have spoken with a large number of those most affected, with those who have been arrested by the French police as being "open to grave suspicion." They assert their innocence. That is their right. One of them, however, said to me: "Monsieur, the raid was held at night with complete dis-

regard to the fact that the French laws prohibit a citizen's home to be entered before 6 a. m.' That is quite true, but war is an exceptional state of affairs and the homes of the people concerned were also something exceptional. The police officer examining the dossiers of those under grave suspicion told me that so far he has sent in about fifty applications for people to be set free. If of the 2,000 people under grave suspicion only two and a half per cent are really innocent— the investigations are still going on— the majority of the remainder have per-

haps also not always respected the hours when it is not allowed to visit the homes of other people. But these are questions concerning the constitution and, moreover', I have no intention of mocking at misery in whatever form it presents itself to me. The French police have declared these people suspects and I am not a policeman but a writer. I emphasize this fact because a literary question now also to be clarified.

You must excuse me for pulling another periodical out of my pocket, but after all I climbed up on to the trans-

e days after the raid. *The demo- d quarter seen from the old har- through a veil of dust and haze.*

 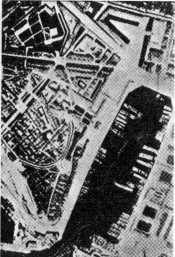

The French plans for the rebuilding. *On the left the old city plan and on the right the new one drawn up on the instructions of the municipal administration of Marseilles a few years ago.*

bordeur in order to read and to look. I find the following in "La Semaine" of 4th February 1943: "Marseilles is a victim of literature." I will quote the end of this longish article:

"That is all", sighed handsome Gino. "Dear old Lisa, even before the war your quarter had lost its prostitutes. When their men were raided, they took to their heels. Everybody was then overtaken by the rumpus, the girls and the apéritifs were then discovered in the rooms at the back behind the shops. Only the better-class houses remained where the gentlemen of the Government and the Town Councillors always went. The opium dens and the sellers of "snow" had disappeared long ago. What was I to do now? Was I to go and work as a coalheaver as Gogo, my old man, had always threatened me when I spent my time in the Rue de la Tour?

Fortunately I then began to do dealings with the Jews. The English pounds and the dollars, all kinds of money, with the printer Milou. I prefer the Jews, who are a bit short-sighted, for you know, to tell the truth, my notes were far from perfect. Meanwhile I shall try to say goodbye to these gentlemen some time or other . . .

But you can tell them, Lisa, that, as the papers say, I know the people who are really responsible. Actually it is the newspapers, the novels, and Pagnol's films with his Raimu and Panisse and all the others dumped on us by the tourists and, finally, the police— that is how it always ends.

That is the truth on my word of honour! Marseilles is literature's biggest victim."

That is a definite assertion made quite calmly and it pleases me to hear it because when I visited Préfet Barraud, I made a similar assertion. I had not yet read the latest number of "La Semaine" and I was talking with the Préfet on the subject of why the harbour quarter of the town had such a bad reputation if in his opinion more harmless than harmful people lived there. It was quite natural for him to refer to literature and I said: "In your opinion, then, Marseilles is a victim of literature?" "You have chosen the right expression," he replied.

I fully agreed and went away but only half an hour later I had changed my mind. For what is literature? "Poetry," our great General Gneisenau said, "is the foundation of States." True, but can poetry bring forth something not in man? It naturally cannot. The background of Marcel Pagnol's works was consequently not a product of the imagination. Various exaggerations may be attributed to that writer, but it is over-estimating a writer when he is considered capable of inventing things which do not already exist at least in their essentials. It must be admitted that in bored and blasé circles, it was "chic" to practise the argot spoken by Pagnol's procurers, prostitutes, seamen and innocent girls. But it was necessary for this language of the criminal classes to exist before it could be raised to the sphere of literature and—perhaps—enriched.

The people of Marseilles accepted the literature on Marseilles and were proud

of it. I am not acquainted with any protest made against this literature.

When you climb to the top of the transbordeur, you can see the Chateau d'If, where Dumas settled one of the fictitious figures he created, the Count of Monte Cristo. Five years after the publication of his novel, Dumas visited Marseilles and discovered that a regular tourist service to the Château d'If was already flourishing. The novelist crossed over to the island on one of the boats and was astonished to be shown the inkpot which the Count of Monte Cristo was supposed to have used. "What did you do, Dumas?" "I naturally bought it immediately!" Well that is the harmless side of the matter, the boastful desire to sell dreams as

regarded the existence of crime as just as natural as the mistral and the sunshine. Pagnol and all the other writers did perhaps gild over this filth and make it romantic, but they did not create it." Far be it from me to give judgement in this question, I feel it only to be my duty to say something about literature's alleged guilt in the case of Marseilles. I do so only because I chance to be the one writer present at the destruction of this favourite scene of criminal literature.

The houses in the neighbourhood of La Major have now been blown up. The tiny church on the edge of the harbour rises in the pure air. The eye can now see across the heaps of débris into space. It is now possible to make

Formerly centres of disease but now green parks. *On the square behind the Exchange in Marseilles there used to be a quarter similar to that in the old harbour. The municipal authorities had it pulled down some years ago. Its place has already been taken by extensive green parks and fountains*

truth, but it is not a completely material harmlessness.

Marseilles has a few crimes which owe their origin to its geographical situation. These are second-class crimes, the smuggling of narcotics and procuring. These crimes, however, involve others in their train, forgers, procurers and perverts flourish so that finally a social problem arises. The drains of the soul are just as important as the drains in the street. But the drains did not exist in either case. The majority of the people of Marseilles

out the hill on which the Greeks erected their Acropolis. It really is true that the beauty dreamt of by M. Baudouin can now blossom here again.

The engineers down below now move off. A cool wind is blowing round the transbordeur. I make up my mind to go, but there is something else I want to say. Witty reporters could make the assertion that Marseilles was a victim of literature because the big raid passed off without an incident of any kind. Had there been a dozen people killed, exchanges of revolver shots, flights

across the roofs, had the catacombs been cleared out with flamethrowers, in short, had there been a Hollywood finale with leaping tongues of fire, the observers would have been more pleased. In this way, however, there was nothing. Everybody went willingly where the police wanted them to go and they did so without making much noise. It was this amazing and unexpected end which so disappointed those people greedy for sensations. The insolent and stubborn apaches just collapsed like a toy balloon on the morning after the carnival. These witty people could not understand that. And that is why they can find no other explanation than that the whole of the criminal quarter was merely a literary fiction.

The truth of the whole affair is very prosaic. No shooting occurred and everything collapsed like stage scenery because this time the vacuum cleaner was just as big as the dustbin. In whichever direction the inhabitants of the quarter looked, they saw steel helmets and automatic weapons and when their eyes passed beyond the cordon of French police, it alighted on the German police.

It was senseless to offer resistance and everything consequently passed off without noise. All this has nothing to do with literature but only with hygiene. When future historians write the history of Marseilles, they will report the remarkable circumstance that here, for the first time, when the old Gothic patrician quarter, which in the 20th century was completely ravaged by shame, was evacuated, the police—both the French and the German police— were employed by the one man organizing the action like a corps of engineers or doctors. The romance of this work lies in its noiselessness and precision. All the love of exaggeration ascribed to Marius of Marseilles died away in the face of this scientific exactness. It would be good for the people of Europe if in this evacuation of a very large criminal quarter they had experienced for the first and last time the silent precision of this, the biggest anti-criminal machine so far, of this dredger of misery.

When I stroll for the last time through these accursed treets, which are dreaming and smelling as they lie in the agony of death, a girl comes timidly towards me. Seeing my uniform, she thinks that I am the commander. She has picked up a small crucifix among the débris and asks me if she can take it with her as a souvenir without being accused of looting. She curtsies and goes. Perhaps it was her intention to fool me, perhaps all the time her loot is concealed under her dress. "You can make any assertion you like about Marseilles," a man well acquainted with the town once told me, "and you can contradict everything. Whatever you say, it will never be possible to prove you wrong."

I insist that this girl is good. Her face shone like a lamp in the midst of this accursed street. I remember the girl in Pagnol's play who remains behind deserted in the harbour of Marseilles. Out at sea the sails are being hoisted for the journey into the new age.

Walther Kiaulehn

Vol. 4, No. 7, First April Number 1943 / SIGNAL / A bi-weekly publication / Editor: Wilhelm Reetz, Deputy Editor: Hugo Mößlang / Signal is published and printed by Deutscher Verlag, Berlin SW 68, Kochstr. 22-26

THE CRUMBLING ALLIANCE

The Axis appeared to be dramatically in disarray during 1943. Italy quit the alliance after the overthrow of Mussolini, and other allies, such as Rumania and Bulgaria, became increasingly nervous as Soviet armies approached their frontiers. They eventually divorced themselves from the Axis, too late to avoid the wrath of the Red Army. To prevent further defections the Propaganda Ministry ordered *Signal* to present as glowing a picture as possible of those states who, *faute de mieux*, remained within the Axis largely due to their proximity to Germany and their relative impotence. In any event, places like Bohemia, Moravia and Slovakia, formerly the constituent parts of Czechoslovakia, were free from aerial bombardment and were simply peaceful places to photograph. The usual fashion and film articles presented by *Signal* all but disappeared, and in their place were published long and tendentious articles without illustrations about why Germany was really winning the war while they were at the same time losing it. We have chosen not to publish many of these, as their similarity of theme makes one reading as useful as a thousand. But the brilliant photography of *Signal* was still apparent in the articles which were illustrated, and the political articles make curious reading now as they must have done for those readers who found sufficient light in their bomb shelters to read Hitler's Wartime Picture Magazine. Toward the end the editorial team of *Signal* chose not to minimize the grave situation but instead suggested the sort of Europe that would appear if Germany lost the war. Articles predicting the Cold War between the Western Allies and the Soviet Union seem prophetic and have a ring of truth to them which is lacking in many of the other 'think-pieces' published by *Signal*. *Signal*, as in its glory years, was as accurate a mirror of life in the Third Reich during the years of retreat. It was a distorted mirror image of life in occupied Europe which revealed almost as much in what it did not state but alluded to obliquely as it did when it openly spoke of triumph for the Axis. When no victories were mentioned, it was a sure sign to the peoples of occupied Europe that the war was nearing an end and their liberation was at hand. The articles also reveal that many of the loftier aims of the Third Reich of a united Europe allied against the United States as well as Communism are still echoed by some European politicians today. It is well to remember that the Third Reich did not die with a whimper in 1945 and is reason enough to record *Signal*'s and Nazi Germany's final years.

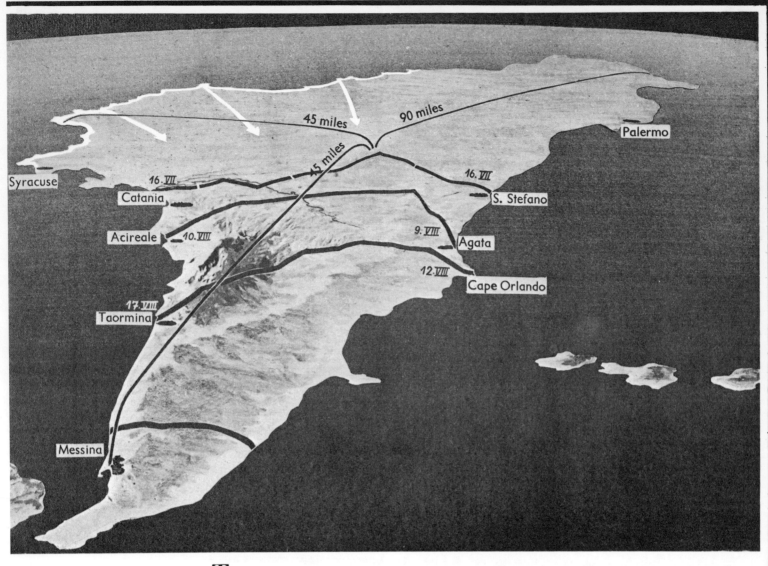

Sicily—a number of comparisons

Two British and American armies were launched against four German divisions on Sicily. Eisenhower's orders were to cut off the Germans in the shortest possible time from Messina, that is, to cut off the retreat to the Continent and to annihilate them. Sicily was to be a German "Dunkirk". But was it?

During the critical phase, the Anglo-American struggle for Sicily, which lasted 39 days, was restricted to one third of the island (1). The above sketch-map shows the successive stages of the fight for this area. In spite of repeated crises, Crete (2) was taken by storm in the thirteen days between 20th May and 1st June 1941. The Ger-

man occupation of Norway (3), an area more than twelve times the size of Sicily, was completed between 9th April and 1st June 1940 with the exception of the action round Narvik which was in German hands again on 10th June. Both these landings are a proof of the efficiency of German troops and arms and of the superiority of German leadership. Dunkirk 1940 was the grand finale to a battle of annihilation. After the Grebbe Line had been penetrated, Holland capitulated on 14th May. On 24th May the annihilation of all the enemy forces still in Artois and Flanders began (4). On 28th May the ring drawn round the remnants of four enemy armies from Ostend to Lille, Armentières and Gravelines was closed.

The Belgian Army capitulated while the fragments of the British Expeditionary Army tried to escape at Dunkirk after an unparalleled defeat in three battles of encirclement (5). On 4th June Dunkirk capitulated with 88,000 prisoners. 26 days after the beginning of the campaign in France, the British had been swept from the Continent and had experienced the Dunkirk catastrophe of which Churchill said that it was "a colossal military disaster". But after more than five weeks of heroic resistance, the German troops down to the last private were able to make an orderly retreat back on to the European mainland. Read our report on the five phases of the Battle of Sicily.

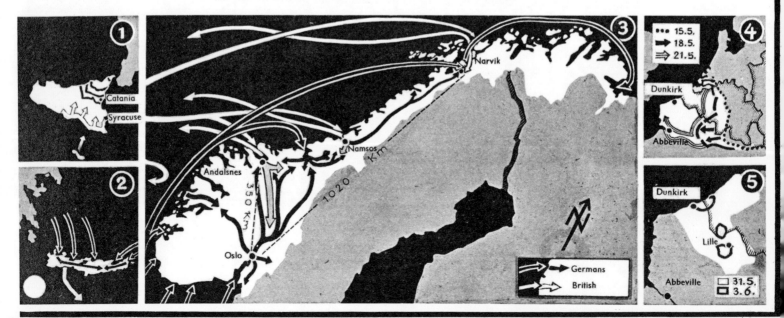

39 days···

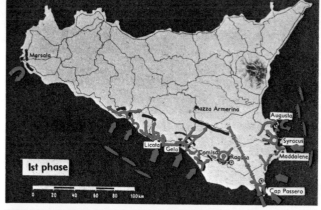

1st phase

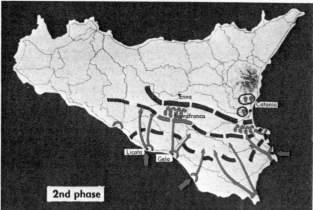

2nd phase

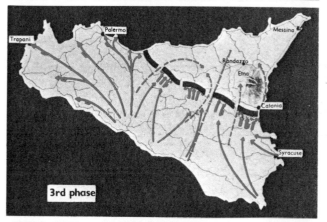

3rd phase

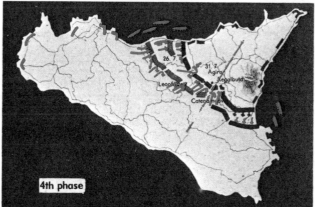

4th phase

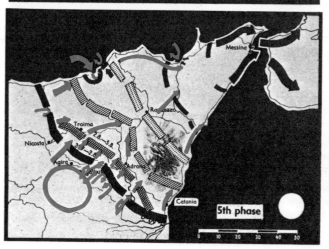

5th phase

1st phase of the fighting 10th to 13th July 1943

During the night of 10th July several groups of enemy ships approached the eastern and southeastern coast of Sicily between Marsala, Cape Passero and Augusta along a broad front. Under cover of the fire from their heavy naval artillery, United States troops simultaneously began to land at various spots along the south coast in the vicinity of Licata and Gela. British divisions disembarked at Syracuse and Cape Passero. Parachutists and airborne troops were also sent into action in the Ragusa-Comiso area.

The struggle of the Anglo-American armies of invasion against Germany's and Italy's advanced guard had begun.

Whilst German and Italian coastal defence troops offered resistance to the invading enemy and immediately engaged him in embittered fighting, the British and Americans continued to land fresh troops at further places along the extensive coastline. The parachutists and air-borne troops landed behind the Axis lines were encircled, annihilated or dispersed by emergency units of the Air Force and Army as soon as they touched the ground. As early as the 10th July, the main body of the "Hermann Göring" Tank Division, which launched an attack in the direction of Gela eastwards on the Gela-Piazza-Amerina road, succeeded in collaboration with a number of Italian units in driving back the Americans who had landed at Gela into a narrow coastal strip and forcing them to take to their ships again with the majority of their strength. In the southeast of the island a unit of the 15th Tank Grenadier Division supported by units of the "Hermann Göring" Tank Division and an Italian division launched an attack against Syracuse. The enemy parachutists who had landed northwest of Syracuse were put out of action.

During the course of the night and the days which followed, the enemy again landed strong contingents of troops including tank units at various places along the coast. Enemy attempts to land at Marsala and Augusta were repulsed with heavy losses.

Under the pressure exerted by the British and American troops, who were continually drawing reinforcements from the bridgeheads, and in order to escape the rain of shells from the heavy naval units off the coast the German and Italian troops withdrew during the succeeding days to prepared positions lying further northwards, all the time fighting delaying rearguard actions. In spite of the stubborn resistance of the British the town and harbour of Augusta and the peninsula of Maddalena were recaptured by units of the 15th Tank Grenadier Division. During fighting for the possession of roads leading northwards through narrow mountain valleys, the German and Italian troops inflicted exceedingly heavy losses on the enemy in elastic warfare. Skilful withdrawals alternating with lightning attacks continually resulted in the cutting off from the main forces and annihilation of enemy advance guards. Once more the armour-piercing weapons of the German troops proved their superiority laying low even the heavy American "Dreadnought" tanks.

In almost uninterrupted day and night fighting, strong bomber, Stuka, fighter and destroyer units of the German Air Force attacked concentrations of enemy troops. columns on the march and disembarkations with annihilating effect. From the beginning of the landing operations until 13th July, the German Air Force sank no less than 20 troop transport ships, cargo boats and merchant vessels totalling 107,500 tons as well as numerous landing boats. 97 ships, 5 cruisers, 2 destroyers and a large number of landing boats were damaged by direct hits from bombs Anti-aircraft guns and aerial combat accounted for 83 enemy planes.

2nd phase of the fighting 14th to 17th July 1943

During the fighting which now followed, the enemy attempted by concentrating his strength not only to force a breach in the Catania Plain but also to capture the area round Enna, the centre of Sicily, by penetrating the right wing of the German defensive front. With this object in view, General Montgomery, who was in command of the British 8th Army in Southeast Sicily, reinforced the British troops held up by the strong German defence in their attack south of Catania by bringing up contingents of freshly landed troops. By the mass employment of parachutists and air-borne units northwest and south of Catania, he attempted to break the resistance of the German troops with an attack in their rear. Battleships, aircraft carriers, cruisers and destroyers were concentrated along the coastline from Augusta to Catania with the object of holding down the German

troops with almost incessant shelling from their heavy guns.

The defenders nevertheless proved in the days to follow that they were able to cope with this superiority in men and materials. The air-borne troops landed northwest and south of Catania were encircled and annihilated before being able to launch their attack. The heavy onslaughts of the British, which now began with strong tank and air support, collapsed in the face of the defenders' resistance with heavy losses after severe and embittered fighting without having reached the Plain of Catania. In only a few days of fighting, the "Hermann Göring" Tank Division alone accounted for 130 enemy tanks and 15 planes at Catania.

The offensive launched to the west by United States troops shared the same fate. General Patton, too, brought

One shell after another *explodes along the enemy's front. It is only at the cost of heavy losses that he can advance at all against the desperate German defence*

and a 3,000 ton steamer as well as damaging a big troop transport ship of 8,000 tons.

4th phase of the fighting
24th to 31st July 1943

Not until 30th July did the British feel strong enough to launch a fresh attack. By outflanking the right wing of the "Hermann Göring" Tank Division lying to the south and southwest of Catania, the enemy attempted to break through in the direction of Regalbuto with the help of strong tank and artillery support. A second group attacked simultaneously in the direction of Catenanuova. Whilst the attack on Regalbuto crumpled in the defensive fire of all weapons before the British were able to reach the town, Catenanuova was lost during the course of embittered fighting. During the night from 31st July to 1st August, the main fighting line was withdrawn to the heights northeast of Catenanuova and Regalbuto, which latter place was abandoned to the enemy.

The enemy strove by every means in his power and by the ruthless employment of his divisions to achieve the aims which he had failed to realize during the previous week's fighting. He consequently regrouped his forces and transferred the centre of his operations to the American sector in the hope that by attacking there with particularly strong spearheads, he would be able to overcome the defenders' resistance and break through eastwards along the coastal road. A second attack by strong motorized and mechanized units was to overrun the troops at Leonforte and Agira, push forward towards the north and join up with the northern group.

Whilst the Americans only skirmished along the northern front with weak forces, they launched a big attack along the coastal road on 25th July. The tank grenadier division fighting there repulsed the attack and threw 'he enemy back in an immediate counterattack. When the enemy attacked again the next day, he met with no opposition.

The mobile German prosecution of the fighting proved its value during the course of the operations which now followed. The most stubborn defence and withdrawals at the appropriate time alternated with lightning attacks.

up reserves from the bridgeheads at Licata and Gela in order to make up for the losses of men and material in the previous fighting. He launched an attack in the Barrafranca area with the object of capturing the town of Enna so as to be able to control and use the roads and railways converging there which were of fundamental importance for the prosecution of the fighting. Although the Americans here sought to carry forward the infantry attack by giving it strong tank and air support and covering it with massed heavy artillery fire, all their efforts did not achieve the anticipated success. They suffered very heavy losses and all their

attacks crumbled in the annihilating fire of the defenders often before the main battle line had been reached.

The chief task of the German Air Force, which gave effective support to the troops fighting on the ground, in this phase of the fighting, too, lay principally in attacks on enemy shipping in the waters surrounding the island. During the period from 14th to 17th July, the German Air Force sank 1 destroyer, 28 troop transport ships, oil tankers, munition ships, supply ships and troop landing ships totalling 94,000 tons. 5 cruisers, 5 destroyers and 53 ships of various kinds were damaged whilst 43 enemy planes were brought down.

ated as being required for the invasion of Sicily was soon exceeded. General Alexander, who directed the operations in Sicily, found it necessary in view of the successful and heroic resistance put up by the defenders to ask the Allied Headquarters for fresh divisions and to transfer them across the sea continually watched over and rendered dangerous by the German Air Force. It was on the sea that the biggest weakness of the British and Americans lay. The enemy's difficulties there increased day by day in consequence of the successful operations of the German naval units and Air Force.

The German Air Force, for example, sank 2 troop transport ships of 14,500 tons and a tanker of 10,000 tons in Sicilian waters whilst 1 cruiser and 1 destroyer as well as 21 ships, most of them of medium tonnage, and innumerable special landing boats were damaged.

A particularly courageous action was carried out by 6 German motor torpedo boats which during the night of 19th to 20th July forced their way in clear weather into the harbour of Syracuse and sank 2 destroyers anchored there

3rd phase of the fighting 18th to 23rd July 1943

The Americans scored a cheap triumph during the third phase of the fighting in Sicily. They occupied the west and northwest of the island, which had been evacuated by the German troops, and took possession of the town of Trapani and Palermo without opposition.

The situation in the east and northeast of the island, however, was very different. Huge forces of mobile and mechanized troops were massed once more with the object of forming two spearheads. The aim of the Americans was to outflank the German 15th Tank Grenadier Division and a number of units from Italian divisions at two places and thus get possession of the roads leading northwards and northeastwards through the mountains via Randazzo to Messina.

The second spearhead was to be the affair of the British. In spite of the defeats inflicted on it during the second phase of the fighting, the British 8th Army was to make another attempt to capture the Plain of Catania along a broad front in order to cut off the German and Italian troops' line of retreat to Messina on the other side of Mount Aetna along the coastal road leading northwards.

But in this phase of the fighting, too,

the enemy was not able to reach his strategic objectives and suffered disproportionately high losses of men and material.

Wherever the enemy attacked, whether in the middle or in the eastern sector of the Sicilian front, the onslaught of his tank units was shattered by the destructive power of the defenders armour-piercing weapons. Did the enemy infantry succeed in places in advancing beyond the outposts and reaching the main fighting line, German and Italian grenadiers nevertheless remained the unquestionable masters of the situation in the hand-to-hand fighting. The nature of the tactics employed in Sicily, the elastic prosecution of the fighting and the many advantages provided by the rugged nature of the country with its narrow mountain passes, made it possible to inflict extremely heavy losses on the attacking enemy with a minimum number of defenders. During the course of the operations from 18th to 23rd July, the enemy was consequently obliged to allow increasingly long periods to elapse between his attacks in order thus not only to regroup his decimated units but also to bring up fresh reserves. The number of divisions estim-

A photographic record. *Methodically, as though on manoeuvres, the last troops fighting in Sicily arrive on the mainland with ferries across the Straits of Messina*

Whilst the enemy offensive along the coast was never able to get going properly in consequence of the delaying rearguard actions fought by the German troops, the second spearhead, that of the Americans in the middle sector, encountered the inflexible determination and stubborn resistance of the German tank grenadiers. Even the assault carried out against the German rearguards at Leonforte compelled the enemy to throw in all his forces. In order to be able to storm Agira, the enemy was obliged once more to regroup his units after the heavy losses they had suffered and to bring up reserves. He then launched the big attack on Agira. After a severe struggle with changing fortunes for both sides, which forced both defenders and attackers to throw in their last reserves, the enemy's attempt to break through to Agira collapsed and the realization of his outflanking movement was frustrated.

Strong bomber and fighter units of the German Air Force were employed over Sicily and participated effectively in the fighting on land. In this phase, too, however, its chief task lay in attacking ships in Sicilian waters and the supply ports in Africa. A 7,000 ton tanker and 3 large merchant ships totalling 20,000 tons were sunk, whilst 36 transport and merchant ships, 1 cruiser and 2 smaller naval units were seriously damaged. 64 enemy planes were shot down by the anti-aircraft defence and in aerial combat.

Small fast boats belonging to the German Navy torpedoed a cruiser and sank an enemy submarine. 7 enemy planes were brought down by A. A. fire from German ships.

5th phase of the fighting 1st to 17th August 1943

Whilst the enemy during the first days of August advanced with only weak forces against the "Hermann Göring" Tank Division in the southern sector and the 29th Tank Grenadier Division in the northern sector, the main enemy attack was now transferred to the middle sector. It was not difficult to guess his intentions. He was trying to gain possession of the roads leading via Troina on the one side and Adrano on the other to Randazzo and Messina. In order to achieve this object, the enemy concentrated his main force in the middle sector in the Nicosia-Agira-Regalbuto area in preparation for a big attack. The German troops together with a number of Italian units now faced their most difficult task during these operations. If they succeeded in repulsing the enemy's attack with its vast superiority of men and material and in gaining time by means of elastic methods of fighting so that the main body could retire, then they would have succeeded in their aim. Conscious of this historic task, the German tank grenadiers resolutely faced the big attack, held it up and continually compelled the enemy to regroup his forces.

The main body of the German and Italian troops meanwhile retired towards the northeast. The enemy pushing forward in pursuit became entangled in wide expanses of dense minefields and thus lost much precious time. Counter-attacks were launched against attempts made by the enemy to hold up the retreat of the German and Italian units by landing troops in their rear. The enemy forces which had landed were encircled, destroyed or thrown back into the sea.

The transference of the troops to the Italian mainland had been going on for days past unhindered by the enemy. The unexcelled courage of the German rearguards, which prevented a more than twentyfold superior enemy from seizing the disembarkation harbours, made it possible to convey all the units fighting in Sicily together with their heavy weapons, tanks, guns, lorries and other equipment across the Straits of Messina to the mainland.

The struggle in Sicily had thus come to an end. During fighting which lasted for 5 weeks, the Army carried out the task allotted to it of acting as an advanced guard and gaining time for the concentration of the main body of their own troops. Only when the history of the war is written will it be possible to pay full tribute to the small but unprecedentedly courageous group of men who in a heroic struggle succeeded in putting out of action more than a third of the fighting strength of a superior enemy.

During the same period, the German Air Force sank and damaged much of the enemy's all-important shipping. 61 transport and merchant ships, most of them carrying men and war material, totalling 290,000 tons were sunk as well as 1 cruiser, 7 destroyers, 3 corvettes and numerous smaller naval vessels. A further 59 cargo and transport ships totalling 278,750 tons were so severely damaged that their loss may be regarded as certain. The other ships set on fire and struck by bombs of all calibres are too numerous to be mentioned.

The achievements of the German Navy, which carried out the tremendous task of withdrawing all the German and Italian troops with their weapons and equipment, nearly 10,000 lorries, 17,000 tons of ammunition, fuel and other supplies as well as more than 4,000 wounded during the first weeks of August were unique in history.

This masterpiece of military organization in the face of a more than fourfold superior enemy force could only be accomplished by troops who had prevented every breach of their lines and every outflanking movement on land, by the heroic deeds of a navy, which carried out the traffic to and from the island almost exclusively with small vessels and protected it on the flanks with light units, and by an air force which participated in the ground fighting with strong bomber and fighter squadrons, engaged the enemy in aerial combat and struck heavy blows at him by sinking and damaging valuable shipping.

Officers and men have thus performed an achievement which will go down in the history of warfare in the same way as a victorious offensive battle.

Vol. 19. First October Number 1943 / SIGNAL / A bi-weekly publication / Editor : Wilhelm Reetz,
Deputy Editor: Hugo Mösslang / Signal is published and printed by Deutscher Verlag, Berlin SW 68,
Kochstrasse 22-26. Copyright under international Copyright Convention / All rights reserved

THE SECRET OF THE MAIN ATTACK

BY LIEUTENANT-COMMANDER RUDOLF KROHNE

The following article from the pen of an expert, who investigates and describes the conditions of naval warfare, reveals the development from the slanting battle order of Epaminondas to the formation of the main attack in modern war

It is probable that history would long ago have ceased to pay any attention to the battle of Leuktra (371 B. C.) during the course of which the Theban general Epaminondas annihilated the attacking Spartan army, if on that occasion he had not made perhaps the great and most amazing discovery in the history of warfare—the slanting battle order. Whilst the front of Epaminondas' army cannot have been more than a few hundred yards long, the German concentration in 1914 was carried out in accordance with the Schlieffen Plan along a breadth of approximately 300 miles until after a series of brilliant initial successes, it was held up by the "Miracle on the Marne." Had Schlieffen's plan been misunderstood or had it not been put into practice consistently? Or was it not possible to apply Epaminondas' simple conception on such a huge scale?—It is certain that modern land fronts—the Germans and their allies in Soviet Russia are fighting along a line extending no less than 2,000 miles—can no longer be established according to Epaminondas' simple principle with any prospect of success. That it is impossible to fight a naval war along the lines of Epaminondas' system is clear to anybody who, for example, takes up a map and compares the theatre of the naval war extending from the Sea of Barent via the Atlantic and the Caribbean Sea round the extremity of South Africa as far as Madagascar with the German front in Russia, which, after all, far surpasses all other previous wars on land in its extent. Has Epaminondas' brilliant idea consequently been relegated to oblivion? No! But in view of the oceanic character of the present war it has undergone a change—the formation of the main attack.

It is only another proof of the oceanic character of this war when the idea of the formation of a main attack continually reoccurs and when Churchill proffers his excuses to the House of Commons by saying that "it is impossible to be strong everywhere." It does not suffice in vast areas, however, to be strong at the decisive point at the right time. Rather does the idea of the formation of a main attack make it essential *to realize already in the planning of the operation which of the modern arms are destined to force the decision*. When they have been determined, it is necessary to ensure superiority in regard to numbers, construction, war economy, training, operations and policy by every means available and to employ it at the right time and at the right spot. Not until then has the formation of a main attack been achieved. Although all the typically "oceanic" land operations of this war provide convincing examples of the formation of a main attack, we shall here confine ourselves to those occurring during the course of the naval war.

Faced by the growing menace from Great Britain and the United States, Japan was confronted with the problem of how and when she would be able as well as how and when she would have to meet the probable attack. Both antagonists possessed strong fleets and advanced bases in the expanse of the Pacific which threatened Japan, whilst their sources of strength were beyond her reach. Japan herself, it is true, had a strong fleet. Its full employment, however, with the object of forcing a decision in the question of naval supremacy as the result of a naval engagement would have involved a considerable risk in view of the relative numerical strengths. But it was impossible to think of capturing the vital areas providing raw materials and the enemy bases of the Philippines, the Strait Settlements, Malay and Burma as long as the British and U.S.A. Fleets at Singapore and Honolulu still formed a menace from the flank.

Aircraft carriers the main base of attack

Such being the situation, Japan early realized that the aircraft carrier was the arm predestined to force a decision in the vast expanses of the Pacific Ocean. For the Japanese Fleet was in a position to provide the essential support for every employment of aircraft carriers in carrying out operations. Should a naval battle against strong enemy forces, however, occur anywhere in the Pacific in order to protect the aircraft carriers, the Japanese Fleet could anticipate that with the help of their torpedo bombers and battle planes, the aircraft carriers would at least be able to establish an equality of strength and even perhaps decide the outcome of the battle in the event of the naval air arm fulfilling the hopes put in it. With the greatest farsightedness and after years of hard work, the Japanese Fleet consequently

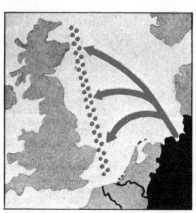

An example of the "slanting battle order." *Following the Schlieffen Plan, the German armies in 1914 were concentrated along a 300 mile long front. The left wing pivoted in the angle formed by the Swiss frontier, whilst the considerably reinforced right wing was to move across Belgium and North France. A gap led to an interruption of the advance, which had been successful until then, and to the French "Miracle on the Marne"*

→

The road leading to the "formation of the main base of attack." *The task facing the German Naval Command was that of creating a main base. Bold rapid action prepared and ensured the submarine offensive against merchant shipping*

At the outbreak of war German ships put out to sea to lay mines off the east coast of Britain. The first step to get out of the "wet triangle" of the Bight of Heligoland had been taken

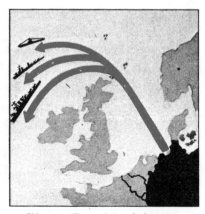

U-boats, auxiliary cruisers and other units took part in an energetic war on merchant shipping in the Atlantic and compelled the British to employ the whole "fleet in being"

Liberty of action was obtained as a result of the brilliant operation which led to the conquest and occupation of Norway. A decisive step had been taken

The result of a correctly established centre of attack

The map shows the result of the correct formation of centres of attack, a conception discussed in the adjoining article "The secret of the main attack." The German Navy today controls the vast areas marked in black on the map. At the southeastern corner of Africa, off Madagascar approximately, it overlaps the area (marked in red) which is controlled by the Japanese fleet. The white dots on a black background represent shipping sunk by German U-boats, whilst the small ships represent the shipping sunk by German auxiliary cruisers from the outbreak of war until Japan's entry into the war   Illustrations: Rudolf Heinisch

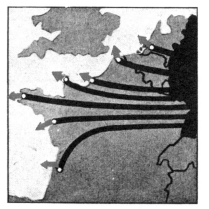

When the Army and Air Force had reached the Atlantic coast, positions had been gained from which the U-boats could operate. U-boats could now exercise a decisive influence on the course of the war

created its naval air arm. It was indefatigably trained at the cost of a considerable number of lives and has always been employed ruthlessly at the right place and at the right time completely taking the enemy by surprise (Pearl Harbour, annihilation of the "Prince of Wales" and the "Repulse" off Kuantan, naval battles of Sumatra and Java). The Japanese naval successes—which of necessity were the preliminary condition and the foundation of all land successes in the India-Pacific war zone—were consequently the result of the farseeing formation of a main driving force for

the attack which was prepared skilfully and with determination and employed in masterly fashion.

Although we must not be surprised that the U.S.A. and Britain sought to represent subsequent events as "signs of having recovered the initiative in the Pacific" and even as "victories," the naval battles off the Solomon Islands, Midway, the successful occupation of the Aleutian Islands Attu and Kiska by Japanese naval forces and the problematical American landing on the Solomons were nevertheless determined to a decisive degree by the resolute action of the Japanese

Fleet. The element of surprise on which the much weakened U.S. naval forces counted in their attacks (Battle of the Coral Sea, Torres Straits, the Solomon Islands), was a failure. Units of the Japanese Navy and the naval air arm were on the spot on each occasion, able and determined to deal heavy blows. On the other hand, the Japanese were successful in occupying the islands at the western end of the Aleutians thus breaking the point of

THE SECRET OF THE MAIN ATTACK

the spear directed from Dutch Harbour against Japan. At the same time, the Japanese Fleet, under unfavourable conditions within range of American planes operating from land bases, unhesitatingly fought a naval battle which the enemy would not accept on the open sea. In consequence of the changed relative strengths and the occupation of bases in various parts of the Pacific, the Japanese were now able to build up their naval strategy on the employment of the entire fleet instead of on the aircraft carrier and to aim at the exercise of naval supremacy.

Improvisation

Compared with the classical and immediately evident example of the formation of an oceanic main attack by the Japanese Fleet, the situation facing the German Fleet was at the outset considerably more involved. In the first place, the German Fleet was forced into war whilst still engaged in the first stages of reconstruction. In the second place, it was essential to extend the naval war resolutely from the hemmed in seas (North Sea and the Baltic) to the oceans and large seas (Arctic Ocean, Atlantic Ocean, Caribbean Sea, Indian Ocean, Mediterranean Sea, Black Sea).

These two facts necessitated extraordinarily rapid and frequent changes of method and thus rendered it difficult for those having had little or no experience in oceanic thinking to form a clear judgement of the naval situation at any given time, or of the results achieved in the German Naval High Command's operations and by the fleet units. And finally, the reticence shown on purpose by the Supreme Command of the German Navy in its communiqués on operations still in progress and on successes gained did not at least make it any easier to form an opinion. But the enemy had to be prevented from obtaining an insight however slight into the German methods and plans.

In the planning of the German Fleet and at the commencement of its construction the chief aim was to create a fleet for waging war on merchant shipping. Its nucleus was to consist of 35,000 ton battleships, 26,000 ton battleships and heavy cruisers. The heroic struggle of the "Bismarck," the sinking of the biggest battleship in the world, "H. M. S. Hood," within the space of a few minutes, the flight of the "Prince of Wales", and, on the other hand, the unprecedented solidity and floating powers of the immobile "Bismarck"—as well as the successes of the heavy German cruisers "Graf Spee," "Admiral Scheer," "Lützow," "Admiral Hipper" and "Prinz Eugen" and of the 26,000 ton battleships "Scharnhorst" and "Gneisenau" under most difficult conditions have proved what a fleet composed in this way would have been capable of achieving.

When Britain began the war before this nucleus of a future German Fleet had been constructed, the German Naval Command found itself faced by an extremely serious situation. Would it succeed in the near future in discovering a new driving force for the attack—and if so, what was it to be? Would it succeed until such time with the forces at its disposal in withstanding the tremendous pressure which it could be anticipated the enemy would bring to bear on the bases in the Bight of Heligoland, un-

favourable in any case for offensive operations, and at least manage to keep the North Sea open? Would it succeed in freeing the German Fleet from the restrictions placed on its movements by the Bight of Heligoland, in obtaining better bases for the employment of the new nucleus to be created and, from the very commencement of the war, in relieving the burden on the land front by launching an immediate and effective attack on British merchant shipping?

Success was only possible as the result of lightning improvisation and transference from one point to another of a main attack with the continual employment of all available means of naval warfare and naval units in brilliant collaboration with the Army and Air Force. The following were the chief methods of attack: offensive minelaying off the East Coast of England by all suitable and available units of the Fleet, offensive war on shipping in the North Sea and the Atlantic, the Indian Ocean and the Pacific; the winning of new bases, the capture of the Norwegian fiords by the German Navy and the capture of the Atlantic Coast by the German Army and Air Force.

In the meantime, a new weapon of attack had been created in the shape of the U-boat warfare on merchant shipping. Whilst U-boat commanders like Prien, Schepke and Endrass resolutely waged a courageous and surprisingly successful U-boat war on merchant shipping with only a small number of submarines, the majority of the U-boats were employed in the extensive and thorough training of young commanders and crews. A large scale U-boat construction programme was also carried out which benefited from the continual exploitation of the valuable war experience already gained. Efficient bases protected against every conceivable kind of attack were constructed at the same time along the coasts which had been captured. Methodically, farsightedly and tenaciously the U-boat warfare on merchant shipping was developed until it became a deadly dangerous weapon of attack in Germany's prosecution of the war at sea. In regard to operations, construction programme, radius of action, level of the nautical and tactical training of the commanders and crews, it has proved itself superior to all the enemy's efforts to create an effective defence. The heavy units of the German Fleet had thus brilliantly carried out their task of covering and preparing the transference of the Navy's main attack to the U-boat arm. They were now free for other tasks. We need here only recall the chessboard move from Brest through the Channel to the North Sea with the object of covering Germany's flank and menacing the Anglo-American sea route to Murmansk and Archangel.

Formation of a combined offensive thrust

The first phase of the struggle in the Mediterranean provides us with a classical example of the combined principal attack repeatedly employed with success by the Tripartite Pact Powers during this war. Not only the German Army, Navy and Air Force but both members of the Axis are fighting in exemplary collaboration in a war zone of very considerable extent (the distance from Gibraltar to Beirut is 960 nautical miles).

In spite of its size, the Mediterranean is geographically and politically an

extremely subdivided "mare clausum." The laws governing the surmounting of maritime space, warfare in confined seas, modern combined land warfare and, finally, policy, here meet and link up together accordingly. The weapons such as destroyers, torpedo boats, motor torpedo-boats and, above all, land planes, which can be employed in the wide expanses of the ocean only under certain conditions, here became of vital importance.

When Italy entered the war in 1940, the British plan was ruthlessly to destroy the fleet of her defeated ally, (Oran, Dakar), to establish communication between the exits of the Mediterranean, which were in the hands of the British, with the help of the British Fleet and the "aircraft carrier" Malta, which was to form the connecting link between Gibraltar and Alexandria, to drive out of the Mediterranean and gradually annihilate the Italian Fleet and Air Force, exert pressure on Greece and Yugoslavia, menace Italy also from the Adriatic side, cut off Germany from the Rumanian oil, exert pressure on Turkey from the Balkans via Crete, Syria, Iraq and Iran, establish a connexion with the Black Sea and the Soviet Union, advance from Egypt through Libya and Tripolitania to French Africa, exert pressure on Spain, annihilate Italy, and close the ring round Germany from Gibraltar to the Soviet Union.

The Italian Navy had for a long time withstood the pressure of British sea-power alone and ensured the reinforcements of the Italian troops in Libya. The Italian troops in Abyssinia had put up a stubborn and desperate resistance without any hope of receiving reinforcements, whilst German policy, conscious of the responsibility resting upon it, strove to save the Balkan peoples from the war which was Britain's aim. The advance of the Axis Powers in Africa began on 24th March 1941. The Balkan countries driven into war by the enemy's agitation were overwhelmingly defeated by the German Army. Yugoslavia and Greece were occupied, Crete was captured, the Aegean Sea was cut off and a valuable air base gained in the Eastern Mediterranean. Turkey remained neutral. The British Fleet and Air Force (Malta) made desperate efforts to hold up German and Italian reinforcements to Africa and to win naval and air supremacy. German U-boats made their appearance in the Mediterranean, sank the "Ark Royal" and the "Barham," whilst Italian motor torpedo-boats sank two battleships in the harbour of Alexandria. British naval supremacy was shaken. British air supremacy was shaken by the incessant heavy Italian and German air attacks on Malta and the complete check placed on that "aircraft carrier" forming the link between Gibraltar and Alexandria. Reinforcements for North Africa were ensured by the Italian and German Navies and Air Forces. After executing a strategical retreat, Field Marshal Rommel launched his second counter-attack against the offensive of the British Eighth Army. Strongly protected British convoys coming from Gibraltar and Alexandria were completely annihilated on many occasions.

The British domination of the Mediterranean had collapsed during this first stage of the struggle. This success was gained as the result of the determined and exemplary collaboration between the armies, navies and air forces of the Axis partners, who smashed the British mastery of the Mediterranean by the formation of a combined main offensive thrust.

In accordance with the law of oceanic warfare, according to which the seas

are never conquered but continually have to be reconquered, these successes gained by the Axis could not clarify the situation once and for all. Their importance was that the planned British flank menace in the Mediterranean had been suppressed whilst the German Army and its allies were fighting out the gigantic struggle on the eastern front in order to annihilate the vast armaments of the Bolshevists and win the extremely valuable sources of food, ores, coal and oil for the further prosecution of the war. *The formation of a combined offensive thrust in the Mediterranean was consequently intended to frustrate Britain's plans until the entire principal attack on the Eastern Front had reached the decisive objectives. Both aims have been achieved.*

The struggle in the Mediterranean has now entered a new stage in consequence of the occupation of French North Africa by British and American naval, air and land forces and the massed advance of strong British units from Egypt. What Britain was unable to achieve alone is now to be attempted for the second time with the help of the United States and the employment of the greatest possible means. To predict the course of the war operations thus commenced would be in accordance neither with the earnestness of the war nor with the purpose of this article. Only this much can now be stated—it is no longer possible to disturb in a decisive manner the successful main offensive thrust on the Eastern Front. The annihilation of the German and Italian units between El Alamein and the Cyrenaica has proved a failure. The intended effect on France has not taken place. The Head of the German State, conscious of the responsibility resting on Germany, had even put up with many difficulties in waging the war in an effort to save French Morocco from becoming involved in hostilities. The American and British attack on French North Africa, which constitutes a violation of international law, has been given a clear and magical answer in the shape of a rapid counter-stroke.

Whatever the outcome of the hostilities in Africa proves to be, our enemies suffered further considerable losses of shipping in connexion with these operations. The war on merchant shipping waged by Germany's U-boats has by no means been thrown off its balance and will only make itself properly felt as the chief weapon of attack in German naval warfare in the future.

A sober consideration of the idea of the offensive thrust shows us that although the fundamental idea proceeding from the vast extent of the war zone is obvious and imperative, the problems which have to be solved and the measures which have to be adopted are extremely various if offensive thrusts are to be carried out and lead to their objectives. *It is always most important to distinguish between what is necessary and what is desirable and in the first place to achieve what is essential.* To carry out what is really a principal attack consequently demands not only imagination and determination, the greatest industriousness and an exemplary talent for organization, perhaps the greatest art in the waging of war, but also the strength of renunciation, the capacity of self-denial—however intolerable the enemy's triumph may appear at times—in order to win successes decisive for the outcome of the war by employing the decisive means at the decisive point at the decisive time.

END

Eia, eia, alalà! Italian mountain troops proclaim their loyalty to National Fascist Italy with the old Fascist greeting   PK. Photograph: War Correspondent Schlickum

IN ITALY

↑ **The end of an Anglo-American tank wedge.** Hundreds of tanks and heavy weapons were either destroyed or captured
PK. Photograph : War Correspondent Lüthge (2)

The march to the rear. Many thousands of British and American troops were forced to surrender during the fighting for Italy ↓

MUSSOLINI the Poet

Benito Mussolini, the Head of the Italian Government, is the author of three plays: "The Hundred Days", "Julius Caesar" and "Cavour", which he wrote in collaboration with Giovacchino Forzano.

In the following we reproduce the third tableau of the third act, the last scene of Mussolini's play "Cavour".

Up to this point, the play, the action of which takes place in 1859, has dealt with the struggle of King Victor Emmanuel and Cavour for the independence and unity of Italy. In the last scene, the author describes the situation which has arisen through Napoleon III, Emperor of the French, not having kept the promise he made to the Italian Government to support them in the fight for Italy's freedom and unity. Before the final scene of the play, the Emperor of the French informs the King of Italy of his changed views.

(The King's headquarters in Montambano. The stage is empty. A candle is burning on the large table. Suddenly the door in the background is flung open and the King enters, followed by Nigra. The King is trembling with excitement. He snatches off his cap and breathes deeply and heavily for a moment. Then, as if suffocated by the warmth of the room, he tears off his cloak and rolls up his sleeves as far as the elbow. With nervous fingers he lights his cigar. Takes a few steps to regain his self-control).

King:

Nigra, fetch the Count. But come back again yourself. (Nigra goes. King sits down, pressing his hands against his temples. Cavour enters, followed by Nigra. He is like a man who has been waiting for hours for a decision affecting his whole life. Extremely agitated. Dares not ask, just as the King dare not speak. Some moments of painful silence. The King draws the copy of the preliminaries from his pocket and offers it to him). Here, take this rubbish! (Cavour grips the paper; reads. His lips quiver. Reads the paper through, sways slightly, tears open his collar).

Cavour:

No! No! A fraud! A deliberate fraud! This Frenchman wants to rob us even of our honour! No! Your Majesty can on no account put your name to this shameful treaty. (King grips the edge of the table as if to break it off). Your Majesty must not make yourself an accessary, an accessary to an — act of treachery against the Italian people! This Italian people has come to us — to us, Your Majesty! The best, the bravest of them have gathered round us.
And shall they now, for their faithfulness, again be delivered up to the Austrian princelings, in order that these gentlemen can revenge themselves on these most faithful people! Is that to be their reward for their faithfulness? Confound it, Your Majesty; such a matter cannot be discussed! Why do we speak at all about this French impertinence! (Points to the paper). That is an insult to everyone of our dead, to everyone of our martyrs!

King:

(Who was trembling at this outburst, now gains a remarkable calm and composure). I feel as you do. It is not my fault, if the Emperor will not continue the fight. But his desires for peace are the result of careful considerations, and I cannot compel him to go to war.

Cavour:

What nonsense! He can go to the Devil, this dish-rag of an Emperor; he is not even a blood relation of the great Napoleon — this crowned mistake of his parents, who sends snivelling telegrams to his wife because he feels depressed! Rotten and nerve-wrecked through his debauchery in Milan, that's what he is! He can go to the Devil and leave us alone! We would rather be slaughtered for Turin and the House of Savoy than remain allied with such a ruffian! (King and Cavour stare at one another). Mazzini, you were right after all! In January of this year Mazzini wrote: ' After the first battle you will be betrayed!' Mazzini — yes, Mazzini is a prophet and I — I am bankrupt. (Sobs choke his voice).

King:

Cavour, you must not say such things. You do not know what you are saying. Do you believe that it is easy for me to remain calm? We have both sacrificed everything for our country — now we must even sacrifice our indignation. We must keep icecold and be guided by our intelligence. We must even be prepared to give way honourably — for the sake of the future; for the future will all belong to us, even though the present may only half belong to us.

Cavour:

I cannot put my name to this shameful document, Sire. (Pauses). Your Majesty, I wish to resign from my position.

King:

(Now also loses his self-control). That's it, is it? Of course! Ha ha! Resignation! That is very convenient for my Ministers — they can settle matters so quickly: hand in their resignation, and they are off! I, on the other hand, cannot resign, cannot desert my post. First of all they are bold enough to embark upon an uncertain enterprise with Us; and then in the most awful moment of responsibility, they leave me alone, alone with my responsibility before the people and before history. (Cavour tries to speak). No — no! So be it! (To Nigra) Count Cavour does not feel well; his nerves are overstrained, he must rest. Accompany him.

Cavour:

(Playing his last card) Just as a Minister must know when he should resign, others — should also know when the time has come to abdicate!

King:

(Trembling with rage) Count, you forget yourself, you are speaking to your King.

Cavour:

(As if he had lost his senses) The Italians know me, me! I am their real King!

King:

(Raving) What? Who is the King here and who is the scoundrel? (He makes as if to throw himself upon Cavour, but stops and then hurries to the door, right, but steps back to the table as Cavour meantime, with a gesture of despair, goes off the stage, centre. Nigra stands as if petrified. Pause. King to Nigra.) Send for Lamarmora at once! (Nigra goes. King fumbles with the cigar which is nearly out. Nigra returns with Lamarmora). General, Count Cavour is not prepared to undertake the responsibility, together with me, for a peace such as Napoleon is going to impose upon us. Consequently he has just resigned. I entrust you, General, with the formation of the new Ministry.

Lamarmora:

Sire, I cannot accept any responsibility which a man like Cavour dares not assume. I would therefore ask Your Majesty to reconsider... (King interrupts him, striking table with his fist).

King:

Lamarmora, too, is suffering with his nerves — he must rest, as well. Let him rest, then — for all I care, here or in Heaven (turns his back on him. Exit Lamarmora. King sits down, then with choking voice to Nigra) Well, did you see that, young man? A splendid thing to be a King, isn't it? But Radetzky, he told me so once already, then, at our meeting after Novara: If you follow this path further, one day you will be all alone. The old man was right; these people now really are leaving me alone — and the country will curse me. (Cavour appears again in the door without the King noticing him. The King, in a sudden mood of rebellion) But that I — I am the one who is right this time, that none of them understand. They don't understand that Italy must not be built up with foreign help!

Cavour:

I understand that.

King:

(Quickly turning) What do you want here? Who called you?

Cavour:

Italy.

King:

(Harshly) You are hearing voices, Count, your nerves are wrecked.

Cavour:

No, Your Majesty, I only hear the call of the future. But in order to prepare the way for this future, I have returned here. Not because I wish to take back my resignation; my task is at an end. I have come for another reason.

King:

(Still with reserve) What reason, Count Cavour, can have led you to return after what has happened?

Cavour:

I wish to beg Your Majesty's forgiveness for my outburst. It is of moment to me that no offensive behaviour towards the — first King of Italy should be associated with my name.

King:

Cavour... are you mad? You say this after having treated me like a dog?

Cavour:

I know that I am of a very excitable nature. But I am honourable enough to admit my mistakes. In Your Majesty I greet today the first King of United Italy. A people that cherishes in their hearts a sacred idea — in their hearts and not in their heads — such a people will march steadily forward through adversity and disappointment — even such terrible disappointments as that (points to the treaty). Even Your Majesty represents a part of the people; you are a great man like the best of our people. Even in this storm you remain on the bridge of the ship of State, even when the crew start to shout and swear. But the ship steers a course through the hurricane towards the sun.

King:

Cavour!

Cavour:

That was all I wished to say, Your Majesty. I count no longer! The helmsman overboard. Another will take my place.

King:

I thank you, Count. Even though we must part — your idea lives on. I will see it through. United Italy will still arise by our efforts — mine and those of the Italian people — without foreign aid!

Cavour:

Yes. Italy is like — God. He exists through Himself alone. (Deep bow; exit. The King gazes after him and then slowly nods).

(Curtain)

The Duce

The Duce, Commander-in-Chief of the Imperial Italian Army, fixes his eyes boldly on the future, and with calm deliberation makes his great decisions which contribute to the creation of a new and better order in Europe. Colour photograph by Elsbeth Heddenhausen

The Berlin State Theater on May 9: a scene from the German premiere of "Cavour", a drama by Mussolini and Forzano. Reading from left to right: Cavour, Princess Clotilde, King Victor Immanuel

IN BERLIN

Glamorous first night of Mussolini's drama

*Dramatic climax: Cavour rejects
the unsatisfactory peace treaty
and announces his resignation*

It would be unfair to Signor Mussolini and would indicate a complete lack of understanding of his personality to assume that his dramatic works are merely a hobby, a means of relaxation. Mussolini knows no idle hours. He is definitely a man of action, given to struggling with life's intricate problems and prophesying new orders. But he is always conscious of his place in the world, always filled with the urge to give an account. For that reason the dramatist Mussolini always chooses only such subjects as reflect his innermost convictions — indeed always the same subjects: the superior statesman in conflict with the destructive powers of reality. This was the case in the drama which portrayed Napoleon's fall after the battle of Waterloo. We find it again in the Julius Cesar tragedy, and in Mussolini's most recent work, "Cavour". The Duce need not stoop, as so many authors of historic dramas are inclined to do, to tamper with the historical truth (not to be confused with accuracy of detail, which is always subject to the rules of the theater). A deep kinship binds him and his heroes; with the experience born of reality he fulfills the flight of their desires, their tribulations and their decisions. With the same clearvision he unmasks the forces of resistance with which his heroes have to contend and to which their earthly exi-

A gay scene in effective contrast to the historic dispute between King Immanuel and Cavour: The Empress dances to the tune of the little piano

stence must give way in order that their spirit live on. Even in their downfall, Napoleon, Cesar and Cavour are greater than the world about them. That is why Mussolini deals not with the victorious moments of such careers but the times of stress for the bases of his dramas. For this reason the drama about Cavour was originally called "Villafranca". For Villafranca, the premature peace with which Napoleon III. betrayed Italy's uniter of the fruits of his ambition, is the critical moment in the life and fate of the great statesman. His greatness — and Mussolini draws him with all the danger, cunning and simplicity which made up the man — succumbed to the immaturity of the time. But the soul of the hero does not parish, and herein lies the greatness of Mussolini's dramatic conception. Cavour's arm is lamed, but he hands the torch on.

Masterful acting and historic characterisation made the performance a unique experience. Werner Krauss, who played the part of Cavour, and Antje Weissgerber in the role of Princess Clotilde

Author Forzano and members of the cast bowing to the storm of applause

The prisoner of Gran Sasso: Benito Mussolini. What are they to do with his gaolers whom they had quickly overpowered? "Set them free!" replies the liberated Duce as he makes for the Fieseler Storch

"Good luck !" At an altitude of 6,000 feet his liberators cheer the Duce. The Storch takes off. Down below in all parts of Italy thousands of Blackshirts are waiting for him, the smith of Rome, the saviour of Italy

They can laugh again

The new agrarian order became a reality: The village elders of an agricultural region listening to the announcement of further transformations of communal estates into independent farms and farming associations

On their own soil again

In the east the farmers are being freed from the kolkhoz system. "Signal" reports on the state of affairs in the second year of the new agrarian order

Men returning from the east never tire of talking about the farmers they saw and observed there. The dull, gloomy expression has disappeared from the faces of both men and women. The farmers have learnt to laugh again. And so the aspect of the country in the east, the vast, fertile land and its people is changing. It is taking on European features, for it is adapting itself once more to the laws of thine and mine of loyalty and faith. He who sows, reaps both for himself and for his own and their needs. A new order created the new fighting Europe that hurled the Red flood back to the east. In the rear of the armies and today securely protected by them, life began anew, was worth living and became the old farmer's life again as known in the east.

A year and a few months have elapsed since a new agrarian order was proclaimed which was the first decisive step towards overcoming the kolkhoz slavery and its principles in opposition to farming traditions and farm property. What is taking place under the new order today is the development of a new prosperity in a country that when it is incorporated with Europe will be able to promise its inhabitants a real farmer's future. And that is the essential point because always and everywhere, even in the east, it is the people that count.

Farmers are at all times and in all places people for whom property and the fruits of hard labour are something holy. They are symbols of the dignity of man, bestowed upon them by Providence and year after year won back with the help of plough and harrow, seed and careful concentration on their work. This, too, like everything else holy and like all human dignity, was stamped out by Bolshevism. One generation was wiped out and another chained to machines like slaves: the farmers had become day labourers without a claim to bread, to fields, to cattle and everything that had been theirs. Nothing had remained their own. "Kolkhoz" was the magic word that had robbed them of the last of their possessions.

At the beginning of this century the Skolypinch agrarian reform had given landed property to the Russian farmers who had been serfs under the Czars up to 1861. During the ten long years land had been allotted to a quarter of the farmers in European Russia to be transformed into independent farms. This farming class was annihilated by the Soviets who took away its land and livestock. But the farmer had to continue to work and slave. He could sow but not reap. The harvest was transported from the fields to the storehouses. With the exception of a few

A village Sunday

Both young and old assemble to dance after a week of work in the fields

The general commanding the eastern troops inspects . . .

The decoration of the bravest. The native units are under the command of the German officer, the "General Commanding the Eastern Troops", General Hellmich. He has complete control of the entire organization from the employment of the troops in the field to the tasks connected with their welfare. Sometimes the general personally distributes awards to men who have shown particular bravery. Our photograph shows Tartar volunteers being decorated by the general

Inspection. The general commanding the eastern troops inspects together with his staff the brave Tartar volunteers who have paraded in front of him for the distribution of awards

P.K. Photographs: War Correspondent Hilmar Pabel

The fighter and his victim. This American Short-Stirling bomber with its crew of twelve could not cope with the German fighter
PK. Photograph: War Correspondent Hubmann

Europe on the way to a new ideology

The problems of the present World War have reduced themselves to a question of destiny—will Europe continue to live? The question can be answered in the affirmative when Europe has human tasks that only Europe, and Europe alone, can fulfil. And there are such tasks. SIGNAL will try to explain them in a series of articles specially written by its scientific editor, Dr Heinz Graupner. This is the first in the series:

WOMAN

AUTONOMOUS IN HER SPHERE

Two cases are on record in which English women were bought by their husbands at the public market in the 19th century. One woman was led to the market with her full consent, a halter around her neck. She was sold for half-a-crown and led three miles away by her new husband to his house. The other woman was bought by an inkeeper in return for a big bottle of gin.

It cannot be supposed that these two instances are typical of woman's social position a hundred years ago, even though woman was regarded as the absolute property of the man in those days. The man ordered even her most personal affairs, forbidding her to go to certain places, see certain people or read certain books. Man asserted his right as the stronger to make woman subject to him.

Even before the dawn of the 19th century, "woman's slavery" began slowly to burst its fetters with the French Revolution. A new ideology, that of equality, began to break through. According to its principles, woman had to be given a better position and more respect. Activated by women themselves, the movement for female emancipation was started.

The struggle waged by the female sex was for equality of rights with men. It meant revolutionizing our whole way of life. This gradually led up to a crisis during recent decades, since it had grown in the soil of liberalism. Although the feminist movement of the last century had certainly broken the "bonds of slavery," it demanded more than this. Among its pioneers, great personal sacrifice was often required in those times, as for instance in the case of the first German woman physician, Dr Tiburtius, who was outside the pale of society, because she worked together with the students in anatomy. She was a favourite subject for ridicule and always produced loud guffaws when her name came up in the Reichstag.

The crux of the feminist movement was to gain material independence from man, an aim which assuredly touched woman closely because of the industrial revolution. Woman became more sure of herself, she was able to demonstrate her ability, a fact which is really quite taken for granted today.

The blue stocking

If woman had moderated her pretentions when this goal had been reached, then perhaps the crisis might have been avoided that such development entailed. But she wanted more; the eternal problem of petticoat government is constantly cropping up in history. Woman longed to be the equal of man in everything. This gave rise to the ludicrous spectacle of the blue stocking, a member of the fair sex who renounces domesticity boasts of scientific knowledge, takes up politics or dabbles with pen and ink. The blue stocking abandoned the ways and appearance of her sex as far as possible, wearing men's clothes, cropping her hair and assuming a generally masculine air. She demanded freedom of selection in science, law and politics. She also toyed with the idea of free love as expressed by the feminist, Anita Augspurg, who found that "a self-respecting woman cannot bring herself to enter into a state of legal marriage."

These are the roots from which feminine emancipation grew. It was unbridled egotism that made such chaotic demands. The ultimate aim was a foothold in the affairs of state together with complete equality of rights in law and in politics.

There are certain primitive tribes where the women have their own language, which they never speak before the menfolk. This is proof of a purely personal feminine world, which touches upon the world of men, but which is not identical with it. This women's language seems to us to be a symbol of the natural demarcation between the two sexes out of the diametrical opposition of which new vigour and strength can perpetually arise for our race.

Even in the best sense of the word, feminine emancipation will not hear of it that there will always be this "woman's language".

Along new paths

But the world over, wherever society has been ordered and there are governments and systems of government, it is man exclusively who has done this work. It is man who has been the productive, producing force. All attempts at setting up female rule have foundered because it is counter to the laws of nature. Women's language would not be understood in the world of men. The United States has placed women on a falsely understood basis of equality, and by this very act admits their inability to be really dynamically creative. Man makes history, woman perpetuates the generations. The blue stocking wanted to leave woman's world and create proprietary rights for herself in man's world. She might be compared with a European child who was allowed to grow up among Chinese, so as to make a Chinese out of it. The result was a sexless creature, who no longer understood woman's language, or wanted to understand it, and who had renounced her own world.

And so the age of liberalism broke the "bonds of slavery" with which woman had been bound to man as part and parcel of his property, but in so doing woman did not attain her true freedom. The attempt at matriarchy ran foul. As a matter of fact, the 19th century brought woman to a new low level in certain social aspects. As a worker, she became a merciless object of capitalistic exploitation. Such a thing as "maternal protection" was unknown. And the idea of free love made her the willing slave of man in a different sense.

When present-day Europe is on the way to a new ideology, and the natural order as planned by the Creator once more has found its place, then a way will also be found along which woman may go, a way expressing the vitality of a new freedom.

Motherhood: triumph of youth

The adult woman, unlike man, must still retain a part of her ability for growth. In other words, she can only attain her full development in motherhood. This burden would not be bearable for a man. But a woman has a natural reserve of strength, and this reserve is what makes of woman's life something akin to the miraculous.

We can perceive this youthfulness, this still not exhausted ability of development, if we place side by side the photographs of a typical man, woman and ten-year-old child. The features distinctly show the similarity between the woman and the child. The impression created by the man's picture is one of greater maturity in keeping with the biological facts of the case.

The comparison of child with woman uncovers the whole secret of woman's productive ability.

The mother of six children has built up her own bodily weight as new substance three times in the course of 20 years. She is only able to do this because from a physical standpoint she is not "finitely" developed herself and can thus use her reserve of developmental power as a vital force for her children.

We see here the primal, creative and greatest function of woman, a work which man, wrapped up in another world, must always be conscious of with respect and even veneration, when he helps to smooth the way of woman to a new freedom, both materially and spiritually.

Wifehood: a new right for woman

The deepest metamorphosis of woman in her social position seems to have occurred, scarcely noticed, in the industrial cities. Unlike the world of the rural population, the world of the industrial worker is divided into two parts. The one is the sphere of man, closed in by the walls of the factory, the other is the home-life, where woman rules in a way that cannot be remarked in the rural home. (That this order has been disarranged in wartime, does not alter the general principle.) The farmer on his farm is the master of life and of work. The city worker leaves the world outside his factory to the province of his wife. She transacts his business for him, is the mistress of the house and has her relatives there. But in the farmer, it is the man's people who are the more important and come to visit the farm the most frequently. The wife's mother, or maternal grandmother, plays a more important part in the city worker's household in bringing up the children than does the mother of the husband.

And so this metamorphosis of woman in a modern industrial community makes

When women leave their sphere... *The American artist, Grand Wood, has called this painting of his "Daughters of the American Revolution," which is one of the leading national women's organizations in the United States. With sarcastic touch, he reproduces the types of female tyrants who rule despotically and irresponsibly over there. In the background hangs the portrait of George Washington, founder of American independence*

itself felt even down to the relatives. It actually spells final release from the confusion of woman's rights to the true world of woman. Matriarchy is being resurrected in a new guise. It leaves to man a rich and fertile field of endeavour, while not limiting or hemming in woman, who can fulfil her biological functions as well as carry out her new and important duties of a managerial and executive nature.

It is here that we must face the big new problems that will loom up especially large when the women who have found war-time employment will stream back into the circle of the home. It is a condition giving rise to conflict. For it is the marriages of the industrial workers, which have led to this new social position for woman, that become grounded on the rocks far oftener than those of artisans, shop-keepers and farmers, where husband and wife live and work in the same world side by side. But the more men realize the new meaning of life which is here given to woman, and the more the women grasp their golden opportunity without turning against the man's interests, then the more easily can the goal be reached.

Natural equality

When it is stated that the feminist movement has opened up practically all vocations to woman, it must yet be remembered that the requirements of each vocation are different. To develop new and suitable vocations for women is one of the most important tasks of the future, which can be solved only when it is coupled with a European ideology in which the ties of nature are taken into proper account.

Typical vocations for women are those in which relations between people can be strengthened and cultivated and in which one's fellow man can be helped. Such professions include the laboratory assistant, the secretary and the nurse. Here women are better than men. The female conductor on a tram or train likes to feel herself as a helper to the public, while the male conductor sets himself up as the authority over the passengers. The housekeeper in a large soldier's home could never be properly replaced by a man. When a crane operator elevates and transports a piece of machinery, the mechanism of the crane and the motors give him pleasure. But a woman in his shoes makes of the same process the union between two workers for the purpose of transporting the piece of machinery.

Light is thrown in this way on the position of man and woman in society. Man is the creative, building principle, he is the architect of our world, he places head before heart. Woman is the connective element, her cleverness comes from the heart rather than from the head. A new matriarchy is being born, although with quite a new connotation; female rule in which woman will reign supreme in her own world. We give a footing of equality to these two poles of life, which have been opposed to one another in the age-old struggle of sex for thousands of years. We do this by grasping at last the natural meaning of the two separate worlds for which they stand and by not trying to force a merger of the two. A creative and harmonious profusion will pour forth from these two sources, constantly renewing and replenishing itself.

TWICE THE SAME THING IS NOT THE SAME THING

In his studies as to woman's position in the future, SIGNAL'S scientific editor, Dr Heinz Graupner, also examines the subject of professions for women. He comes to the conclusion that one of the most important tasks of the future in Europe will be to find new and suitable vocations for women. He demonstrates by means of a trenchant example the types of vocations that are suitable for women. He states that while a crane operator, whether man or woman, has the same work to do, the brain processes involved are quite divergent with the two sexes. In the transport work that a man operator does with his crane, he is animated by satisfaction in his method of organization, and by its quick and precise functioning; perhaps he is pleased, too, in the play of cable, chains and his own manly strength. Illustration above.) But the woman for her part is filled with pleasure in helping, in looking after loads, in passing them on to others who need what she is helping to transport. In this example given by Dr Graupner, one sees the natural differences between man and woman. On this basis, he reaches the conclusion that while man and woman have equal rights, it is only on the foundation of their natural biological attributes. To place this theoretical knowledge in practical use is one of the biggest and most worthwhile tasks with which the scientists, the technicians and the statesmen of Europe are faced

At the frontier of Europe
PK. Photograph: Lieutenant Frentz

Pull away the chocks
— night operations!

The Ju 88 has taken its bombs on board, the humming of the propeller changes to a loud droning. Lit up by the floodlight on the taking-off ground the hubs of the engines which are running at full speed look like circles of glistening fabric. And now the giant metal bird glides down the landing-ground; it rises and disappears into the night. One after the other the bombers take off on their flight against Britain which was relying on a lull in the German attacks on the island after the beginning of hostilities on the eastern front   Photographs: PK. Stempka

REICHS-RUNDFUNK

European Service

To hear your Continental Programme in English from the European Service of the Reichsrundfunk, tune in to:

Calais I   on 582 kilocycles (514 metres)
Calais II and, until 8.15 p. m.   on 995 kilocycles (301.6 metres)
In addition, after 7 p. m. British Summer Time the following short-wave station can be heard:

DXM   on 7270 kilocycles (41.27 metres)

News bulletins are broadcast at the following times (all British Summer Time):
    6:30 a. m., 1:30 p. m., 2:30 p. m., 6:30 p. m.
    8:30 p. m., 9:30 p. m., 10:30 p. m., 11:30 p. m.

William Joyce (otherwise known as Lord Haw-Haw) broadcasts daily following the news at 10:30 p. m. and 1:30 p. m.

In addition to the standard stations and wavelengths given above, the following stations are employed at various times of the day:

Deutschlandsender   on 191 kilocycles (1571 metres) at 6:30 a. m.
Luxemburg   on 232 kilocycles (1293 metres) at 6:30 a. m.
                        1:30 p. m., 2:30 p. m., 8:30 p. m.
Friesland   on 160 kilocycles (1875 metres) at 6:30 a. m.
                        7:30 a. m., 1:30 p. m., 2:30 p. m.,
                        5:30 p. m., 6:30 p. m., 7:30 p. m.,
                        8:30 p. m., 9:30 p. m.
Bremen   on 758 kilocycles (396 metres) at 6:30 a. m.
                        7:30 a. m., 1:30 p. m., 2:30 p. m.,
                        5:30 p. m., 6:30 p. m., 7:30 p. m.,
                        8:30 p. m., 9:30 p. m.
Breslau   on 950 kilocycles (316 metres) and
Cologne   on 658 kilocycles (456 metres) at 10:30 p. m.
                        11:30 p. m., and 12:15 a. m.

Finally the following shortwave stations are employed in addition:

DXJ   on 7240 kilocycles (41.44 metres) at 5:30 p. m.
                  and 6:30 p. m.
DXZ   on 9570 kilocycles (31.35 metres) at 7:40 p. m.
                  and 8:30 p. m.
DXT   on 15230 kilocycles (19.70 metres) at 1:30 p. m.
DJL   on 15110 kilocycles (19.85 metres) at 2:30 p. m.

Special feature programmes are broadcast at 7:30 a. m., 5:15 p. m., 7:40 p. m. and 8:30 p. m.

The German War Communiqué is read at speed 2:30, 3:30, 4:30 and (at dictation speed) 4:45 p. m.

Deutschlandsender
on 1571 metres or 191 kilocycles

Daily (with the exception of Sundays)
        17.15—18.30 Late afternoon concert with concert music of four centuries.
Sunday: 20.15—21.00 Musical treasures.
Monday: 20.15—21.00 Concert with well-known soloists arranged by Professor Michael Raucheisen, who also takes part.
Friday: 21.00—22.00 Musical plays or short histories of music with musical illustrations.

Man's surroundings tomorrow:

Where shall we live?

For hundreds of years European domestic architecture has been living on numerous old styles but has invented no new style characteristic of the age. Will it now find its own style?

Made by a village carpenter. A cupboard of dull larch wood. The village smith of the same place made the iron hinges, the square inlays are solid. A piece of furniture of self-evident beauty

Shall we live like this? *The corner of an architect's room. The cupboard is at the same time an object of utility and domestic furniture. The arabesque of the upper left hand corner, reminiscent of Rococo ornaments, does not seem to harmonize well with the expression of the whole, and the chair on the right is still flirting with the peasant style. All the same one notices a commendable originality*

→

Spiral staircase in a country house. *Made of natural wood from the neighbourhood with all the charm of its grain and branches. The layman might think that it was built without much constructive calculation but here particularly the saving of space yet assurance of comfort in the width and height of the steps, as well as harmony of all the parts, are only achieved by exact calculation*

A door which one remembers. *This hall door is reminiscent of no earlier period. It is not a door separating one room from another but it creates a unity both externally and internally*

What was planned:

Visiting their future home. *They are fascinated most of all by the cosy sitting- and dining-corners of the living-room. Especially attractive is the solid wooden settle-bench the seat of which can be tipped up. Each one of them has his own plans for what can be stowed away there*

Living conditions today demand more adaptability and the sacrifice of the so-called conventional suites of furniture which are only rarely within the individual's means and seldom satisfy the demands of space. The ideal furniture permits a free and easy arrangement, can be used in different rooms if the family moves to a different house and, last but not least, can easily be added to and supplemented when the family grows. Another important consideration is that the household furniture should be independent of the annual dictates of fashion. It is not necessary that craftsmen and manufacturers should bring out new models every "season."

The housewife's pride: a handsome china cabinet . . .

The boys' room. *The furniture is simple, solid and friendly. It is fun to keep the place in order. The lad has plenty of room and quiet for doing his homework and good light for it too. The bed is a real boy's bed: well-sprung and strong. It has a heavy brown woollen blanket (boys shouldn't lie on the bed in their clothes but they do all the same) and a hard-wearing checked pillow (in case Willy uses brilliantine) . . .*

. . . and the china: *The shape is simple and beautiful, neither showy nor lacking in originality. The picture shows two coffee sets: on the right a "fancy service," ornate and unpractical—on the left a set which does not threaten to fall over at the least provocation. Its charm is in its pleasing and sensible form and not in an extravagant design. Therefore it will always retain its beauty*

becomes a reality:

Evening at home. *The children romp on the soft carpet. The father is occupied with the paper, the mother with her needlework. The daughters are poring over their books. The table is placed in the corner in accordance with an ancient German custom. It was not until the 19th century that the love of "cold splendour" brought it into the middle of the room, completely spoiling the proportions*

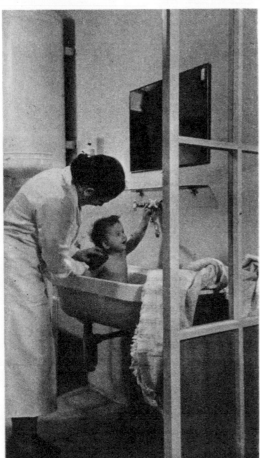

Johnny's little paradise. *In the deep bathlike basin which the family normally uses as a wash-basin the little fellow kicks about to his heart's content. Beside the baby's bath stands the table on which he is dressed. The electric geyser provides hot water in a few minutes for the bath*

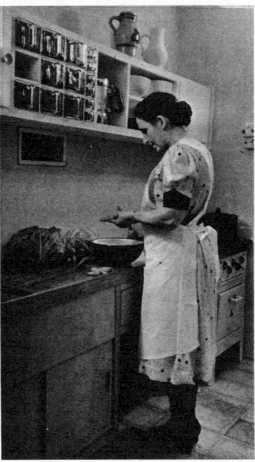

The kitchen is small—*on purpose. Long distance running belongs to the sports grounds. The equipment is convenient, modern and complete; every detail was carefully planned and tested. A small refrigerator is used for storing food-stuffs. The meals are handed in through a hatch in the wall*

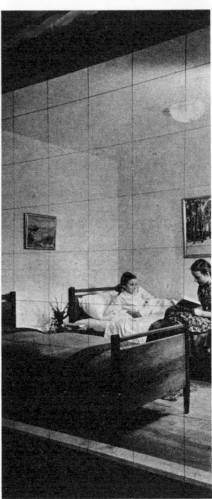

The girls' room. *The beds are made of plain larch-wood, less attractive in appearance but excellent to sleep in. And girls sleep well at this age especially when they can look forward to all the little joys of a family breakfast-table such as is found in every real home*

Question: Has Germany a programme for which she is fighting? Answer: What the German soldier is defending is not a programme. It is the very substance of his existence, the richness and variety of his civil life in peacetime. What he desires to acquire by victory, however, is the fulfilment of the claim that an individual shall be respected for his own self. This, too, is not a programme but an idea, to explain which SIGNAL publishes the following pages

WHAT WE ARE FIGHTING FOR

Wilhelm Leibl:
The three
women in the
church (1881)

The theme of this number is what Germany is fighting for. The picture by the Munich painter Wilhelm Leibl, portraying the three women in the church as they can be seen in that part of the country, has been placed at the beginning. The aim of the following pages is to show what we are and what we possess, what is indispensable and sacred to us

THINGS THAT MAKE LIFE WORTH LIVING FOR US

His ear concentrated on the sound, which the hands mould with delicacy of feeling, Herbert von Karajan faces the orchestra

IN THE SPIRIT OF THE PRESENT AGE

Scarcely five years have passed since a new orchestra conductor made his appearance in Berlin. He first conducted a concert by the Philharmonic Orchestra and subsequently in the State Opera House a classic and polished "Fidelio," a glowing "Tristan" and a performance of the "Mastersingers" which was full of buffoonery and vitality. It was immediately realized that "the" new conductor had arrived, the representative of the younger generation, who with outstanding ability and musical fanaticism subjected the old scores to the clear, bright light of the present age. The new name was that of Herbert von Karajan—today it is known throughout the whole of the musical world.

At that time, the young conductor's career, although short, had been rapid. Salzburg, the musical Mozart town, is his home. He studied at Vienna. After a few years at the theatre in Ulm, he went to Aix-la-Chapelle in 1934 at the age of twenty-six. Here he became the successor of Peter Raabe as the town's General Director of Music. He was not only in charge of the opera but also of the concert organization and an excellent choir. From Aix-la-Chapelle, already, he made his influence felt abroad—he made a profound impression at Amsterdam when he conducted that city's Philharmonic Orchestra as well as at Brussels where he led his Aix-la-Chapelle choir in a performance of Bach's Mass in B-flat.

Since then the radius of his influence has increased. In 1941, Paris acclaimed his "Tristan" with enthusiasm a performance of which he gave with the full Berlin State Opera House orchestra. Never before had a performance with such orchestral polish and such intense dramatic inspiration been experienced in Paris. He had previously been acclaimed in Budapest and Madrid, Rome, Milan and Florence as a great interpreter of German symphonic music.

Whether he is conducting an opera or a concert, Karajan always does so by heart. Without the help of the score, he communicates his conception of the music—whether it be a Mozart symphony or the gigantic apparatus of Strauss' "Elektra"—to the orchestra down to the slightest detail. He possesses a choice feeling for tone which varies between the sharpest contrasts and the most delicate nuances flooding even works we have heard many times before with a surprising freshness. This youthful, elastic man, who plays on the orchestra with calm and sometimes even with apparently negligent movements, at other times, however, with movements full of concentrated willpower, as though on an instrument, is like a medium through which tremendous forces flow. He is not overpowered by them, but controls, binds and restrains them only to release them later in a volcanic outburst. He is the master of the mysterious magic of the primeval forces which are the creative power of our age.

Collected, at attention for the first note, Karajan takes up the baton ...

... With restraining hands he holds back the insistent crescendo ...

... now letting the sound pour forth with freedom of movement

With a nod, the serious cantilina of a solo instrument is brought into prominence

In brilliant scherzo, the left encourages a sparkling cadence

The far-off brass instruments are led with light hand

Ever new nuances of tone are spun from the orchestra like invisible silken strands

All forces are unleashed. The conductor abandons himself to the ecstasy of sound

Masterfully co-ordinated by the gesture of the conductor, the symphony draws to its finale

At work before the rehearsal. Herbert von Karajan discusses the score with his first violin, Siegfried Borries

What we are fighting for:

For man's right to culture

The problem of the masses is the special problem of our age.

In the plutocratic countries, the number of those people having any part in the benefits of culture has become increasingly small. On the other hand, the wretched products of the proletarian cult in the Soviet Union have proved that the nation's need for culture cannot be satisfied by levelling processes and standardization.

It is consequently one of the most important of Europe's war aims that every worker should have at his disposal sufficient leisure time to be able to shape his life so that it is not completely filled out by the dreariness of offices and factories. This need for culture benefiting every individual and every family appears to us no less important than the struggle for a just wage which is essential for providing security and removing that uncertainty which more than anything else has rendered people homeless in great towns. By this means alone is it possible to give talented and ambitious people opportunities for advancement. We are consequently opposed to both standardization and class supremacy.

The right of talented people to receive training is the logical continuation of the right to work which must be the basis of any new social order in Europe. Ability must be the deciding factor and not class, money or profit. The capable individual must be able to occupy by his efforts the place for which he is fitted. That appears to us to be the expression of real culture. It was a fundamental mistake of previous socialist movements to instigate the people to make claims without simultaneously stating that every claim could justifiably be attained only as the result of improved performance. There, however, where the capable individual is cast back into the hopelessness of proletarian existence, social justice can never hold sway. We are passionately opposed to such a system.

Two examples among many: A Beethoven concerto played by a State orchestra conducted by Wilhelm Furtwängler during the lunch hour in a big German industrial plant. One of the German pleasure steamers which give the less well-to do the opportunity to appreciate the beauties of the world which are otherwise available only to the favoured few

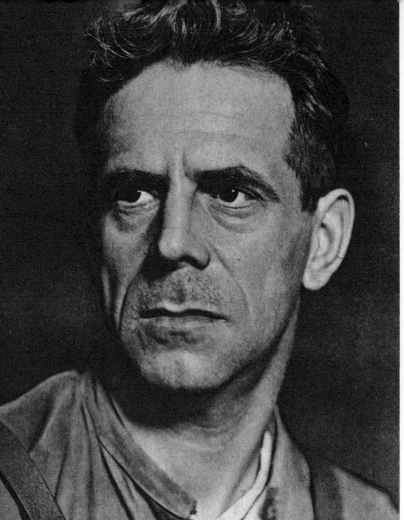

For the final solution of the question regarding the worker's standing

The chief point at issue in this war is the question regarding the individual of the future.

Will this individual be the servant of machinery or of money? Or will he, on the other hand, be the master of machinery and capital? That is the great question now raised in this world struggle.

Not only for the rule of the machine, the characteristic feature of the Soviet Union, but also for the mastery of capital in the British and American plutocracies, the working man is a proletarian.

The rule of capital and of the money market is founded on the uncertainty in the existences of millions of people. On the other hand, the aim of Marxism and of Sovietism is to make the proletariate a thing of permanence. Both Sovietism and the plutocracies have tried to construct an ideology of human ideals based upon a mistake in the social system. In every country capitalism has deprived the worker of his rights, rendered him homeless and made him antagonistic to his people. Sovietism has done the same but by the reverse process. In the vast areas of the Soviet Union, man has been reduced to the state of a slave of machinery and a Stachanov proletarian without rights and without a just wage.

We, on the contrary, aim at social security for the working man; Only he can bear the honourable name of worker who possesses both for himself and his family the security of a definite wage, comfort during the last years of his life, help in cases of illness, a pension should he be injured, benefits for motherhood, and also knows that in the event of his decease, provision will be made for his wife and children.

Insecurity is characteristic of the proletarian system whether it be in the shape of the wage struggles and unemployment in the capitalist countries or in that of debasement to the level of cattle which is first sent to work at one place and then to another as in the Soviet Union.

On the other hand, we are fighting for the individual's security in the community of the people. That is the most important aim of our European struggle.

hese **four pictures symbolize** the path leading the worker to a secure existence which
s already been trodden in Germany where, by the outbreak of this war, a large proportion
everything which turned the worker into a proletarian had already been suppressed. The
rman worker has a legal claim to work, an adequate wage, sick treatment, medical care,
lidays and an old age pension. As far as possible, the factories have provided sanitary

installations, clean and sunny recreation rooms and no less clean and sunny
workshops. Besides all this, kindergartens have been established by the State
or by private concerns. Continuation schools can be found everywhere. The
gifted can there gain by their work both the right and the opportunity to climb
the social ladder. The most important thing, however, is: (see the following page)

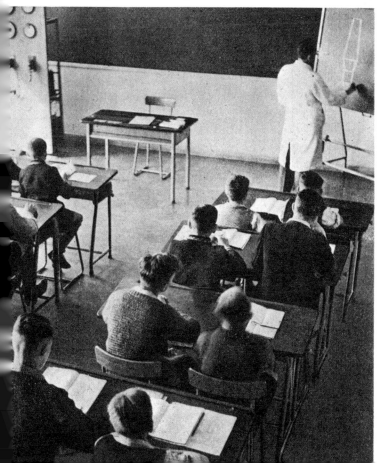

Fiodr Ivanov is a Russian. Since the beginning of the eastern campaign numerous members of this people have volunteered to take part as soldiers, farmers or mechanics in the liberation of their native land from Sovietism. The Russians, who had been cut off from the rest of the Continent by the wall of Bolshevism, have thus joined in the fight for the liberation of Europe. Their conception of Germany derived from more than twenty-five years of Bolshevist propaganda is undergoing a complete revision

Tatashvill is a Georgian. His people, which numbers about two millions, inhabits the southwest of the Caucasus. For the most part, they have retained their traditional Christianity. Ever since 1801, when they were annexed by the Russian Empire, they have fought again and again for freedom or for genuine autonomy. Before the First World War many of the Georgians hoped that the Russian Socialists would bring about a change and give them their liberty. They were bitterly disappointed by Bolshevism and Stalin, who is himself a Georgian, and are now fighting with dogged enthusiasm against the Soviets

Vladimir Maximenko is a Ukrainian and thus belongs to the second largest people in the Soviet Union. The total number of Ukrainians is something more than 40 millions. The cold, unnatural theory of Sovietism is entirely foreign to the deeply optimistic nature of this vivacious people living in the fertile black earth country. There is a lively tendency in the Ukraine towards both economic and intellectual incorporation in Europe. It has now come to the surface again as strong and vigorous as ever. Ukrainian soldiers have always fought courageously against Bolshevism

For the rights of their peoples

Sigerbai Kusherbai is from Turkestan. The Turkomans, including Usbeks, Kirghiz, Kalmucks, Kasachs, Tadshaiks, Karakalpaks and hordes of other names, settled in the vast territory stretching from the Caspian Sea to Pamir and to the borders of China. The Turkomans number between 25 and 30 million people. A recent census taken by the Soviets numbers them at less than half this figure, but these statistics were dictated by political intentions. Today many of the Turkomans, who never willingly submitted to the Soviet system for national reasons, are fighting with the Germans

Idris Shakirov is a Volga Tartar. His people, which lives on the Upper Volga, numbers approximately four millions. In spite of close contact with the Russians when it was exposed for many years to intense attempts at Russianization, this people has defended its national individuality and its own religion with conscious obstinacy and preserved its national integrity intact. Like their cousins in the Crimea, the Volga Tartars have taken advantage of the opportunity offered by the great international conflict of our day and are fighting for the rights of their people

Hasmik Nasarian is an Armenian. This tiny people of approximately 2 millions has retained Christianity ; it was the first people in the east to adopt this religion to which it is consequently particularly attached. There have always been religious martyrs among the Armenians so it is easy to understand that the Armenians are natural enemies of Bolshevism and that especially large numbers of deserters come from the Armenian divisions as convinced antagonists of the Red Army. As soldiers, they are grim and steadfast, as grim as their history and as steadfast as their loyalty to their own tradition

Timer Gallamov is a Crimean Tartar. The Crimean Tartars settled in the Crimea at the time of the Golden Horde. They are Mohammedans and, like all Islamic peoples, have always fought to preserve their national customs against all foreign influences. Bolshevism went so far as to grant them on paper the autonomy they demanded, but this was never realized. During the struggle for their rights, many Tartars were banished to Siberia. In consequence, the percentage of Crimean Tartars, who have joined the volunteer units from the eastern terrories is especially high

Vassili Kigorovitch is a Ruthenian. The Ruthenians, numbering about eight millions, played a special rôle even in the Grand Duchy of Lithuania. Later the intellectuals were absorbed by the Poles and Russians, so that today the nation has more the character of a peasant people. As far back as the First World War, however, the Ruthenians remembered their individuality and, in spite of all the attempts of the Soviets, this national consciousness remained awake. Today, with the doors of freedom open to them, they are proving particularly receptive to European tendencies

Alexei Sovichenko is a Cossack. He thus belongs to the warlike community of the east. Although the Cossack lands suffered exceptionally during the Civil War in 1917, and though the Bolshevists destroyed the last remnants of Cossack independence, what are known as the "Cossack Armies" have preserved intact the laws of Cossack tradition. Once they lived on the banks of the Don, the Terek, the Kuban and the Volga as farmers, but now they are fighting as volunteers with the Germans in the hope that one day they will be able to live there under their own laws once more

The volunteer units from the eastern territories personify the natural rights of over 160 peoples who lost their individuality when forcibly banded together as the Bolshevist U.S.S.R. SIGNAL here introduces 12 examples

PK. Photographs: War Correspondents Pabel, Grimm, Frenske, Modl, Arndt, Kirsche, Mittelstaedt, Knaack

S. Havibakshi is an Aserbeidjan. He is wearing the award for wounds. This mountaineer people from the Northern Caucasus is famous for its horsemen and marksmen. For years it has waged bitter warfare against Bolshevism of which it was the declared enemy from its earliest days. It withdrew before the overwhelming terror into remote mountain valleys without giving up the struggle. When the Germans came, the Aserbeidjans greeted them as liberators and joined them by the hundred. When the Caucasas was evacuated, many families followed in the Germans' train

Machmet Hadaiuhov is a North Caucasian. His tiny people of slightly more than 150,000 inhabitants are Mohammedans. When the North Caucasian territory was occupied by German troops in 1942, it transpired that the Soviet rule had been particularly violent there. Numerous North Caucasians accompanied the German Army when it evacuated the country again. They are freedom-loving mountaineers who have been to a certain extent pressed into the North Caucasian industries by the Soviets, though they take every opportunity to evade this oppression. The North Caucasians are excellent marksmen

Ivan Kulkaanen is a Carelian. The Finnish linguistic group in the Soviet Union numbers about 4 million people. The Finns and Carelians on Soviet soil do not differ racially from their brothers in Finland. The division line between the Russian and Finnish racial areas runs approximately along the Murmansk Railway. The frontiers of the Carelian Soviet Republic had been intentionally so drawn that the Carelians and Finns formed a minority. Today the Carelians are fighting with heart and soul side by side with their people against Bolshevism

Professor Wolfgang Liebeneiner:

A new form of art

The development of the German film

In the midst of war the German film has followed a path which must be considered as having resulted in the development of a new art of the film. At the beginning of the war, the general opinion was that the Muses would be silenced by the noise of battle. It soon appeared, however, that the Muses were a sort of spiritual battalion of the geniuses. Signal here produces an article on the subject by Professor Wolfgang Liebeneiner who was shortly appointed production chief of the Ufa Film Company

A work of art and a style are not rooted in the formation of a theory but in the formation of life The theorists can subsequently trace its origin, give it a name and assign it a place in the history of that branch of art.

The film is not in the fortunate position of a theatrical performance, which sweeps past us and then belongs irrevocably to the past. It is both the strength and the weakness of the film that, like a piece of sculpture, it is made of lasting material and does not alter its shape. A film, however, cannot wait like other works of art to be "discovered." A film artist cannot say like the composer of a symphony, which is first greeted with cat-calls, that he will be understood later. No, the organization of a film production is far too complicated for the film not to be produced immediately.

That fact makes it obligatory for us to pay more attention to success. At the same time, it prevents us from becoming estranged from life. But this working for success is also to blame for a large number of the obstacles which have hindered the film in its development as a real art. It is quite wrong to put the blame on the technical nature of the film—a phrase which is unfortunately still too often thoughtlessly repeated.

Film technics can accomplish a very great deal. All sorts of tricks are possible, time can be bridged and the illusion of space can be produced. By means of pictures shown in associative succession, the progress of feelings can be made visible—a process brought to the pitch of mastery in the silent film. Film technics can do a great deal, but alone they can do nothing. Only when film technics are employed to carry out a poetic idea are they more than a mechanical plaything. The poetic content of a film always decides its value. It is as yet, however, by no means certain which form of the poetical film idea contains its immortality, the script or the actual film strip. If there is no apparatus, the film merely

THE BIG TEST Three young actors are playing their first leading rôle before the camera. They are Harald Holberg with Ingrid Lutz (above) and again Harald Holberg with Lisca Malbran: (below) — the usual film story of the man between two girls — three entirely new faces. In the following pages SIGNAL describes their big camera test

The chief producer of the Ufa company: Professor Wolfgang Liebeneiner with Johannes Heesters, the star of the Ufa film "Großstadtmelodie", during an interval in the shooting

exists as a strip just like a musical score. A drama or a symphony, it is true, are also dependent to a considerable degree on their production. It does not matter how abominably bad Beethoven's ninth symphony is played, it still remains what it is. What, however, is the permanent feature of a film? The film strip, on which a performance at a definite time is recorded, or the poetic creation on which the performance is based? If our script writers were to take the trouble to give their film scripts an equally literary form as that of a theatrical play, we should then have a beginning from which a film could be made in a hundred years' time with the help of new technical devices and given a new interpretation by other people.

It is very difficult to control words. Film people must consequently not be reproached with tackling the solution of this problem only timidly and slowly and even with having invented for years past all sorts of theories in order to close their eyes to this task. Just remember the history of the film! What a bad reputation it used to have!

The great change has come. The art of the film has established itself. Just as during the Renaissance the Medici and other prominent persons in the Italian states gave contracts to artists and let them go to work with their road already planned out for them, orders for films are given to us in Germany today. I have been in Rome and in Florence and everybody will agree with me that those artists, who worked there carrying out orders for the state or for some Maecenas or other, did not produce the worst works of art. In their works they have lived until long after their own age. That is why we film people are happy today to have been given a clear and precise task and we are proud that in fulfilling that task we have been given a free hand.

With every plan, however, we must ask ourselves whether it can stand the test when compared with what those men, who will one day see the film, have experienced in the war. We have seen the news reels and been amazed at the courage, the selflessness and the spirit of sacrifice with which our brothers are fighting at the front. We are, therefore, trying to play our part in real life in the same way as those men who are prepared to sacrifice their lives for it. That is the all-important revolution which has taken place in the German film. Even our methods of expression have been enriched by this experience. We have discovered with what simple means, if only they are used properly, the most magnificent effects can be obtained.

The films made recently are the best testimony that a film art has really begun to develop here. Its object is to inspire everything which has to do with films. It consciously follows the opposite path to that along which the film industry used to work. That path formerly used to lead to external things, to coarse, spectacular effects. Now, however, it follows the path leading to the soul . . .

"Not so imperial, please!" With this exclamation the producer, Boleslav Barlog (right), interrupted the filming. He now shows the three young artistes, who are playing their first leading rôles, how to act with natural simplicity

Even climbing stairs is an art! *It is more difficult to walk in front of the camera than anywhere else. But the audience should not notice it*

The big test

Stars for the first time

Ufa has entrusted the chief rôles in one of its films to young, inexperienced actors thus giving them a chance to show their ability. This experiment touches an old problem: should young artistes be presented in big parts or should they be allowed to climb the ladder slowly? There is much to be said for and against both theories. The only way to come to a clear conclusion is by making the experiment. Today it is one of the principles of German film producers to present young actors in all types of parts. In this way abilities often come to life which were not even suspected in the beginning. A young player with a talent for tragedy suddenly gives a convincing performance in a comic part. This method of discovering talent aims at preserving actors from being condemned to one-sidedness by incorporating one special type all their lives. But above all the producers want to avoid the wastage of great undiscovered talents.

Not a break-down — merely a torn stocking
...and a quick, skilful darn during the shooting with
the smiling stone statues in Sans-Souci as spectators →

Ingrid Lutze used to be a dancer. *She went straight to the films and was given a few small parts. Now she has been given her first big rôle as an actress*

Lisca Malbran is 17! *She was trained in the Ufa Studio for Young Actors and is now appearing before the camera for the first time in her life. Her acting reveals all the nonchalance of youth*

is is how to run! *Barlog demonstrates until* actor's every movement is quite natural

Running for their future! *Success in the examination depends on this scene too*

ONE OF THEM

Portrait of a Cossack

Cossacks are fighting on the Eastern Front. Fearless men, fighters, decorated with the infantry assault badge, the red ribbon of the winter campaign and the green ribbon of the fighting Eastern peoples. SIGNAL interviews one of them

He is a Terek Cossack, born in 1915, and a former lieutenant in the Soviet army in which he served as from March, 1940. With seven of his men, he gave himself up as German prisoner in August, 1941, at Jelnja, east of Smolensk. He remained only two days in the prison camp at Roslawl. He then immediately asked to be used in the German Army.

His manly, bold demand must have made a good impression. At any rate, he was sent along with other Cossack officers to a camp west of the old Soviet frontier. Like-minded men banded themselves together there and formed a Cossack company. Dominated by a fanatical love of freedom, they asked to be placed in active service. They were under the command of a major, a Cossack like themselves. Then came a Don Cossack colonel, who had gone over to the side of the Germans with his cavalry regiment. He organized the Cossacks. The unit became more solid all the time, more dependable, more eager. They wanted to fight against the Bolshevists. The old hate was burning in them. They had not forgotten the punitive expeditions which had pushed forward from Moscow to their frontier-lands, and the massacres that had taken place there. A free life in their free Cossack homeland—the distant dream, the fair-flowering ideal, the poignant longing of every Cossack, regardless of antecedents and district, whether the Don, Kuban, Terek, Volga, or Siberia. The piercing glance, the sharp nose, the fur cap, the sure seat in the saddle, ability at trailing, hard fighting, riding with wild abandon—the dream-world of every Cossack.

He is one of them—a lieutenant now in a Cossack battalion that is seeing fighting in the middle sector of the Eastern Front.

20 grow into 300

Back in 1941, he found it very boring to be in a training camp. He asked to be transferred to a ski battalion. He was taken on together with 20 others. Behind their horses, they pulled the skiers of the chasseur battalions. During the severe winter of 1942, they fought against the Belov unit, which had penetrated the German lines. He began his fight against parachutists, air-borne brigades, guerrillas and fanatical, dispersed troops. Together with 20 others, he operated with the German units. He emerged from these engagements with more than 300 Cossacks. For the Cossacks among the ranks of the enemy, who had penetrated the lines or been dispersed, heard of the Cossacks in the German units fighting their forest warfare among the dense undergrowth. They came over to the Germans singly and by the dozen—but come they did.

The numbers of the Cossacks increased. The divisions had their own companies. The various armies organized their own battalions. The army high command stepped in, and a regiment was formed. He, however, who had been decorated in the meantime with the green ribbon for bravery and the Eastern medal of the winter campaign, was promoted to lieutenant. He was a leader among leaders. A man

among men. A warrior among warriors. He was given a company, which he called the *Eskadron*. The men were all Cossacks like himself.

They are all the same as he is

They are all the same as he is. They are big fellows with shining eyes, sure and dependable. They won't let the Germans down. They won't desert. They are pleased with their lot.

Every German regards them as equals. Man to man, they are imbued with mutual confidence and respect. In a big operation in the autumn of 1942, they took 1,400 men prisoner in one week. Like bloodhounds, they scented out the bandits in hiding in the woods. Like a clean man detests filth, so the Cossacks regard their enemy. They are masters facing slaves. They have weapons, horses, ammunition. They are living as they used to live in their homeland before the Bolshevists came. They maintain order and discipline amongst themselves.

Meaning of life

He told us about his home country once. About the beautiful womenfolk with their jet-black hair and flashing eyes. About the horses. About the steppe. About the hate for the Bolshevist foe. His facial expression denotes courage. His strong hands held ours. They squeezed hard when he promised anything. We sensed this and we trusted him. These men are our friends, truly and in honour bound. He, the Cossack from Terek, talked about his own land and of the common ties of loyalty. He spoke of Czarism as if it were a fairy-tale, and of Bolshevism as of a nightmare. Freedom and the steppe are synonymous. Moscow, emboldened by Stalin, tried to destroy the privileges of the steppe. Destructive orgies were to exterminate the Cossacks. They failed. In 1936, Stalin even attempted to restore these privileges in part—a sign of his weakness. Contempt and hate were reflected in the eyes of the Cossack Freedom; the meaning underlying talk. Fighting; the method of achieving it. Victory; the ultimate result. Hate; the dynamo. Faith; the desire of the heart.

We listen to the Cossacks singing in the evening. Their songs voice their love of the far-off homeland.

When the machine guns go rat-tat-tat, the grenades pockmark the earth, the tanks lumber relentlessly forward, these men lie beside us, brave fighters for their Cossack freedom.

These units, fired with hate and burning passion, are our valuable auxiliaries. We esteem these Cossacks highly, not as mercenaries, but as soldiers filled with the ideal of freedom for Eastern Europe.

All this was told to us by the Cossack lieutenant, born on the Terek, decorated with German medals, speaking Russian, feeling as a European.

We know that these Cossacks have understood us as to the meaning of this war—its goal is freedom!

By PK. War Correspondent Dr Joachim Fischer

"All hands on deck!" The commander of destroyer inspects the units which have paraded on the gunwale for the ceremony the presentation of the Iron Cross

PK. Photograph: War Correspondent Lagema

New colours- traditional honour

The second anniversary of the foundation of the French Volunteer Legion fighting against Bolshevism

"In the name of the Marshal", *General Bridoux handed to the French Volunteer Legion against Bolshevism the new colours presented by Marshal Pétain. They are to be the pattern for the new fighting colours of the future forces of the French State*

There has never been a break in the glorious tradition of the French Army. As early as the summer of 1941 many of the best soldiers of France recognized it as their task to join the front protecting Europe in the east. This was the origin of the French Volunteer Legion against Bolshevism which celebrated the second anniversary of its foundation a few weeks ago. On this occasion in the Invalides in Paris a solemn High Mass was celebrated for its 211 fallen. After the service in the court of honour of the Hôtel des Invalides a flag was blessed. As a sign that the military honour of France is the honour of the Legion, to use the words of the Marshal, the colours were handed to it which are to be the pattern for the future French Army flag.

50 legionaries were decorated for their heroic part in the fighting on the battlefront of Europe. Relatives of fallen legionaries were handed diplomas of honour and decorations for bravery in the name of the Supreme Commander of the German Forces.

At sunset a deputation of legionaries lowered the new colours of the Legion before the tomb of the Unknown Warrior—an action symbolical of their confession of faith in the traditional honour of the nation.

Pride fills the Parisians *as the bearers of the future of France march up the Champs Elysées to honour their fallen camrades at the tomb of the Unknown Warrior*

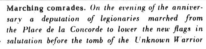

"In memoriam." Captain Dupuis. a veteran from the eastern front, hands to the relatives of legionaries fallen in the east, the Croix de Guerre Légionnaire and the Médaille Militaire

Marching comrades. On the evening of the anniversary a deputation of legionaries marched from the Place de la Concorde to lower the new flags in salutation before the tomb of the Unknown Warrior

gh Mass in the Dôme des Invalides. The white ss on the red and blue field wreathed round with old flags of the Grande Armée and combined h the flags of all the nations fighting against lshevism points to the signification of the ceremony

PK. Photograph:
Front Correspondents Pabel, Zucca

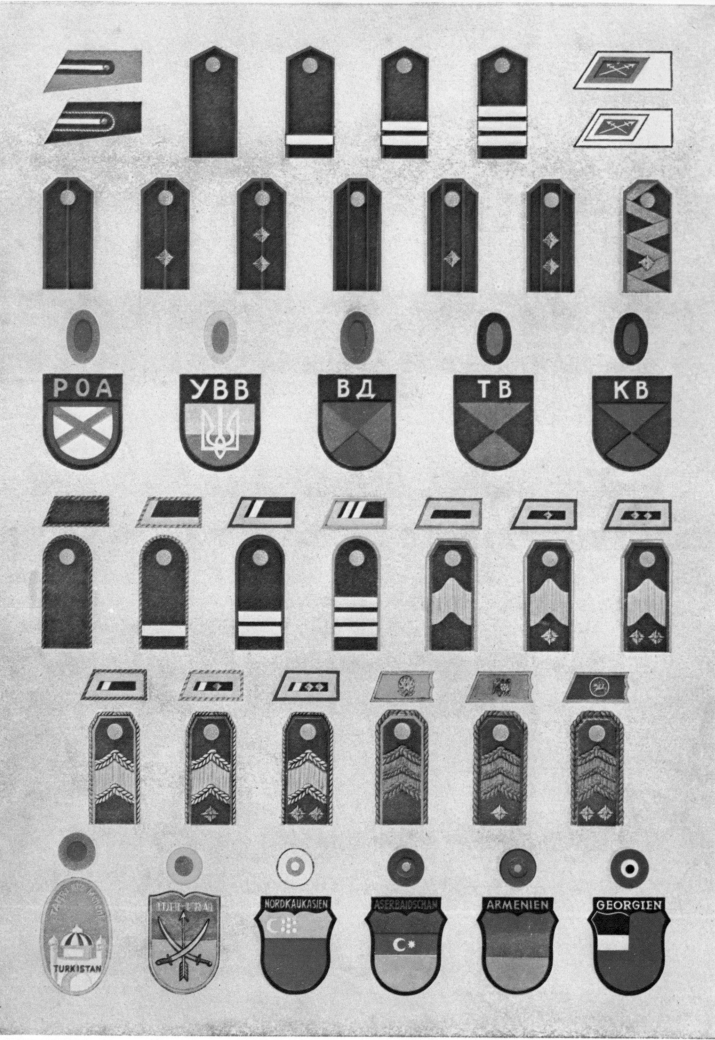

Ranks of the Eastern Volunteers

I. Russian, Ukrainian and Cossack units

1st row: Patches of the Russian and Ukrainian Army of Liberation: Men (above), officers (below); Shoulder straps of the Russian Army of Liberation and the Cossack units: Volunteer, Lance-Corporal, Corporal, Sergeant. Patches of the Cossack units: Men (above), officers (below)

2nd row: 2nd Lieutenant, Lieutenant, Captain, Major, Lieutenant-Colonel, Colonel, Lieutenant-General. (The badges worn by a Major-General and a General are not shown here)

3rd row: Sleeve badges and cockades: Russian Army of Liberation, Ukrainian Army of Liberation, Don Cossacks, Terek Cossacks, Kuban Cossacks

II. Turkestan, Caucasian and Volga-Tartar units

1st row: Patches and shoulder straps: Volunteer in the Turkestan Legion, Lance-Corporal in the Volga-Tartar Legion, Corporal in the North Caucasian Legion, Sergeant in the Aserbeidjan Legion, 2nd Lieutenant in the Armenian Legion, Lieutenant in the Georgian Legion, Captain in the Georgian Legion

2nd row: Major in the Turkestan Legion, Lieutenant-Colonel in the Volga-Tartar Legion, Colonel in the North Caucasian Legion, Major-General in the Aserbeidjan Legion, Lieutenant-General in the Armenian Legion, General in the Georgian Legion. (The patches of the Generals in the Turkestan, Volga-Tartar and North Caucasian Legions are not shown here)

3rd row: Cuffs and cockades: Turkestan Legion, Volga-Tartar Legion, North Caucasian Legion, Aserbeidjan Legion, Armenian Legion and Georgian Legion

The Tartars sound their bugles . . . The guard of the Volunteers parades in front of a khan's castle from the Turkish period (17th century)

AN ARMY:

. . . and everything attaching to it

Everywhere it has been employed, the Army of the Volunteer Units formed by the eastern peoples has proved its mettle in the struggle against the Soviets. Behind the front, however, the native volunteer units indulge in all the activities of troops not actually engaged in the fighting for the moment. SIGNAL also describes this side of the volunteers' life

Two flags—one struggle. The Volunteers are proud that every morning at sunrise they can hoist their own colours in their camp beside the Reich War Colours. They have ra:lied beneath their symbol of the struggle cohich is blue and red

PK. Photograph: War Correspondent Artur Grimm

In the general's presence. The General-in-Command of the Eastern Troops personally convinces himself of the standard of training reached by his legionaries. Turkestan volunteers are here explaining to him how to use a grenade thrower   PK. Photograph: War Correspondent Kintscher

Decorations for bravery and merit awarded to the eastern peoples. Medal for Bravery, Second Class in Gold. Medal for Bravery, First Class in Gold. Medal for Merit, Second Class in Silver. Medal for Merit, First Class in Silver. Medal for Bravery, Second Class in Bronze.

At a concert in Prague: the Deputy Reich Protector, Reinhard Heydrich, on his right his wife

THE HERITAGE

"Signal" publishes in this number several articles on that part of the Greater German Reich which as the Protectorate of Bohemia and Moravia occupies within the Reich a unique political position of world interest. These articles commence on pages 4 and 5 with a description of the Protectorate's geographical position and the general historical consequences following from it. The next article brings us to the present day by giving an account of Reinhard Heydrich, the Deputy Reich Protector of Bohemia and Moravia who was assassinated in Prague in the early summer of 1942. What he achieved in the short period of his activity was consecrated by his death as the foundation stone of a project of organization which, like a heritage, pledges both Germans and Czechs

It is doubtful if anybody but a German or a Czech would know what is meant when the statement is made that President Hacha revived the tradition of St Wenceslas when he placed Bohemia and Moravia under the protection of the German Reich. Wenceslas was the Bohemian King who a thousand years ago in 929, was stabbed to death by his brother because he had resolved to convert his country to Christianity. To be a Christian meant in those days to be a German. Polygamy, slavery, plunder and murder were the order of the day at the foot of the Castle when Wenceslas made his resolve.

On 4th January 1942, Reinhard Heydrich, the German who only a few weeks before had been presented with the keys of St Wesceslas' Chapel by the Czech President, Dr Hacha, died as the result of an attempt on his life carried out under the instructions of enemy international wirepullers. The order to assassinate him came from London, but from Czechs just as it had been Czechs who murdered Wenceslas. They carried out the orders, landed by parachute in Bohemia and Moravia and committed the murder because they were opposed to order and in favour of darkness.

Reinhard Heydrich was in Prague for less than a year. He arrived there in September 1941 and was killed in June 1942 on a morning early in summer just as he was about to drive to the Prague Castle unmindful of danger for he had a good conscience.

Vaclav Stoces wrote in the "Narodny Prace" of 7th June: "The physical ideal of the German man incorporated by the murdered statesman was completed by the ideal soul and mental

Heydrich's death-mask. *The cast was taken by the Prague sculptor, Professor Rotter*

attitude which entirely filled his personality. A fine man both in his person and his personality—such was the human profile of the murdered man."

Heydrich possessed the virtue of the real man—inoffensiveness. He did not spurn danger, but he never believed that he was exposed to danger in the Protectorate. He had naturally thought of death, even of a sudden death—he had discussed the possibility of it even once with his friend and successor Daluege—but he never anticipated meeting his death in Prague.

Heydrich knew his murderers. For several days they saluted him when his car came to the bend in the road which was to prove fatal to him. Heydrich returned the salute, because he thought the men working on the road at the bend were labourers.

The Chief of the Security Police and General in the Police Force might have employed every available means of protecting himself, yet he disdained them and moved through Prague without escort, because he was conscious of having done only good to the Czech people. When he came, profiteering, illicit trade and treachery had been flourishing. The working people were in danger and going short. Heydrich acted energetically and he was pleased that among the guilty people he laid his hands on, there was scarcely a single workman.

Nor did his murderers belong to the working class. They were idlers and émigrés who had been sent over from London and dropped on to Bohemian soil by parachute because no Czech worker would have raised a hand against the S.S.Obergruppenführer. It would be varnishing over the facts to say that

A chivalrous fighter as statesman, as air pilot on the eastern and western fronts and as man—
the sportsman Reinhard Heydrich was a good swordsman too. He was one of the best European fencers

the foreign people felt affection for him, but the undeniable truth is that the people placed their confidence in this tall, fair-haired man.

At the time of his assassination, the measures he had ordered to be adopted for the benefit of the Czech people were just taking shape. The fact that they were not delayed is proof of the dispassion of the Germans.

On 18th October 1942 the Prague "Moldaulände"—whence one has the most beautiful view of the Prague Castle (Hradshin—was renamed the "Reinhard Heydrich Ufer." S.S. Gruppenführer and Secretary of State Karl Hermann Frank made an important speech on that occasion which was dedicated to the memory of the dead man.

In it he said: "And now I would like to address a few words to the Czech intellectual classes in general. We have so far adopted a strict attitude towards the Czech intelligentzia. We have done so because 90 % of the political enemies of the Reich, the people who helped Heydrich's assassins and the enemy's agents, belonged to the Czech intelligentzia."

The speaker clearly distinguished between the creative spiritual forces of the Czech people, the doctors and engineers, officials and technicians, writers, artists and well-meaning teachers and that destructive set of Czech intellectuals supporting what they call the "Czechoslovakian State Council with its seat in London." Heydrich, too, had declared war on these intellectuals because being unable or unwilling to earn a living as honest citizens they had led the better part of the Czech people into the paths of a venturesome foreign policy, plunged them into misfortune and finally tried to instigate them to murder and revolt.

The political megalomaniacs who led the Czech people to the edge of destruction are living in London and feeding on the fat of the land because it is intended that they shall continue to betray their own people in the service of Powers hostile to Europe and because they have volunteered to do so.

Nature's best gifts to man are a happy disposition and sound common sense. With these two gifts one can survive the blows dealt by fate such as illness and poverty. An evil disposition and too little common sense are a curse because they lead to a gloomy view of things and open false perspectives.

This curse, however, had been set by nature on that part of the Czech intelligentzia which had caused the diligent population in Bohemia and Moravia to lose all their friends, who tolerated the immense riches of the Pechek and helped to increase them but left the people, from whom this intelligentzia originated after all, in a state of unemployment and poverty.

When in the midst of war Heydrich received a deputation of Czech workers in the Prague Castle—this was the first occasion that Czech workers had ever set foot in the Castle's reception-rooms for those in power during the 20 years of the Czech democratic republican régime had never received workers—he questioned them regarding their anxieties and wishes. Among other things the workers mentioned that many of them after years of unemployment in the former Czechoslovakia had now obtained work again

as the result of the increased economic prosperity since 1939. These men, formerly unemployed, had not been able to buy shoes during the period when they had no work. Now, however, when they had work, these people found it difficult to purchase shoes in consequence of the rationing system during the war. Just imagine that in the country of the world-famous Bata shoe factories, the many Czech workers were unable to get solid footwear! A proof that the régime of a degenerate intellectual class was bad and asocial. S. S. Obergruppenführer Heydrich provided the workers with the necessary shoes in the midst of war.

The Czech political intellectuals had looked towards France, Britain and America in spite of the fact that the statistics on Czech export trade plainly showed that Germany provided the biggest market for the products of Czech industry. There is no law and there can be no law binding a people to a hypocritical friendship with its partners in trade. A policy, however, and an intellectual class which condemn their own people to be the declared enemies of their partners in trade are a bad policy and a rotten intellectual class. It is a blessing for the people when war is declared on such an intellectual class.

At the same time, however, Heydrich held out his hand to the working people. After his assassination a charitable action was carried out which he had arranged some months before his death. At the Protector's expense 7,500 Czech industrial workers were sent for a holiday to the best Bohemian resorts.

After Heydrich's successor, General Daluege, had convinced himself that Heydrich's assassination had not been desired by the Czech workers, it would have been contrary to the murdered man's wishes not to carry out this charitable action. This holiday for the workers was symbolic. Only a proportion of the workers could participate. The murdered man did not consider himself as a philanthropist. As a Socialist he wished to say to the workers: This will be your right when at some time in the future social justice has been established among you.

Heydrich very soon recognized what had been sapping the energies of the Czech people in the past, namely, the contrast between the yearnings of the working people and its misguided intellectuals who were striving to lead the people along false paths. The Czech people had not been given any opportunity of deciding its own style of life. The transference and application of western ideals which, moreover, had been misunderstood, could not bring happiness to the Czech people. It is only when a people develops its own intelligentzia that it can find the manner of life which best suits it. The people must be able to say to its intellectuals that it is wrong to think what cannot be lived. The people must clearly recognize the dangers threatening it from a misguided intelligentsia. For it to be able to do so it must above all live in tranquillity. That was Heydrich's resolve and that this peace which alone guarantees the development of a real and genuine manner of life for the Czech people, shall never again be disturbed by revolver shots is the heritage bequeathed by the assassin's victim.

THE "OLD MAN"

Heydrich's successor, S.S. Oberstgruppenführer and Generaloberst of the Police Kurt Daluege

Heydrich's successor as Deputy Reich Protector is a powerfully built Silesian. There is an old proverb which says that the best Berliners come from Silesia. Kurt Daluege made his home in Berlin by choice. It is surprising to hear that a man of such outspoken soldierly character should have worked as an engineer. The Generaloberst has many engineering feats to

ficient to prove how efficiently he dealt with it. Today Daluege has under his command in the Order Police three million police troops consisting of town police forces, country police, fire brigade police, anti-aircraft police, technical emergency police, voluntary fire brigades and other auxiliary police organizations. In addition he holds the office of Reich Protector. It

The Generaloberst in private life

Right: the happy father with Frau Daluege and their youngest child. Below: the three elder children, the "boys"

his credit, among others the technical exploitation and canalization of the industrial district of Velten to the north of Berlin. Later on he entered the service of the city of Berlin as engineer. But even in those days he shared his time between duty and inclination. As part-time officer of the Reichswehr he was introduced to the staff work which occupies most of his time today.

Daluege was one of the oldest and most popular leaders of the Storm Troopers in Berlin. As a member of the Prussian Diet he was the mouthpiece of the National Socialists for the Police. It was natural, therefore, to entrust to him the re-organization of the Prussian police. A special task was reserved for the police for they had to provide the majority of the leaders in the event of the re-introduction of general military service. Military training for the police was Daluege's principal task and the fact that 190 former German police officers, today officers in the Armed Forces, have been awarded the Knight's Cross is suf-

is clear that in these circumstances it is almost impossible to speak of a private life. He spends a great part of his leisure working in aeroplanes or cars. He hurries back and forth between Prague and Berlin and between the fronts where his troops are fighting. He is the happy father of a family and an enthusiastic hunter. The public rarely sees anything of his family life, of his wife and his four children. The Generaloberst lives a retired life and his wife works quietly for her favourite task, the care of large families. It is very rare that Daluege's colleagues meet their superior, the "old man" as they call him, socially, that is enjoying a glass in the evening when recollections of bygone struggles are revived and when the sudden fire in the eyes of the heavy phlegmatic giant show how much pleasure he finds in the manly and rough life of the hunter.

S.S. Oberstgruppenführer and Generaloberst der Polizei Daluege, Deputy Reich Protector in Bohemia and Moravia
PK. Photograph : Front Correspondent Weidenbau

A VISIT TO THE CASTLE

In these pages "Signal" shows the joint residence of the Reich Protector and the Czech President and gives a short description of the modern interplay of self-administration and State control

The fortified castle overlooking the Moldau was the ancient seat of the German emperors. Rudolf II, the friend of the alchemists and the great art collector, was the only one of the Habsburgs to reside in Prague. The others took up their residence in Vienna. Maria Theresa, however, saved the old castle from ruin, and the structures she added gave the mountain the flat, massive lines of the classical period of architecture. Until then the Gothic style had prevailed, all the lines rose sheer into the sky. Now, the buildings are broad and have something of the character of a barracks, but high up in the grey clouds, the Gothic filigree still jubilates and the green Baroque roof of the cathedral tower smiles like a chubby-cheeked rogue over the heavy walls down on the river.

The Castle is the official residence of the highest representative of the Greater German Reich in Bohemia and Moravia — the Reich Protector. The President of the Protectorate also has his residence in the Castle building.

From the Mathiastor in the court of honour the German and Czech colours are flown together. For the duration of the war there are no so-called guards of honour in Germany, but Prague is an exception to this rule. Two sentries are posted before the artistically wrought entrance to the court of honour.

This gateway is opened only for the Reich Protector and the President. A guard of honour stands to arms when General Daluege or President Hacha enters. Then, in honour of the President, a guard of honour of the Czech Government troops presents

In St Wenceslas' Square in Prague. A demonstration by the Czech population against the wire-pullers behind the murder of Reinhard Heydrich. The Czech population swore fidelity to the Reich

The Deputy Reich Protector Generaloberst Daluege in conversation with the President Hacha in the Castle

The Secretary of State to the Reich Protector S. S. Gruppenführer K. H. Frank and Frau Frank at a reception given by the President. On the left the Czech Minister Moravec

arms in the rear castle yard where his offices are situated. When the representative of the Reich and of the Czech people are entertaining official guests the entrance to the court of honour is opened for them too.

This rigid ceremonial in the lonely rambling castle courtyard is a very solemn expression of the dignity of the Reich.

The Protector occupies very few rooms in the castle, a private office, the offices of his adjutants as well as a conference room and a dining-room. The latter contains a large painting by a Czech master while in the wings occupied by the Czech President, German art treasures are hung.

The Reich Protector's permanent representative is S.S. Gruppenführer and Secretary of State Karl Hermann Frank whose official residence is at the Czernin Palace a few minutes away from the Castle. This magnificent building also houses the Reich Protector's Office. In the time of the former Czechoslovakia, the Foreign Ministry was accommodated in the Czernin Palace. Here is the point of contact between the German Reich and the Czech Government. The Reich Protector is immediately subordinate to the Führer of the German Reich.

The Reich Protector's Office is a supreme Reich authority, that is to say that it is on the same footing as the Reich Ministries and has not the character, for example, of a government of one of the German states. Its decisions are therefore Reich decisions. The government of the Czech people is absolutely autonomous on questions of culture. That it differs from the Government of a German state is proved by the existence of the Czech Ministry of Popular Enlightenment which also deals with questions of autonomous Czech culture. The countries of Bohemia and Moravia have been divided into seven administrative regions. Even the parish authorities belong to the sphere of influence of the heads of these units. The administration is a modern combination of autonomy and state control, a system that guarantees the development of productive personalities. General Heydrich, the late Reich Protector, was himself responsible for the introduction of this modern German administration. It was one of his last outstanding official acts. If this liberal form of administration proves a success it can but promote the mutual advantages of the other parts of the Greater German Reich and the Protectorate.

The residence of the Reich
Protector of Bohemia and Moravia

When the Protectorate of Bohemia and Moravia was established the Castle of Prague was selected as the official seat of the Reich Protector. Czech soldiers (below) daily mount guard beside the German soldiers (above)

The flags
flown from the Castle of Prague

The Reich service flag and the standard of the President with the arms of Bohemia and Moravia

THE ASPECT OF THE MODERN BATTLE

Note on the colour impressions of the fighting in the East by war artist PK. Walter Gotschke

"Signal" was the first periodical in the world to publish colour photos taken by its front correspondents directly on the battlefield. The accounts of those who witnessed the battle are supplemented by colour photography to an extent which until now had been considered impossible. "Signal" has nevertheless not refrained from sending the artist to the front along with the photographer. The reason is this. Even a colour camera fitted with every conceivable device cannot render the artist's eye superfluous. Only the colour photograph together with the artist's impressions on the battlefield afford an approximately correct picture of the modern battle. The camera lens has an inexorable range and an objectivity at its disposal not granted to the human eye. The human eye controls every impression of colour. It tones down many a strong impression reproduced by the colour camera and, on the other hand, registers others such as lightning, the glow of fire, and smoke more clearly.

"Signal's" photographers have often published colour photographs of tank battles in burning villages. Scarcely one of these photographs, however, is so thrilling in its grimness as the artist's impressions of tanks passing through the burning village (page 23). The photographer does not take such photographs because they offer him too few details. The artist's eye, on the other hand, wide open in terror, preserves the memory of the journey through the sea of flames. It is a snapshot such as is also taken by the camera and yet the artist's memory, although less exact than a colour photograph, thrills and excites, whilst the person examining the picture is told just as much, possibly even more, than by the colour photograph. The artist's inferiority when compared with the colour camera is his subjectivity, which at the same time is also his strength and his superiority. The human eye, however, has a sovereign advantage over every man-made apparatus by the fact that it can be employed at any time and under all circumstances. The colour camera cannot reproduce the night battle with its ghostly play of colours as enthrallingly as the artist.

The colour photograph is an unimpeachable document. If the reader of "Signal" compares earlier colour photographs with the artist's picture, he will discover to his astonishment that the artist's apparent exaggerations are due to his omissions. The human eye is

The machine-gunner on the topmost iron plate of a German assault gun protects the gunners during the battle

During the battle a mach because he has noticed upon the fire of this M

always attracted during the battle in the first place to the men, even when the men are accompanied by machines. The colour photograph shows both in their objectively correct relationship whereby the machine seems to dominate the battlefield. The truth is, however, that man gives the modern battle also its shape. He is the master of everything which is unleashed on the battlefield. The totality of war springs from the will of man. It is his will also which makes him capable of the deeds of heroism and comradeship here depicted by "Signal's" artist.

A German assault gun has joined in the battle being fought by the infantry. This modern weapon enables the general to get near to the dream of Napoleon who wished for the direct participation of the artillery in the front line as decisive for the outcome of the battle.

So that the men inside the armour-plated gun can do their duty, they are accompanied by a machine-gunner who lies on the topmost iron plate of the armour-plating. His only protection is his weapon and the cold-bloodedness with which he uses it. Next to his M.G. lies ready to hand the flag which he spreads out when the dive-bombers join in the battle. The flag tells the pilot of the dive-bomber who is friend and who is foe. During the engagement, through which "Signal's" artist went, three machinegunners were wounded on one single assault gun. Without hesitation others took the wounded men's places,

...ner leaps on to a moving German assault gun
...comrade has been wounded. It possibly depends
...ether the battle can be decided at this point or not

brought their comrades to safety and took
over the protection of the gunners until
the battle was victoriously concluded.

It would have been necessary to seek
out these scenes laboriously from colour
photos of the battle. To the artist they
seemed to be the most profound of
thousands of separate impressions. They
showed him the triumph of man over all
force and so, after the battle, he committed them to paper for the glori-
fication of man.

PK. Front Correspondent: W. Kiaulehn

"Without hesitation others took
the wounded men's place . . ."

In the following pages, "Signal" compares the documentary value of the colour photograph with that of painting. War Artist PK. Gotschke's reports were made during the battle of encirclement at Viasma. Above: Tanks and German infantry repulse a night attempt made by the Soviets to break out of the pocket. Below: German tanks storming through a burning Russian village ⟶

THE ALLEGORY OF THE SNOWBALL...

By Emanuel Moravec

The position of Bohemia and Moravia in the past and in this war

E. Moravec, who held the rank of colonel in the former Czechoslovakian General Staff, has for many years been recognized as a military writer of repute. Since the establishment of the Protectorate of Bohemia and Moravia, Colonel Emanuel Moravec has addressed himself to the Czechs as the champion of the conception of the Reich both in speeches and publications. In January 1942 he became a member of the Government of the Protectorate occupying the posts of Minister of Education and Head of the Office for Popular Enlightenment. When this office was subsequently converted into a Ministry, E. Moravec was appointed Minister of Popular Enlightenment. President Hacha has also entrusted the control of the training of the youth of the Czech people to E. Moravec. By his literary works and broadcast lectures, his activity as a reformer of the Czech educational system and his achievements as head of the propagandistic enlightenment, Moravec has done much to further the spiritual amalgamation of Bohemia and Moravia with the Reich

I. From Rome to the Habsburgs

The Mediterranean Sea, as the state's chief line of communication, formed the centre of the old Roman Empire. Only a third of the territories ruled over by Rome lay on European soil, the greater part was in Africa and Asia. The maritime character of the Roman Empire caused it to establish its north-eastern frontier on the Continent with the help of the largest ancient European line of communication, that formed by the Rhine and Danube. That was a mistake which many Roman Emperors realized. As soldiers, they were of the same opinion as Napoleon centuries later who said that a river can only be successfully defended if you have a good bridgehead on the other bank. But the warlike Germanic tribes lived on the other bank of the Rhine and Danube. The principal natural fortress causing all the Roman thrusts northwards into the territories occupied by the Germanic tribes was the Ercynian Forest. The citadel of this natural Germanic fortress against Rome was the "Bohemian Basin," which included the upper reaches of the Elbe and its tributaries. This European watershed lay right on the southern edge of the "Bohemian Basin" and nearest to the Danube. From here, too, the Germanic tribes had their shortest route across the Roman province Noricum to the Adriatic. (Sketch 1.)

Charlemagne's strategic instinct

When the Roman Empire had collapsed before the Germanic onslaughts in the fifth century, the Germanic tribes advanced towards the south and south-west and partially evacuated the area between the Vistula, Elbe and Danube as well as the "Bohemian Basin." The "Slav"*) tribes now moved into these relatively empty areas in Central Europe under the pressure exerted from the east by the Mongols. "Slav" tribes, which later assumed the name Czechs after their unification by the Primislides, occupied the "Bohemian Basin" during the 7th century. This "Slav" people, the one which had penetrated farthest towards Southwestern Europe, became the nearest neighbour to the Germanic empire just being founded which had assumed the protection and extension of Catholic Christianity. (Sketch 2.)

It is an old sociological axiom that out-of-date peoples and states succumb to new ideas. Such ideas give young peoples, however, great creative strength. Christianity, which had undermined the Roman Empire, provided the Germanic peoples with the ideological impetus to create the first Continental European state, the Holy Roman Empire

of the German Nation, which was founded by Charlemagne in Western and Central Europe at the commencement of the 9th century.

The "Slav"-Mongolian territories lay to the east of Charlemagne's empire. In the Hungarian plains Charlemagne left the old Roman frontier formed by the middle reaches of the Danube as a barrier against the Mongols whilst he created a new frontier against the "Slavs" extending along the Elbe 250 miles eastwards of the old Roman Rhine frontier

Without being in possession of any exact maps, Charlemagne instinctively realized that his empire could only withstand the pressure from the east if it included the citadel of the Ercynian Forest formed by the "Bohemian Basin" as well as the "Carpathian Gate," the great line of communication between the Baltic territories and the Danubian steppes occupied by the Mongols. The "Bohemian Basin" and the "Carpathian Gate" were inhabited by Czech tribes which under the leadership of the far-sighted Primislides became the Reich's allies against the Mongols and were also the first "Slavs" to adopt Christianity. At the beginning of the 9th century Bohemia and Moravia became autonomous parts of the Holy Roman Empire of the German Nation. The Bohemian kings were also among the seven Electors of the Reich who elected the German Emperor.

Two frontiers — an old problem

In the time of Charlemagne the political centre of the German Reich lay on the Rhine. Later when the frontiers of the Reich had advanced eastwards as far as the Oder and in Prussia as far as Memel, Prague, the capital of the Kingdom of Bohemia, became the capital of the Reich and the Imperial residence. It was in this town, too, which was situated in the middle of the "Bohemian Basin," that the first university in the German Reich was founded. (Sketch 3.)

The Habsburg dynasty, which inherited the Bohemian crown after the Luxemburgs, not only bore the Imperial title in the German Reich but also ruled in Spain and Italy at the commencement of modern times. In the west it was opposed by France and in the east by Poland and the Ottoman Empire which formed a similar threat to Europe as the Mongols and the Bolshevists. The seat of anti-European intrigue was then in Paris. France even conspired with the Turks against the German Reich.

During the first half of the 16th century when the Turks had advanced as far as Vienna and Graz, the "Bohemian Basin" formed the strategic basis towards the south-east during the long struggle which ensued. A hundred years later it also formed the strategic basis towards the north-west when the

German Emperor was forced to defend himself during the 30 Years' War against the Protestants who were supported by the French and Swedes.

The "Bohemian Basin" played an even more important part at the beginning of the 19th century. It is a not uninteresting fact that during his campaigns in Eastern Europe Napoleon never marched through this basin. Only in 1805 did he penetrate the Carpathian Gate from the south-west in order to fight the Battle of Austerlitz. It was from the "Bohemian Basin" that he was dealt the heaviest blow in 1813. It was in this area that Schwarzenberg concentrated the army which almost cut off Napoleon's retreat at Leipzig. (Sketch 4.)

It is equally significant that the struggle for mastery in the German Reich between Prussia and Austria was decided when the Prussian troops defeated the Austrians at Königgrätz in 1866 and the Prussians thereupon occupied both the "Bohemian Basin" and the "Carpathian Gate." After the German question had been settled during the second half of the 19th century, the Austrian Emperors made Bohemia and Moravia into a strategic base against the Balkans and Russia. It was here that German and Czech initiative and hard work created the foundation for Austrian industry. Czech blood had to a great degree been intermingled with German blood in consequence of having belonged to the German Reich for a thousand years. The Slav language had remained but both spirit and character had become harder, tougher, more creative and more industrious. Inseparably linked to the Germans by culture and blood, the Czechs had become estranged from all other "Slavs" who had been subjected to the influences of different admixtures of blood.

II. Britain Intervenes

When the British had succeeded in annihilating the navies of all the states of Europe and finally, with Prussia's help, in crushing Napoleon, it was clear that after 1,500 years of liberty Europe had come under the economic and political servitude of a new naval power which in its ruthless colonial policy of exploitation was comparable to the Semitic Carthago of ancient times.

A century after Napoleon, Britain realized that in Europe the Triple Alliance between Germany, Austria and Italy under Berlin's leadership was achieving a supremacy over France and Russia whose strength was sapped by her internal politics. They consequently decided to deal a blow. The first World War ended with the Treaty of Versailles which was intended to renew Britain's domination of Europe. The British had not forgotten Bismarck's words that he who was master of Bohemia was also the master of Europe. The "Bohemian Basin" was doubly important for Britain because the greater part of the industry of the Habsburg monarchy was concentrated there. This industry had to come under British and French control and consequently an artificial state in the shape of the Czechoslovakian Republic, which became the servile vassal of Britain and France, was created by the Treaty of Versailles.

Men who were completely subservient to the Western Democracies and hostile to the German Reich were placed at the head of this new political creation. For the first time since Charlemagne the "Bohemian Basin" had become part of a power combination exclusively directed against the Reich. From the year 1918 onwards nearly 120,000,000 inhabitants of the eastern part of Central Europe were the vassals of Britain and France.

In the eastern part of Central Europe, which had succumbed to British influence, there was only very little

strategic industry. Whilst Germany in 1937 produced 36 million tons of iron and steel, British-French Eastern Europe, which had twice as many inhabitants as Germany, produced something under 9 million tons. Of this, 4,000,000 tons of iron and steel were produced in Czechoslovakia and 1,000,000 in Austria. It was on that account that Germany referred to Czechoslovakia as the Anglo-French armoury in Central Europe. Poland, which in both population and area was twice as big as Czechoslovakia, produced only 2,000,000 tons of iron and steel annually, that is to say, only half as much as Czechoslovakia. These figures suffice to show what strategic importance Czechoslovakia and Austria possessed for Anglo-French hegemony in Central Europe.

The backbone of the Anglo-French colony in Central Europe

Apart from Czechoslovakia and Austria, there were ten states (Poland, Esthonia, Latvia, Lithuania, Rumania, Hungary, Yugoslavia, Bulgaria, Greece and Albania) in Anglo-French Eastern Europe which were agrarian. These ten states produced 79 pounds of iron and steel per head of the population in 1929 as opposed to 550 pounds in Germany. At that time Soviet Russia, too, was agrarian. It produced 66 pounds of iron and steel per head of the population.

From 1929 to 1937 the production of iron and steel in Germany rose by 20 %, in Czechoslovakia by 10 % and in the other eleven states in Anglo-French Eastern Europe by 5 %. In Soviet Russia, however, it rose by 270 % whilst in France it sank by nearly 20 %.

The political development was in accordance with this fact. France was no longer able to provide her Eastern European colonies with economic support.

*) Research has shown that the appellation "Slav" and its derivative "Slavonic" are not based on racial or anthropological considerations but designate a linguistic family. During the course of this article the word "Slav" when employed to describe national or racial characteristics has been provided with quotation marks.

When Hitler assumed power in 1933, France refused to grasp the hand of peace he proffered and in 1935 concluded an alliance with Soviet Russia. The effect on the balance of power was that the Anglo-French spheres of influence in the eastern part of Central Europe with their 120,000,000 inhabitants were now outposts of the Soviet Union. This was primarily true of Czechoslovakia which country together with France concluded an alliance with the Soviet Union in 1935 with Britain's consent. (Sketch 5.)

The Soviet "aircraft-carrier" becomes a part of the Reich

Britain and France behaved at that time very arrogantly towards National Socialist Germany. The British Empire numbered more than 500 million inhabitants, the French Empire nearly 120 millions, the Anglo-French spheres of influence in the eastern part of Central Europe 120 millions as already mentioned and Soviet Russia 180 millions. Germany faced this tremendously superior encircling menace with only 65 million inhabitants and an army in the process of organization. At home she had to overcome much poverty artificially caused by the economic measures adopted by the enemy. What prospects of victory could Hitler have in such circumstances?

Britain, however, failed to recognize the strength of National Socialist Germany and when Adolf Hitler proceeded to unite the German people, she prematurely played a number of welltried trumps. According to British calculations Germany would not be able to fight a big war until 1942. By that time Britain would have completed her armament programme whilst France, who was behindhand with her programme, and Soviet Russia would then have finished arming. The British aristocracy finally wished to play off Germany against Soviet Russia but in such a way that Britain's power over Europe should not suffer by it. The all too strong Soviet-French bloc was dangerous to Britain particularly where India and China were concerned.

What Britain and France considered impossible now became reality. Adolf Hitler came to an agreement with Benito Mussolini concerning the organization of the future Europe and in 1938 Austria was incorporated in the Reich. This was a gift to the Reich of 7 million inhabitants and one million tons of iron and steel annually. Strategically, however, it was far more. Adolf Hitler, who recognized the danger threatening from the east, quite openly followed in the footsteps of Charle-

magne who in 796 had advanced in an easterly direction along the Danube and the Drave and established the "Marches of the Avars." Charlemagne had thus established a flank position to the south of the "Bohemian Basin" into which he penetrated in 805 with the object of reducing the Czechs and their princes to obedience and inducing them to form an alliance.

Adolf Hitler's Greater German Reich also required a strategically sound frontier against the democratic-Bolshevist east. The chief strategic rôle was here played by Czechoslovakia who was industrially strong and politically completely subservient to Britain. This state, it is true, had a population of 15½ millions of whom only half, however, were Czechs. Of the remaining half, 50 % were Germans while the other 50 % was composed of Slovaks, Hungarians, Ruthenians and Poles. Internally this vassal of Great Britain was very weak. Its German population wished to become a part of the Reich whilst the Hungarians wished to be incorporated in Hungary and the Slovaks were striving for independence.

After Austria's incorporation in the Reich Hitler began protecting the interests of these Germans and at the same time commenced a forceful political attack on Czechoslovakia as Soviet Russia's "aircraft-carrier." He was here helped by anti-Soviet aristocratic circles in Britain. Exhausted by the half-Communist "Popular Front," France clung to the British policy which had "magnanimously" guaranteed her eastern frontier. This diplomatic struggle closed at the end of September 1938 with a complete victory for Adolf Hitler who won from Czechoslovakia the Sudeten areas inhabited by Germans. This meant, however, that he had acquired the mountains forming the boundary of the "Bohemian Basin." With the consent of Britain and France, the "Bohemian Basin" now ceased to be an advanced fortress of the democratic-Bolshevist east against Germany. But it was not a part of the Greater German Reich as it always had been for the last 1,000 years.

This came about, however, when Slovakia declared herself independent and Bohemia and Moravia, forming a wedge in the Greater German Reich and deserted by all their former allies and friends, asked for the protection of the Reich through their President, Dr Emil Hacha. The old unity of the Greater German Reich was thus reestablished in March 1939. The whole of the "Bohemian Basin" as well as the Carpathian Gate were then incorporated in the Reich.

III. Bohemia and Moravia in the Greater German Reich

The attitude of the Czech people was like that of school children who return unwillingly to school after having been given holidays for some unexpected cause. The Czechs, too, thought at first that an injustice had been done them when the territories they inhabited were again incorporated in the Greater German Reich. In their heart of hearts, however, they felt that Czech "independence" as it had been called and which had scarcely lasted twenty years had been dependent on the favour of Britain and France and was actually an unnatural phenomenon. Their blood felt the call of the Reich.

The President, Dr Hacha, acted in the same way as the Primislides in the 9th century when the Reich gave them and their people the political choice of either becoming an autonomous part of the German Reich or of being over-

whelmed as an advanced outpost of the backward east. President Dr Hacha's example was the Czech Prince Wenceslas who in spite of the resistance made by the heathen aristocracy in the 10th century renewed his attempts to establish a unification with the Reich and lost his life in pursuing this wise policy. After being canonized Wenceslas later became the national patron saint of the Bohemian Kingdom. After Slovakia had established her independence in March 1939, Bohemia and Moravia, which had accepted the protection of the Greater German Reich, had an area of not quite 20,000 square miles and a population of 7½ millions.

The most important fact was that as the result of the incorporation of Austria, Bohemia and Moravia into the Reich, its position in regard to democratic-Soviet Eastern Europe had been

1 Bohemia and Moravia on the frontier of the Roman Empire, the key position of the Germanic tribes, which could not be taken

《 *Frontier of the Roman Empire in the 2nd century A.D.*

▨ *Frontier of the territories inhabited by Germanic tribes*

◉ *Ercynian Forest with the Bohemian Basin*

🜍 *European watershed*

⬇ *Direction of the Germanic thrust towards the Mediterranean*

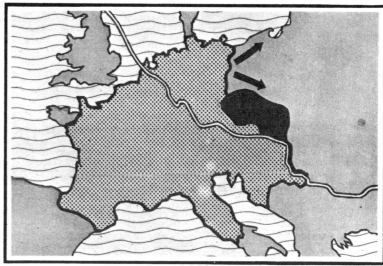

2 Bohemia and Moravia on the edge of the first "Continental Europe" with which it has to ally

《 *Frontier of the Roman Empire*

▨ *Frontier of Charlemagne's empire at the beginning of the 9th century*

■ *Bohemia and Moravia inhabited by Czech tribes*

➡ *Direction of the German colonization on the Baltic*

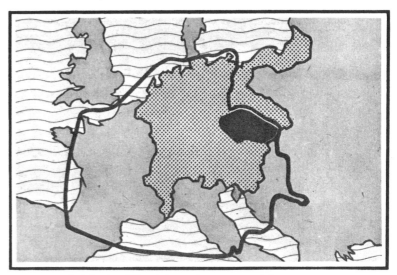

3 Bohemia and Moravia form an important part of the German Reich in the late Middle Ages. Prague is the imperial seat

❴ *Frontier of Charlemagne's empire*

▨ *Frontier at the beginning of the 15th century*

■ *The territories of Bohemia and Moravia*

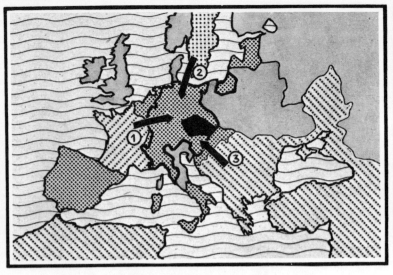

4 Bohemia and Moravia in modern times as a strategic basis against attacks from outside and inside

⟨ *Frontier of the Reich*

⋮⋮⋮ *Sweden*

▦ *Countries under Habsburg rule*

╲ *Ottoman Empire*

╱╱ *France*

➡ *Concentrated attack by the enemy against the Reich 1 = France, 2 = Sweden 3 = Turkey*

5 Bohemia and Moravia after the Dictate of Versailles included for the first time for more than 1,000 years in a coalition aginst the Reich

« *England and France with the countries under their influence*

╲ *Anglo-French spheres of influence in the eastern part of Central Europe*

╱╱ *Anti-German Anglo-French-Soviet coalition*

➡ *Directions of the concentrated attack on the Reich 1. = England, 2. = France, 3. = Poland, 4. = Little Entente 5. = Soviet Russia*

■ *Bohemia and Moravia in coalition against the Reich for the first time in more than a thousand years*

considerably consolidated. Slovakia had at the same time become the Reich's ally. In this way the Anglo-French colony in Central Europe during the period March 1938 to March 1939 lost 20 million inhabitants in the former Czechoslovakia and the former Austria as well as 60 % of its armament industry and the major part of the means of communication in the south between Poland, the Danubian area and the Balkans. The Reich acquired an annual production of nearly 5 million tons of iron and steel as well as a very valuable armament industry. The dense railway net in Bohemia and Moravia greatly improved the Reich's strategic resources both against Poland and the Danubian area. The Reich gained a direct connexion from Nuremberg via Prague to Breslau, from Berlin via Prague to Vienna and from Breslau via Brno to Vienna and, more important still, it came into possession of important Central European railway junctions. Adjoining Bohemia and Moravia was Slovakia which embraced Poland from the south in the same way as East Prussia did from the north.

The fate of Poland was sealed in the hour when Bohemia and Moravia were incorporated in the Reich. As long as Czechoslovakia existed, Prussian Silesia and East Prussia were strategically dead areas condemned to a defensive retreat in the event of a possible war against the Western Democracies and their eastern Allies. After Czechoslovakia had ceased to exist, Prussian Silesia and East Prussia became bases from which offensive actions could be launched by the Reich in an easterly direction. The railways of Bohemia and Moravia without doubt contributed considerably to Poland's rapid defeat. Before the outbreak of this war the Greater German Reich completed by the Protectorate of Bohemia and Moravia and strengthened by its ally, Slovakia, had a total population of 90 millions and an area of nearly 266,000 square miles. When Poland succumbed on the seventeenth day of war, the Reich bloc together with Slovakia covered an area of 340,000 square miles, and had a population of 110 millions.

The war potential of the "Bohemian Basin"

Towards the end of 1939 the Reich had a peaceful front in the east extending from Villach via Bratislava to Lupkov and from there along the new Soviet frontier as far as the mouth of the Memel. At that time Yugoslavia, Hungary, Rumania and Russia, too, were all political riddles. The "Bohemian Basin" and the "Carpathian Gate" were of the greatest importance behind this peaceful eastern front on account of their production and their transport facilities. Industry in the Protectorate had the same value as the industry of the Austro-Hungarian monarchy during the first World War. In this connexion, too, the fact was important that together with Austrian and Polish industry they had formed a full third of Anglo-French industry on European soil.

During the years 1938 and 1939 the Reich had acquired a new strategic base in the east and south-east. It had here increased its area by 96,000 square miles and its population by 45 millions, that is to say as much as by the area and population of France who was opposed to the Reich in the west.

In 1940, as a result of the campaigns against Norway, France and her Allies, the Reich had acquired another very advantageous strategic base against Britain along the Atlantic coast. At the same time it was further strengthened by its new ally, Italy, with the result that a second front was thus established against Britain in the Mediterranean which now ceased to be Britain's line of communication to India.

Bohemia and Moravia had already proved to be a strong fortress of the Reich against the east and now that Italy had joined the Reich, the Protectorate provided fresh transport connexions with the new ally in the south via Prague to Linz and via Brno to Vienna. These new communications were not only of great importance for supplying Italy with coal but also for sending reinforcements to the new African front where German units also subsequently joined in the fighting.

During the course of 1940 the Reich occupied territories in Norway and Western Europe having an area of 293,000 square miles and a population of 55 millions. The Reich together with Italy and the newly conquered territories began the year 1941 as a compact European unit with an area of almost 780,000 square miles and a population of 210 millions. Between 1938 and the summer of 1940 Britain had lost both militarily and politically territories in Europe having an area of 585,000 square miles and a population of 145 millions.

Then came the year 1941 in which the Reich gained allies (Rumania, Hungary, Finland and Bulgaria) in Europe with 40 million inhabitants and an area of 312,000 square miles. In the Balkans Yugoslavia and Greece were conquered which together have an area of 150,000 square miles and a population of 22 millions. Before the campaign against Soviet Russia anti-British Europe had an area of 1,240,000 square miles and a population of more than 270 millions. At that time Bohemia and Moravia formed an important junction of means of communication behind the anti-Soviet front just as it had done against Poland during the 1939 campaign. The distance from the frontier of the Protectorate to the Soviet frontier was not quite 190 miles. When in the autumn of 1941 the front had been pushed forward more than 600 miles farther eastwards, Bohemia and Moravia as an inseparable part of the Reich formed the centre of the New Europe. This New Europe acquired further regions in the east having an area of something more than 500,000 square miles and a population of 65 millions. It thus increased to a total area of 1,760,000 square miles and a population of 325 millions.

During 1942 the New Europe extended further towards the east and acquired another 156,000 square miles with a population of 25 millions and in the west an area of 94,000 square miles with a French population numbering 13 millions when Adolf Hitler was forced to occupy the south of France after the British and Americans ha dinvaded North Africa. Towards the end of 1942 anti-British Europe thus formed a bloc having a total area of 2,012,000 square miles with a population of. more than 360 millions.

Since the time when Britain sold the Czechs thinking thus to gain time for its armaments, the Reich has deprived her in Europe of territories having an area of 1,800,000 square miles and a population of 290 millions. Britain who betrayed the Czechs in Munich had not only lost her position in Europe but had also lost her world Empire when she was forced to appeal to Bolshevist Russia and to Roosevelt's imperialistic America for help in her dire need. The snowball which Chamberlain had treacherously fashioned in Munich now developed into a huge avalanche rumbling down the mountainside formed by Europe and threatening to smash the British Empire to atoms. Fate has taken revenge on Britain for the Czechs.

The allegory of the snowball

Bismarck was right when he said that the master of Bohemia was also the master of Europe. After the World War the British recalled Bismarck's words but by 1938 they had forgotten what they knew in 1918. They thought that strategic conditions in Central Europe would not be greatly altered if they surrendered the "Bohemian Basin" to the Greater German Reich for a certain period. But they were very much mistaken. Like Charlemagne, Adolf Hitler established in good time a base capable of offering resistance to the puzzling east. Britain is now suffering the consequences of her treachery.

In their propaganda broadcasts the Soviets have also admitted that the light and heavy weapons coming from Bohemia and Moravia are causing them a lot of trouble. The factories in the Protectorate are still working under full pressure. The Czech worker, who in spite of restrictions resulting from the war has experienced practical Socialism since the creation of the Protectorate, has made it his ambition to contribute to the victory of the Young Europe by the work of his hands.

Lovely, well-groomed hair

thanks to

Dralle

Lohse Uralt Lavendel

The clean, refreshing fragrance

It is no longer possible to manufacture Lohse Uralt Lavendel in unlimited quantities but it is still obtainable in its original pure quality. If you use it carefully, it will last a long time for a few drops are enough to provide refreshing coolness for quite a while. And we recommend it, for surroundings full of perfume and freshness make life much pleasanter and work much easier

KHASANA

PERI KHASANA

WORLD FAMOUS COSMETICS

Dr. Korthaus

DR. KORTHAUS   FRANKFURT A.M.

PERI

BOHN

As smooth and shining

as silk is the nib of every

Kaweco-Pen

that is why the *Kaweco* moves so easily across the paper

Ask to see the modern *Kaweco* writing materials at any stationer's

The Protectorate in Greater Germany

"All the rivers of Bohemia flow into Germany"

Anybody who studies the geographical position of the Protectorate of Bohemia and Moravia on the map will realize that it forms a natural constituent part of the territory which the German people has occupied as its lebensraum for centuries. Bohemia and Moravia consequently belong geographically and economically no less than politically and historically to the Greater German Reich.

Geography teaches us that the mountain ranges which skirt Bohemia and Moravia (Erzgebirge, Bohemian Forest and Sudeten Range) are Central German mountain ranges and that the plateau of Central Bohemia is connected towards the south with the Vienna basin. On the other hand, the Carpathians extend between Bohemia and Moravia on the one side and Slovakia and Hungary on the other. The Central German mountain ranges are crossed by so numerous passes that the traveller on foot scarcely feels that he is surmounting an obstacle. No less than the mountains and plains of the Protectorate, its rivers, too, belong to German territory as a whole. An old proverb has it that all the rivers of Bohemia flow into Germany. These rivers do actually strive to reach the Elbe or they flow towards the Oder and the Danube, in any case, in whichever direction, to main rivers which are vital arteries of the regions occupied by the Germans.

The greatest geographer in Europe during the Renaissance, the Italian Eneas Silvio Piccolomini, who was subsequently Pope Pius II, wrote: "The whole of Bohemia, Moravia and Silesia lies within the limits of the territory over which German culture extends... All the towns are of a purely German character. The style of the settlements and farms is the same for Germans, Czechs and Moravians, and the same is also true of the shape of the houses." Anybody who crosses the mountain ranges of Central Germany can convince himself of that fact. He will easily be able to see for himself that the same culture lives in the towns of post-war Germany as lives in the towns of the Protectorate such as Prague, Brno, Iglau, Pilsen, Eger etc.

That Bohemia and Moravia form a part of Germany's lebensraum as a whole is also demonstrated by the traffic net which has been built up. No less than 13 railway lines connect Bohemia and Moravia with Northern and Southern Germany. They are the lines Budweis-Linz, Budweis-Znaim, Pilsen-Eger, Prague-Saaz, Prague-Leitmeritz, Turnau-Gablonz, Starkenbach-Trautenau, Senftenberg-Morava-Ostrava, Cadca-Jablunca, Vienna-Brno and Vienna-Znaim. Until recently the mountain range on the frontier between Moravia and Slovakia was not traversed by a single railway line.

As railway lines, as we know, are only laid between regions where economic conditions call for an exchange between natural resources and manufactured goods, the artificial traffic net of Bohemia and Moravia bears testimony also to the economic links between the Protectorate and the adjoining German territories.

The great extent to which even the former Czechoslovakia was economically dependent upon post-war Germany and Austria—with which countries it sought, as is well known, to have as little to do as possible — is proved particularly impressively by the trade statistics of the year 1932, the last year before the National Socialist assumption of power. Whilst Czechoslovakia's imports from post-war Germany amounted to 1,173 million crowns and her exports to post-war Germany amounted to 1,198 million crowns and even a tiny country like Austria exported goods to Czechoslovakia to a total value of 1,031 million crowns, Czech exports via the Elbe and free zone of Hamburg to non-German countries amounted to only 675 million crowns.

As a result of the incorporation of the Protectorate in the Greater German Reich, its trade and industry have increased considerably because industry and agriculture in the southeast of Germany between Vienna, Breslau, Dresden, Hof, Passau and Linz form a natural supplement to one another. Unemployment in the Sudetenland, over-population in Prague and the remoteness of Linz will never appear again whilst Vienna has once more been given the Moravian and Silesian hinterland with its raw materials which it so grievously lacked after the Peace of St Germain.

The reincorporation of Bohemia and Moravia into the Reich was not without importance for Germany from the strategical point of view, for every state must strive to establish an equable balance between the length of its frontiers and its area. The length of the frontiers of the Reich was diminished from 4,670 miles to 3,640 miles as the result of the incorporation of the Protectorate. The Greater German Reich thus now had a frontier shorter than that of the smallest German Reich in 1920, the length of which was 4,000 miles. The population of the Greater German Reich when compared with the Germany of Versailles had risen by about 26 millions to a total of approximately 86 millions.

The prototype of a distorted state, however, was provided by the former Czechoslovakia concerning which country it was said not unjustifiably that it had the shape of a crocodile with its jaws towards Germany. One of the results of this abnormal frontier was the tremendous expenditure in Czechoslovakia on the Army and the frontier police which per head of the population was the heaviest burden in the whole of Europe. In consequence of the dissolution of the former Czechoslovakia and the establishment of the Protectorate of Bohemia and Moravia, the Czech people has once more returned into the community of the German Reich and Bohemia and Moravia have again become a part of the geo-political unit in the middle of the Continent.

The solution of the vital problem of a thousand years has thus led back to the natural geographical and racial foundations of the course of history

FRANKFORT-ON-THE-ODER

SILESIA

BRESLAU

HIRSCHBERG SUDETEN

ISER
RIESENGEBIRGE
REICHENBERG
GABLONZ

ODER

OPPELN

NEISSE

GLEIWITZ

LEITMERITZ

TRAUTENAU

GLATZ

TROPPAU

RATIBOR

VISTULA

PRAGUE ELBE

MORAVSKA
TREBOVA

ODER

MORAVSKA
OSTRAVA

DEUTSCH BROD

OLMÜTZ

PRERAU

WEST BESKID

PROTECTORATE OF
BOHEMIA AND MORAVIA

MOLDAU

IGLAU

BRNO

WHITE MOUNTAINS

BUDWEIS

ZNAIM

LITTLE CARPATHIANS

SLOVAKIA

AUSTRIA

DANUBE VIENNA

PRESSBURG

LINZ

After the dissolution of the Czechoslovakian State in 1939, the Protectorate of Bohemia and Moravia was established. The map shows its natural position within the Greater German territories. The red dotted line shows the extent of Czechoslovakia until 1939

in this part of Central Europe. The law operating here can again be recognized and has once more become effective.

The whole course of history clearly demonstrates the fact that whenever the Czech people drew away from the German people or even turned against it, this action always proved its undoing. Whenever the Czechs formed an integral part of the territories surrounding them, their country prospered. Its weal and woe has always depended upon its attitude towards Germany. In all the epochs of its economic and cultural prosperity, the Czech people has been within the union of German states and formed a part of the Reich. It was borne upward on the rising tide of the Germanic peoples in general and of the German nation in particular. German influence has never hampered but always furthered the development of the Czech nation and the economic consolidation of its existence as a people.

An old tradition: The guard in its brilliantly coloured uniforms creates an atmosphere of splendour around the Regent of Hungary

Admiral Nikolaus Horthy von Nagybanya, Regent of the Kingdom of Hungary

Very frank and assured, the commanding personality of Horthy dominated the interview with the "Signal's" reporter. Since 1920 Horthy has been at the head of the government of his country. Although he is 72 years of age, he has a certain vigour and vivacity which lend weight to his movements and his utterances. The detachment and the almost imperceptible humour of the "grand seigneur" reveal a mature and very kindly nature

THE
WATCH
ON THE
DANUBE

Hungary's excellently trained and splendidly equipped army has another important task besides the protection of the country from foreign threats or tutelage. It guarantees the independence of the country and at the same time assures unhampered trade between Central and South-east Europe, between Greater Germany and the Balkan States. On this trade, of which the Danube is the most important thoroughfare, the new European order is based

"How long does the train take to get to Budapest? A whole night? Where shall we stay? Shall we see Regent Horthy?" Peasants from the districts which fell to Hungary after the Arbitration of Vienna discuss their trip to the capital

Right: Great preparations are made for the trip. Shimmering white and red costumes are taken out of their chests. There are as many as 70 embroidered ribbons worked into the skirt and apron, significantly called "ruha" (dress), worn by many of the women

Left: The picture shows them going down the village street to the station. The only luggage they carry is a small wicker basket

Part of Hungary again!

In Budapest: they go for their first walk through the rainwashed asphalt streets. Passers-by and even the policeman turn to look at the unusual costumes that had not been seen in the capital for 20 years

The great thrill for the young peasant girl: 3 days in the city, 3 days strolling about among the palaces and museums, and past the shop windows

In the evening the flags of the peasants are illuminated by the searchlights of the City Theatre. The audience in their enthusiasm applaud the peasants who have acted the traditional plays of their native district. (Picture below)

"Europe must be wiped out... *Tanks 30 feet high raze Berlin mercilessly to the ground, crushing walls, men, women and children beneath them... In Copenhagen there are no survivors. Stockholm is as silent as the grave. While the clouds of gas are de cending over Paris, tho population flees to take refuge in the Underground... But all in vain! Bolshevism deals its blow. Paris and France are extinguished. One year suffices to annihilate the Continent with its 350 million inhabitants... The peoples of Europe are deported to Siberia...*

From the "Trust for the destruction of Europe," a book by the Soviet journalist Ilia Ehrenburg published in England and the U.S.A.

See the colour pages following :

THE WAR AIM OF THE CONTINENT

A theme certain to interest the whole world but which cannot be broached without a few introductory remarks to explain the situation

Looking back, the first shots in this war were provoked by a purely local quarrel. The bone of contention was a certain Corridor and a certain Free City of Danzig. It was a matter of the revision of a frontier in which every nation with a sense of honour was deeply interested. Documents prove how easily this revision could have been carried out in a peaceful manner without wounding any feelings.

Why, in spite of all, were the first shots in this war fired in the north of Europe, on the German-Polish frontier? Why did this strip of territory and this city of less than 200,000 inhabitants set alight the flame which a few careful hands could easily have extinguished and which has now become a conflagration spreading over the five continents and the seven seas. Is not the lack of proportion between the cause and the effect of such a monstrous historical phenomenon enough to shake one's belief in mankind? Or have we put the question badly? Should we not rather ask whether the Corridor and Danzig are really the cause or merely the occasion of this war?

A world-wide struggle

It is a fact that in 1939 Britain gave as the reason for war her desire to protect the smaller states and in the same year France declared her anxiety for her own safety. A little later, beyond the ocean, the United States felt threatened by a Germany which was involved in one of the bitterest struggles in its history taking place before its very frontiers.

But these war motives or war aims scarcely justify the magnitude of the struggle. They have been refuted or explained by confiscated archives. To a certain extent these explanations have something satisfactory about them. When people see that Britain meant neither Poland nor Denmark, neither Norway nor Holland, neither Belgium nor France and neither Greece nor Yugoslavia when she declared war but the maintenance of the European balance of power in her own favour and the freedom of the seas as she understands it, the realists of the 20th century are facing facts to which it is easy for them to define their attitude. They understand too that a French Government which sees the country's centre of gravity abroad, and in Britain at that, cannot avoid going to war. Meanwhile Lend and Lease Acts and other diplomatic-military actions have revealed the real war aims of the U.S.A. The American policy to obtain control of bases is slowly materializing and is obviously a move on the way to world dominion in the future, while the monopoly for the building of bombers, about which "Signal" published a report recently, points to the fact that it is to be a policy of air supremacy. Clearest of all are the real war aims of the Soviets who for 26 years have made no attempt to disguise their plans for world revolution which they have

partly realized in exemplary fashion on their western frontier whenever the opportunity offered itself.

Germany's war aim, too, has been clearly revealed. The Germans maintain that they are fighting for the fruits of their internal revolution which has solved the problem of the century for them, the social problem. This revolution has brought them into deadly combat with the modern forms of human enslavement, Capitalism and Bolshevism, and placed them in the forefront of an intellectual struggle involving the whole world.

That brings the war aims on to another plane: the United States have plans for world domination against which the British Empire is on the defensive. The Soviets are trying to create a Bolshevist empire. Germany, the bulwark of Europe and the world against the threat of Bolshevism, is holding the front in the east and defending herself like Japan in the west who is fighting for her historical claim to leadership in the Pacific against the tyranny of foreign interests.

The demands of the hour

Seen from this point of view the question of the Corridor and Danzig vanish into thin air, for such causes are in proportion to the effects of this world-wide struggle. At the same time, however, the relentlessness of what the hour demands from the living becomes clear as crystal. The whole universe is involved in a dispute from which there is no escape and which must be faced. It has to be coolly considered and weighed up. Even the most idyllic spots on this earth will be involved and everyone must be prepared for questions of life and death which have to be answered precisely and quickly. It is just like an examination: the candidate is given a quarter of an hour and what he thinks of afterwards is of no avail.

If fate were to ask the European Continent about its attitude and aims in this universal struggle (and we believe that this question has already been asked), what would Europe answer?

One thing is certain: It would fail miserably in this examination were it to bring before the Supreme Court of world history all the details of its internal affairs. Minor problems are solved automatically according to the lines laid down by the main verdict. But in order to secure a favourable main verdict, Europe must have a strong case, and she has it.

The case is made up of sober facts; it is an argument that has been fought and suffered for with bravery and industry, with wisdom and tears and with the blood of every nation of this hemisphere throughout its history. It is the outcome of the natural and dynamic development of history—it is the path leading to the synthesis of Europe's power.

On the four pages following, "Signal" attempts to give details on this theme.

Whither
is Europe going?

A question to the history of the Continent—and the answer in five pictures

In the middle of the 9th century when Charlemagne's Reich, the first Central European Empire, decayed, Europe broke up into the scene of innumerable miniature struggles, for in the minor empires that came into being the previous vassals became supreme lords at the cost of the various central powers. The rivalry between the different houses was the beginning of the struggle to form the society, economics and State of Europe

In the early years of the struggle against the East the outlines of a national German state were visible although it did not become a reality until a thousand years later. Meanwhile France, with the Ile de France as its centre, overcame its vassals and stabilized the state during the Hundred Years' War with England. At the same time Spain was acquiring strength by defeating the Moors. But on the whole, the Middle Ages, resounding to the march of mercenary soldiers, were drawing to a close

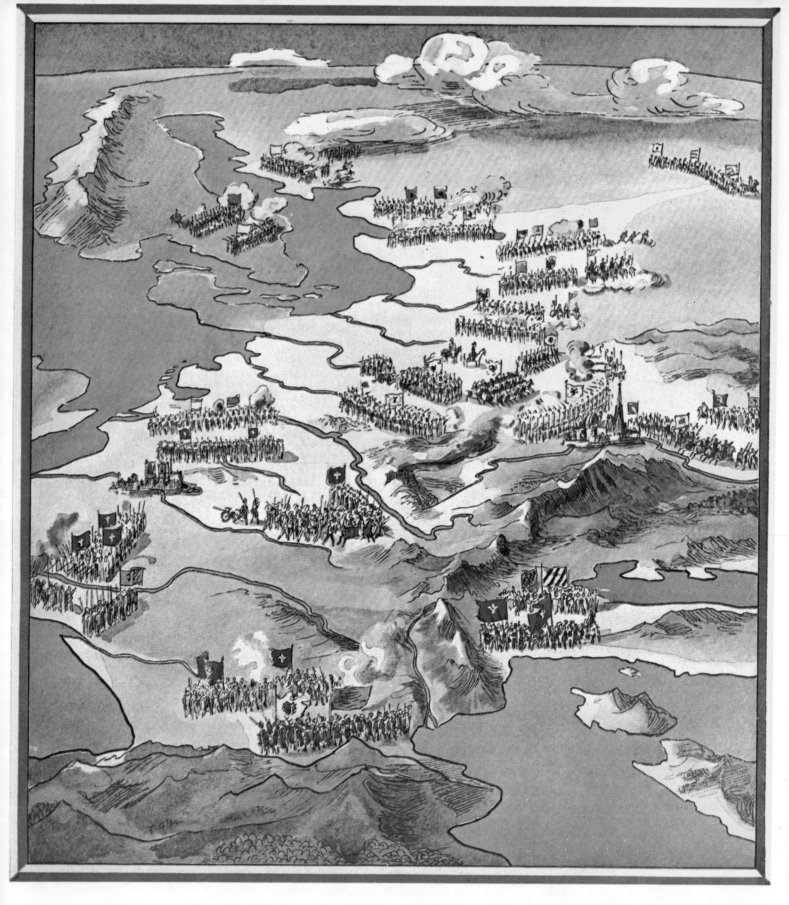

The great turning-point

The turning-point between the Middle Ages and modern times was also the hour of birth of the Continental idea. Whilst European explorer impetus and courage discover the wide areas of the earth, it simultaneously outlines the frontiers of the Continent and teaches us for the first time to look upon it as a cultural, economic and political unit. Europe has become a home. Whilst in the Italy of the Renaissance period the intellectual torch of antiquity is again being kindled in order to throw a new light on universal space and mankind, the Portuguese, Spanish, Dutch and French are conquering the world for western culture. But this enormous and unique achievement in the history of humanity appears to grudge its performer his own perfection: The heart of Europe is bleeding from the blows dealt by the first social struggles of

reorganization during the Peasants' Wars. The commencing world trade develops new friction and civil life becomes a war-influencing factor. The ceaseless fighting for new territory gains, moreover, a fresh impulse resulting from tragical religious differences. The great turning-point will not allow a great unity. Even the next step which Europe must inevitably take, that is the step towards the reorganization of peoples and states, leads only to a dynastical allotment of the Continent. For two centuries it will continue to groan from the results of heritage and Cabinet wars. On the other hand, the island on its outskirts, England, will realize its unique maritime position and, by skilfully betraying one Continental power to the other, will inherit all of them. Therefore, Europe stands — still divided into more than 200 sovereign states — on the threshhold of modern history

The last stage

At the beginning of the latest period of history, too, Europe has placed a milestone. The obsolete forms were wiped away by the French Revolution and its great son tried to create a Continental State out of the ruins. Napoleon recognized the necessity but fate forbad him to accomplish his plan. He cleared the way along which European history was to advance from the idea of the dynastic principle to that of the national state. Napoleon recruited his legions from the first levée en masse of the peoples of Europe which, however, began to be inflamed with national enthusiasm. A century of struggles for national unity followed during which the number of sovereign states sank from 200 to 20. While this simplification was in process the spirit it liberated created the magnificent tools of civilization. And while Europe was occupied with her own affairs the rest of the goods of the earth were being newly distributed for the technical age brought with it a new grouping of all political powers. The first World War for which considerations of foreign policy were chiefly responsible was the result. These considerations decided the issue and contrary to its own interests split the Continent into an uneasy conglomeration of 36 states. Meanwhile grossraum economy was beginning. Europe with its 8 additional states barricaded itself behind the unsurmountable walls of mutual distrust and rearmament and remained inferior to the rest of the world in economics and politics. But from the East came the menace of Bolshevism that appeared like a new storm threatening the whole world.

The final decision

The heavy damages suffered by almost all the States of Europe, the victors not excepted, during the first World War were a profitable lesson from fate to the Continent showing that in future capital and oil, wool and rubber, coal and iron which had assumed an incomparably greater importance in wartime played a decisive rôle in history like traditional questions of frontiers and sovereignity. The sequence of interminable economic crises between 1918 and 1938 are a proof of this fact. Has Europe understood or is the old rivalry between the 36 States continuing while the development of world history is confronting continent with continent? It is continuing. Only the most profoundly affected European States, that is Germany and Italy, recognize the first demand of the hour, the dangers of West and East. They are modernizing their conception of technics and capital, of socialism and society and within their frontiers are solving the problems of the time in exemplary fashion. It is one of the most tragic things in European history that at this moment the smouldering passions of the world should flare up for a second time and try to plunge Europe into chaos. Today, now that the Axis has established its outposts along all the coasts and frontiers of Europe and now that she has been forced to oppose Bolshevist imperialism in arms revealing in the attack the extent of the danger, the powers of Europe who look forward to the future with confidence have recognized the second demand of the hour, the dynamic demand of European history and have formed a common front regardless of frontiers. The road to the synthesis of Europe has been opened up—perhaps for the last time.

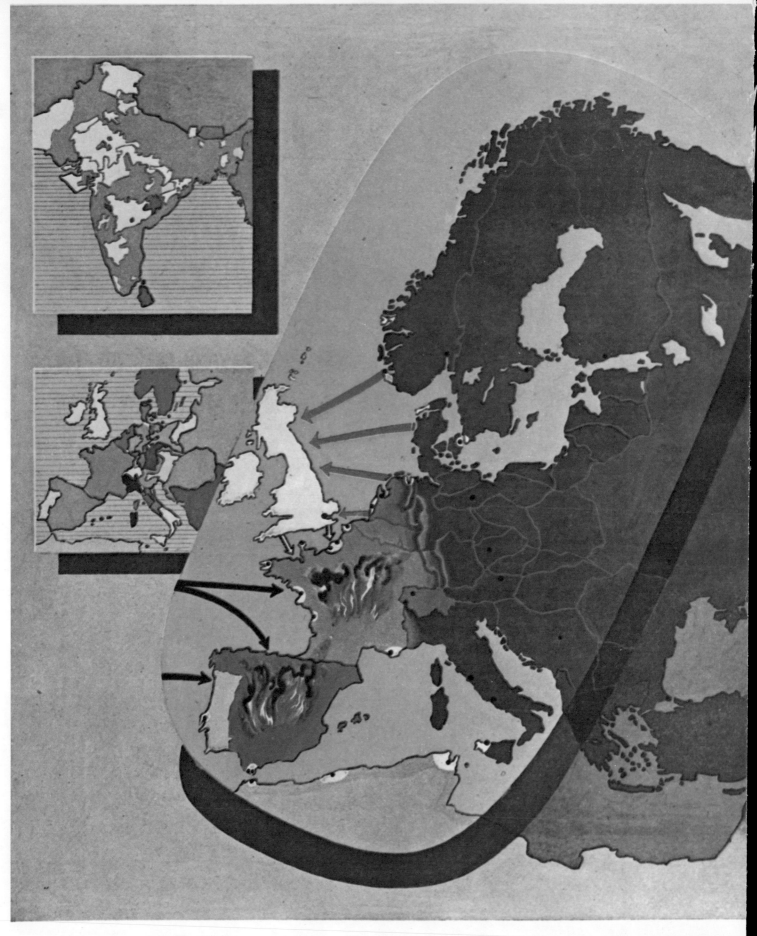

Europe — the theatre of a third World War

1 **India today.** Britain's traditional policy is founded on the axiom "divide et impera." Britain has rigorously applied the principle in India of splitting up a vast continent and has thereby condemned the peoples of India to impotence. The fact cannot be shown on the map that apart from splitting up India as a state, Britain has been aiming at undermining India's spiritual unity by continually fanning the flames of the conflict between the Moslems and the Hindus

2 **Europe around 1850.** For centuries Britain's policy in Europe has been founded on the same principles as those applied in India. Britain wishes to divide the unity of Europe in as many states as possible all hostile to one another. In view of the present world situation, the only result would be that such a Europe would become an easy prey for the Soviet Union

3 **A future theatre of war?** Were the Soviets become the master of Europe, the Continent wo automatically be condemned to become the theatre third World War. The map shows how British, Soviet even American interests would necessarily cut across another in Europe and lead to a new and frightful con the consequence of which would be that the peoples of rope were completely reduced to misery. The struggle v begin for the bases on the Atlantic, rapidly spread a Western Europe and subsequently also across Central Eu